Walter Herdeg 1980

With his grandson
Mit seinem Enkel
Avec son petit-fils

42 YEARS OF GRAPHIS COVERS

AN ANTHOLOGY OF GRAPHIS COVERS

EINE SAMMLUNG DER GRAPHIS UMSCHLÄGE

RECUEIL DES COUVERTURES DE GRAPHIS

Edited by/Herausgegeben von/Réalisé par

B. Martin Pedersen

Editor and Art Director: B. Martin Pedersen
Assistant Editor: Joan Lüssi
Project Manager: Annette Crandall
Designers: Marino Bianchera, Martin Byland
Art Assistant: Walter Zuber

GRAPHIS PRESS CORP, ZÜRICH (SWITZERLAND)

GRAPHIS U.S. INC., NEW YORK, N.Y. (USA)

GRAPHIS PUBLICATIONS

GRAPHIS, International bi-monthly journal of graphic art and photography
GRAPHIS DESIGN ANNUAL, The international annual on design and illustration
PHOTOGRAPHIS, The international annual of photography
GRAPHIS POSTERS, The international annual on poster art
GRAPHIS PACKAGING VOL. 4, An international survey of packaging design
GRAPHIS DIAGRAMS VOL. 2, The graphic visualization of abstract, technical and statistical facts and functions
GRAPHIS COVERS, An anthology of all GRAPHIS covers with artists' short biographies and indexes of all GRAPHIS issues
GRAPHIS ANNUAL REPORTS, An international compilation of the best designed annual reports
ARCHIGRAPHIA, Architectural and environmental graphics
FILM + TV GRAPHICS 2, An international survey of the art of film animation

GRAPHIS-PUBLIKATIONEN

GRAPHIS, Die internationale Zweimonatszeitschrift für Graphik und Photographie
GRAPHIS DESIGN ANNUAL, Das internationale Jahrbuch über Design und Illustration
PHOTOGRAPHIS, Das internationale Jahrbuch der Photographie
GRAPHIS POSTERS, Das internationale Jahrbuch der Plakatkunst
GRAPHIS PACKUNGEN BAND 4, Internationaler Überblick der Packungsgestaltung
GRAPHIS DIAGRAMS BAND 2, Die graphische Darstellung abstrakter, technischer und statistischer Daten und Fakten
GRAPHIS COVERS, Eine Sammlung aller GRAPHIS-Umschläge mit Informationen über die Künstler und
   Inhaltsübersichten aller Ausgaben der Zeitschrift GRAPHIS
GRAPHIS ANNUAL REPORTS, Ein internationaler Überblick der Gestaltung von Jahresberichten
ARCHIGRAPHIA, Architektur- und Umweltgraphik
FILM + TV GRAPHICS 2, Ein internationaler Überblick über die Kunst des Animationsfilms

PUBLICATIONS GRAPHIS

GRAPHIS, La magazine bimestrielle internationale de l'arts graphiques et de la photographie appliqués
GRAPHIS ANNUAL, L'annuel international du design et de l'illustration
PHOTOGRAPHIS, L'annuel international de la photographie appliquée
GRAPHIS POSTERS, L'annuel international de l'affiche
GRAPHIS PACKAGING VOL. 4, Panorama international de l'art de l'emballage
GRAPHIS DIAGRAMS VOL. 2, La représentation graphique de faits et donnés abstraits, techniques et statistiques
GRAPHIS COVERS, Recueil de toutes les couvertures de GRAPHIS avec des notices biographiques des artistes
   et récapitulatif des index annuels du magazine GRAPHIS.
GRAPHIS ANNUAL REPORTS, Panorama international du design de rapports annuels d'entreprises
ARCHIGRAPHIA, La création graphique appliquée à l'architecture et à l'environnement
FILM + TV GRAPHICS 2, Panorama international du cinéma d'animation

PUBLICATION No. 187 (ISBN 3-85709-422-2)
© Copyright under Universal Copyright Convention
Copyright 1987 by Graphis Press Corp., 107 Dufourstrasse, 8008 Zurich, Switzerland/
Graphis U.S. Inc., 141 Lexington Avenue, New York, N.Y. 10016, USA
No part of this book may be reproduced in any form without written permission of the publisher
Printed in Japan by Dai Nippon
Typeset in Switzerland by Setzerei Heller, Zurich
Typefaces: Garamond ITC Light Condensed, Futura Extra Bold

CONTENTS INHALT SOMMAIRE

1935

Climbing in the Dolomites

Auf Klettertour in den Dolomiten

Escaladant les Dolomites

It so happened that when I was first apprised of the plans for this book I was occupying my mind with Indian painting of past centuries, and had just read the words of B.N. Goswamy, Professor of Art History at the Punjab University, Chandigarh: "It would seem that as far as facts are concerned Indian painting is a world of silence in which one has to strain one's ears to be able to pick up the whispers coming from the past." Indian painting and the covers of GRAPHIS publications may seem to be worlds apart; yet I was at once struck by a certain parallelism. The covers of GRAPHIS in the Walter Herdeg era also come to us out of a world of silence, especially as that era is now over. The magazine covers appeared regularly every two months over a period of forty-two years, they surprised and delighted and impressed and intrigued many who were far from the scene of their genesis and who could know very little about the mechanisms of their conception and production. True, people occasionally came from far off to investigate the source from which the magazine emanated, but on the whole visitors were few. A good proportion of them were Americans, and they mostly came expecting to meet up with a numerous editorial staff, big studios full of busy creative minds, and probably some printing facilities attached. They were taken aback to find only a few dull offices sporadically occupied by a handful of layouters, penpushers and secretaries. In fact, it was a pretty still center if you like, and now that Walter Herdeg has unobtrusively withdrawn from it, anyone who contemplates the 246 issues of the magazine and the many books he edited and designed, here represented by as many striking covers, must surely feel as I do that this great oeuvre, just like Indian painting, comes to us, however powerfully, out of a big silence.

The silence is admittedly not quite of the same character as the Indian one. The artists of the subcontinent are conspicuous by their anonymity – they never signed their works. The covers reproduced in this book all bear the names of their artists, and a prestigious muster it is, including Munch and Picasso as well as Steinberg or Glaser. The silence here lies not in a lack of names, but rather in the comparative obscurity in which such a brilliant parade of twentieth-century art and design came into being.

I have a right to say this, seeing that for forty-odd years I was very close to the heart of the mystery. Before the first number of GRAPHIS appeared, Dr Walter Amstutz consulted me on the name to be given to the new magazine – even if the one I preferred was not chosen. For the next twenty years I translated and edited texts for the magazine, after which I quitted the engineering world in which I had for so long been a successful impostor and joined the editorial staff. Now I was really, personally, at the said still center. I could hear the creative heart ticking over. Even so, I had, like Professor Goswamy, to strain my ears, for it ticked very softly.

This had a lot to do with the character of Walter Herdeg, who was by nature of a retiring disposition, one who, though never averse to recognition, hated the spotlights and feared nothing more than having to make speeches. This attitude seemed to affect his environment. Many of his closest collaborators kept themselves to themselves, not volunteering much information, each busied with his own small realm. The milieu was never very communicative. Of course, helpers were needed to manage the formidable amount of work. Some of these were known as Assistant Editors, normally young designers, and I am still full of admiration for what they accomplished. Most of them stayed only for two or three years, but they must have learned a good deal, for many were very successful when they left. I need only mention Paul Arthur, who made a name as a magazine editor and designer in Canada, or Ken Baynes, who rose to be one of Britain's best writers on graphic design. This series of notable successes came to an abrupt end when I arrived.

But since Walter Herdeg remained honestly convinced that he needed a right hand, one or two further assistants followed after I had become merely a part of the furniture. Yet it would be futile to look for their influence in the covers. All in all, quite a few people came to GRAPHIS firmly believing that they would play an active part in the shaping of this prestigious magazine, that they would, cloistered with the gray eminence himself, share in his decisions, becoming important agents in a great ferment of creative teamwork. They never did. Though symbiosis might seem to work modestly for a while, it always petered out. The right hands slowly realized that they would never have much say in things. Frustration overtook them, and one by one they fell by the wayside.

I was the only one whose collaboration lasted all of the forty-two years spanned by these covers, and that is in fact my sole qualification for writing these prefatory comments. If I survived so long, it was partly because I had no graphic design background and therefore no right whatever to question the verdicts of one whose experience and knowledge were vastly superior to my own. I accordingly concentrated more on the literary aspects of the job. I think I also shared with Walter Herdeg a certain quality bordering on obduracy – a touch of stiffness in the spine. In forty-two years of cooperation, although our relationship mellowed, we never got round to calling each other by our Christian names. Now in our age we both have bad backs; his prevents him from playing his beloved golf, and mine looks like vetoing my addiction to gardening.

It is in a way something of a paradox that the covers of GRAPHIS should have taken on such importance. For the magazine differed from most others in never really depending on its covers. It was rather too expensive to attract many impulsive buyers on newsstands. Its readers were instead primarily subscribers, and for long periods its circulation fluctuated around the 20000 mark. So the eye-catching qualities were only a secondary consideration. Yet the covers did catch the eye, and became one of the hallmarks of the magazine. And the publishers recognized this: the corridors of the GRAPHIS offices are lined with the whole gallery of them, proudly exhibited to visitors.

The procuring of the covers was a fairly straightforward mechanism. Suitable designs would sometimes be found in the material sent in by a contributor for a major article. The editor was always on the lookout, among the masses of work that passed through his hands, for motifs that would make a good cover. Often he was able to give exact instructions for what he wanted, based on some facet of the artist's work. Covers were also invited, and there were some painful moments when the packages sent in by artists were opened and the results of their endeavors failed to satisfy the editor's expectations. But there was never any shortage of cover designs. There was a steady flow of them, submitted often speculatively by artists and designers who could think of no higher beatitude than having their work on the front of GRAPHIS. Some of them were even willing to take over the costs of color reproduction. Because of this competition, and because the publicity value of an appearance on GRAPHIS was so great, no fee was ever paid for a cover design. This astonishing fact even includes the Picassos – through the good offices of Daniel-Henry Kahnweiler, Picasso gave his personal consent, and no payment was made. As a propitiatory gesture to those whose work was not accepted, articles occasionally appeared presenting the best of the unpublished covers - and many of them were hardly inferior to those used.

Once a project was accepted, a formidable effort was made to achieve optimum reproduction quality. Usually the GRAPHIS title and number had to be stripped in by the staff in the studio, and a designer might be employed for days on the lettering, trying out ever new variants on foil. In some cases as many as twelve different colors were assayed. When No 91 was completed, Ben Nicholson sent the complimentary comment that he could not have done the titling better himself. Great experimentation was also expended on getting the title in No 140 just right, as part of the pattern of torn posters. And when No 185 had already been printed, the white lettering was found not to be the non plus ultra, and a designer had to paint in the final pink at least for the exhibition copy.

Anyone who surveys the cover pageant will note how it reflects the changing tastes of graphic design over nearly half a century. The transitions are admittedly not distinct - the poetic and painterly works of earlier years, for instance, jostle the new informative clarity of the sixties for quite a time. Some designs have of course dated, but it is surprising, too, to find some that seem to have been done before their time - the Tarzan of No 171, for instance, still strikingly modern. No less imposing is the fact that all conceivable art forms are represented here: pen and crayon drawings, oils and acrylics, lithographs, etchings, aquatints, woodcuts and linocuts, photographs, three-dimensional artefacts - the whole gamut. This catholicity in forms of expression is paralleled by a catholicity of taste: Walter Herdeg was quick to recognize quality wherever it appeared, and in spite of a certain reserve - he hesitated lest No 195 should offend the sensibilities of some readers - he was always quite open to new and even audacious departures provided he saw the glint of beauty and talent in them.

The book jackets that are also included in this volume differ to some extent from the magazine covers, those for PHOTOGRAPHIS or the packaging books, say, revealing a much stricter stylistic line. They were selected and reproduced, however, with the same meticulous esthetic criteria and the same untiring devotion to quality.

The covers fascinated the GRAPHIS readership, and they also fascinated the staff who had to deal with them. We repeatedly stood in the corridors comparing them and picking out our own favorites, as readers of this book will now be able to do themselves. It is really invidious, in the face of such riches, to mention single works, but some were delighted, say, by Günther Kieser's original Arcimboldesque composition (No 184), some by the technical skill of Braldt Bralds' cats (No 215). Others admired the subtle chromatic mastery of James McMullan's revolver (No 213), the symbolism of Roger Hane's winged boot (No 167), the mysterious nostalgia of Richard Hess' station (No 178) or Etienne Delessert's matches (No 208), while Saul Steinberg's female head (No 123) always commanded general admiration. So much for a few pot-shots - the reader can take it from here himself.

The covers meant a lot to me, as it became the rule for me to write brief commentaries on them. Little information was normally forthcoming. I withdrew into my office and for a few hours indulged in an intense tête-à-tête with the artist's image. This was a small corner in which I could deploy my own imagination and my own reactions to design. No doubt I occasionally injected into the pictures thoughts that had never occurred to the artists; but I greatly enjoyed the philosophic ambivalence of André François, for instance, or the teasing implications of Roland Topor or Eugène Mihaesco. And these sessions taught me something: that every one of these covers has more in it than meets the eye.

One might have expected that there would be a lot of anecdotes to recount about the origins of these covers. For instance that the Polish poster artist Franek Starowieyski, asked to do a cover when on a visit to Zurich, went out and bought paper and colors, retired to his hotel and came back next morning with the finished design (No 157). But asked for more, past collaborators look blank. Legends were never able to spread, because each person was working in his own small compartment. Walter Herdeg no doubt has a few tales to tell; but this book is meant to be a surprise for him, and so we cannot consult him.

A word in closing about the man who chose and in a sense fathered all these covers. They will serve very well to symbolize his achievement: the enormous fund of experience, taste, judgement, and sheer hard work that went into what he did, the unflaggingly high esthetic standards, but also the stimulating and inspiring influence he had on the graphic design of the twentieth century. It is true that he was a solo performer, that he was rather withdrawn in his method of working. There is much in what I have said above about these covers coming to us out of a world of silence. But no silence I know of was ever more eloquent.

Stanley Mason, the author of this introduction, was born in Canada, in 1917. He is British citizen and has been living in Switzerland for many years. From 1963 until 1983 he worked as Assistant Editor with Graphis Press. Since then he has been working as writer and freelance translator.

1954

Fishing at the Rhine

Beim Fischen am Rhein

A la pêche au bord du Rhin

1963

Der Zufall wollte es, dass ich mich mit indischer Malerei aus früheren Jahrhunderten befasste, als ich von diesem Buchprojekt erfuhr und gerade folgenden Ausspruch von B.N. Goswamy, Professor für Kunstgeschichte an der Universität in Chandigarh, gelesen hatte: «Was Tatsachen angeht, ist die indische Malerei eine Welt der Stille, in der man die Ohren spitzen muss, um das Flüstern der Vergangenheit zu vernehmen.» Nun mag es scheinen, dass zwischen indischer Malerei und den GRAPHIS-Umschlägen Welten liegen; dennoch fielen mir sogleich einige Parallelen auf. Die GRAPHIS-Umschläge aus der Ära von Walter Herdeg sprechen auch aus einer Welt der Stille zu uns, zumal diese Ära mittlerweile vorüber ist. Die Zeitschriftenumschläge erschienen zweiundvierzig Jahre lang regelmässig alle zwei Monate; sie überraschten, erfreuten und beeindruckten viele, die weit vom Schauplatz ihrer Entstehung lebten und nur sehr wenig über die Mechanismen ihrer Konzipierung und Herstellung wissen konnten. Zwar reisten gelegentlich Leute von weit her, um sich die Wiege dieser Zeitschrift anzusehen, aber im grossen und ganzen gab es wenige Besucher. Die meisten waren Amerikaner, die gewöhnlich ein grosses Redaktionsteam erwarteten, geräumige Studios voller geschäftiger, kreativer Köpfe und daran angeschlossen vielleicht noch eine Druckerei. Sie waren enttäuscht, nur ein paar graue Büros vorzufinden, in denen verstreut einige Mitarbeiter sassen. Es war in der Tat ein recht stilles Zentrum; und jetzt, da sich Walter Herdeg unauffällig zurückgezogen hat, fühlt wie ich sicherlich jeder, der die 246 von ihm redigierten und gestalteten Nummern der Zeitschrift und die vielen Bücher betrachtet (die hier durch die entsprechenden Umschläge vertreten sind), dass sein grossartiges Œuvre, ganz wie die indische Malerei, aus einer tiefen Stille heraus kraftvoll zu uns dringt.

Aber diese Stille ist anderer Art als die indische. Die Künstler des Subkontinents fallen durch ihre Anonymität auf - sie signierten ihre Werke nie. Die in diesem Buch gezeigten Umschläge tragen alle die Namen ihrer Schöpfer und stellen eine ansehnliche Sammlung dar. Es sind sowohl Munch und Picasso wie auch Steinberg und Glaser vertreten. Die Stille beruht hier nicht auf Namenlosigkeit, sondern auf der geheimnisvollen Entstehungsgeschichte einer solch herrlichen Parade zeitgenössischer Kunst.

Ich darf dies mit Recht behaupten, da ich über vierzig Jahre lang dem Kern des Geheimnisses sehr nahe war. Vor dem Erscheinen der ersten Nummer von GRAPHIS zog mich Dr. Walter Amstutz bezüglich eines Namens für die neue Zeitschrift zu Rate. Der von mir vorgezogene Titel wurde am Ende nicht gewählt, aber während der nächsten zwanzig Jahre übersetzte und redigierte ich Texte für die Zeitschrift, und schliesslich kehrte ich der technischen Welt, in der ich lange Zeit so etwas wie ein «Hochstapler» gewesen war, den Rücken und trat dem redaktionellen Team bei. Nun befand ich mich wirklich selbst am erwähnten stillen Mittelpunkt. Ich konnte das schöpferische Herz schlagen hören. Doch wie Professor Goswamy musste ich die Ohren spitzen, denn es schlug sehr leise.

Dies hatte viel mit dem Charakter von Walter Herdeg zu tun, der ein zurückhaltendes Naturell besitzt, und obwohl er sich immer über Anerkennung freut, scheut er das Rampenlicht und fürchtet nichts mehr, als Reden halten zu müssen. Diese Haltung schien sich auf sein Umfeld zu übertragen. Viele seiner engsten Mitarbeiter waren recht zugeknöpft und gaben unaufgefordert nur wenig von sich. Jeder arbeitete in seinem eigenen kleinen Reich still vor sich hin. Das Klima war nie sehr kommunikativ. Natürlich waren Helfer nötig, um das ansehnliche Arbeitspensum bewältigen zu können. Unter diesen gab es einige Assistant Editors,

junge Designer gewöhnlich, und ich bin immer noch voller Bewunderung angesichts ihrer Leistungen. Die meisten blieben nur zwei oder drei Jahre, aber sie müssen wohl eine Menge gelernt haben, denn viele waren später sehr erfolgreich. Ich brauche nur Paul Arthur zu erwähnen, der sich in Kanada einen Namen als Redakteur und Designer einer Zeitschrift gemacht hat; oder Ken Baynes, einen der grössten Experten auf dem Gebiet des Graphik-Designs in Grossbritannien.

Da Walter Herdeg immer noch der ehrlichen Überzeugung war, er brauche eine rechte Hand, folgten ein oder zwei weitere Assistenten, nachdem ich bereits zum Inventar gehörte. Doch es wäre sinnlos, in den Umschlägen nach ihrem Einfluss suchen zu wollen. Alles in allem kamen recht viele Leute zu GRAPHIS im festen Glauben, dass sie eine aktive Rolle in der Gestaltung dieser angesehenen Zeitschrift spielen würden; dass sie, in engem Einvernehmen mit der grauen Eminenz persönlich, an seinen Entscheidungen teilhaben und wichtige Agenten in einem grossartigen Gärungsprozess kreativer Teamarbeit sein würden. Doch soweit kam es nie. Obwohl eine Symbiose manchmal in bescheidenem Rahmen zu funktionieren schien, verlief sie schliesslich immer im Sand. Die «rechten Hände» begriffen allmählich, dass sie niemals viel zu sagen haben würden. Frustration überkam sie, und einer nach dem andern blieben sie auf der Strecke.

Ich war der einzige, dessen Mitarbeit alle durch diese Umschlagseiten dokumentierten zweiundvierzig Jahre überdauerte, und das ist auch meine einzige Qualifikation für das Verfassen dieser einleitenden Worte. Wenn ich so lange durchgehalten habe, liegt es teils daran, dass ich keine Ausbildung in Graphik-Design hatte und somit auch nicht das Recht, das Urteilsvermögen eines Menschen in Frage zu stellen, dessen Erfahrung und Wissen so überlegen sind. Ich konzentrierte mich mehr auf die literarischen Aspekte. Ich glaube, ich hatte mit Walter Herdeg auch einen gewissen an Halsstarrigkeit grenzenden Charakterzug gemeinsam - eine Tendenz zu einem steifen Rückgrat. In unserer zweiundvierzigjährigen Zusammenarbeit kamen wir uns zwar näher, aber wir brachten es nie soweit, uns beim Vornamen zu nennen. Heute, im Alter, haben wir beide Rückenprobleme; ihn hindern sie manchmal daran, seinem geliebten Golf zu frönen, und die meinen scheinen gegen meine Leidenschaft fürs Gärtnern Einspruch zu erheben.

Eigentlich ist es paradox, dass die Umschläge von GRAPHIS so berühmt geworden sind. Denn die Zeitschrift unterschied sich just dadurch von allen andern, dass sie nicht von der Wirksamkeit ihrer Umschläge abhing. Sie war eigentlich zu teuer, um viele Spontankäufer am Zeitungsstand anzulocken. Ihre Leserschaft bestand hauptsächlich aus Abonnenten, und lange zählte die Auflage etwa 20000 Exemplare. Das Blickfang-Attribut war somit nur ein sekundäres Moment. Doch die Umschläge fielen ins Auge und wurden ein inhärentes Merkmal der Zeitschrift. Die Herausgeber erkannten dies: die Gänge der GRAPHIS-Büros sind mit der gesamten Umschlaggalerie tapeziert und präsentieren sich stolz den Besuchern.

Das Beschaffen der Umschlagentwürfe gestaltete sich relativ einfach. Es kam manchmal vor, dass sich beim Material, das ein Künstler für einen grösseren Artikel eingesandt hatte, passende Werke befanden. Walter Herdeg war unter der Unmenge von Arbeiten, die durch seine Hände gingen, immer auf der Suche nach Motiven für einen gelungenen Umschlag. Häufig konnte er bezüglich seiner Wünsche auch genaue Instruktionen geben, die auf einem Teilaspekt im Werk des Künstlers basierten. Manchmal wurden Künstler auch eingeladen, Umschläge zu entwerfen, und gelegentlich entstanden peinliche Momente, wenn die eingesandten Pakete geöffnet wurden und das Resultat der Bemühungen den Erwartungen des Herausgebers nicht entsprach. Aber es herrschte nie ein Mangel an Umschlagentwürfen. Sie strömten unablässig herein und wurden oft auf gut Glück von Künstlern und Designern eingesandt, die sich sehnlichst wünschten, ihre Arbeit auf der Titelseite von GRAPHIS zu sehen. Einige waren sogar gewillt, die Kosten für die Farbreproduktion zu übernehmen. Dank dieser Wettbewerbssituation und der grossen Werbewirksamkeit eines GRAPHIS-Umschlages wurde nie ein Honorar für einen Entwurf bezahlt. Diese erstaunliche Tatsache trifft sogar für die Picassos zu – durch die Vermittlung von Daniel-Henry Kahnweiler gab Picasso seine Zustimmung, und es erfolgte keine Zahlung. Als versöhnliche Geste jenen gegenüber, deren Werke nicht angenommen waren, erschienen von Zeit zu Zeit Artikel mit den besten unveröffentlichten Umschlagentwürfen – und viele standen den verwendeten Arbeiten kaum nach.

War ein Projekt einmal für gut befunden worden, unternahm man ungeheure Anstrengungen, um eine optimale Wiedergabequalität zu erzielen. Gewöhnlich mussten Name und Nummer von GRAPHIS von den Mitarbeitern im Studio eingepasst werden, und ein Designer war manchmal tagelang mit der Schrift beschäftigt und probierte immer wieder neue Varianten auf Folie aus. In einigen Fällen wurden bis zu zwölf verschiedene Farben geprüft. Als das Heft Nr. 91 erschien, erhielten wir von Ben Nicholson das grosse Kompliment, er hätte die Titelschrift selber nicht besser gestalten können. Intensiv wurde auch daran gearbeitet, den Titel der Nr. 140 als Teil eines Musters von zerrissenen Plakaten zu gestalten, und als Nr. 185 bereits gedruckt worden war, befand man die weisse Schrift nicht als das Nonplusultra: ein Designer musste wenigstens beim Ausstellungsexemplar das definitive Rosa hineinmalen.

Jeder, der das Defilee der Umschläge ansieht, wird feststellen, dass es das wechselnde Stilempfinden im Graphik-Design während nahezu eines halben Jahrhunderts widerspiegelt. Die Übergänge sind allerdings nicht eindeutig – die poetischen und malerischen Werke der früheren Jahre zum Beispiel stehen recht lange neben der neuen, informativen Klarheit der sechziger Jahre. Manche Graphiken sind natürlich veraltet, aber es finden sich erstaunlicherweise auch einige, die ihrer Zeit weit voraus waren – der Tarzan von Nr. 171 zum Beispiel, der noch verblüffend modern wirkt. Nicht weniger eindrucksvoll ist die Tatsache, dass alle nur erdenklichen Kunstformen vertreten sind. Feder- und Kreidezeichnungen, Öl- und Acrylbilder, Lithographien, Radierungen, Aquatinten, Holz- und Linolschnitte, Photographien, dreidimensionale Kunstwerke – die ganze Palette. Diese Universalität der Ausdrucksformen entspricht einer Universalität des Stils: Walter Herdeg erkannte Qualität sofort, und trotz einer gewissen Zurückhaltung – er zögerte bei der Nr. 195, weil er fürchtete, sie könne das Feingefühl einiger Leser verletzen – war er neuen und selbst gewagten Tendenzen gegenüber sehr aufgeschlossen, vorausgesetzt, er entdeckte darin einen Schimmer von Schönheit und Talent.

Die Umschläge der Jahrbücher unterscheiden sich in gewissem Masse von den Zeitschriftenumschlägen; jene für PHOTOGRAPHIS oder die Packungsbücher z.B. verfolgen eine viel strengere stilistische Linie. Sie wurden allerdings nach denselben ästhetischen Kriterien und mit demselben Qualitätsanspruch ausgewählt und reproduziert.

Die Umschläge zogen die Leserschaft von GRAPHIS in den Bann, und sie faszinierten auch die Belegschaft, die sich mit ihnen befasste. Oft standen wir in den Gängen herum, verglichen sie und wählten unsere Lieblingsstücke aus, wie es die Leser dieses Buches nun selbst auch tun können. Es erscheint eigentlich fast gehässig, angesichts solcher Reichtümer einzelne Werke hervorzuheben, aber einige waren beispielsweise entzückt von Günther Kiesers origineller arcimboldohafter Komposition (Nr. 184), andere von der technischen Brillanz von Braldt Bralds' Katzen (Nr. 215). Wieder andere bewunderten die subtile Beherrschung des Farbenspiels in James McMullans Revolver (Nr. 213), den Symbolismus von Roger Hanes' «beflügeltem» Stiefel (Nr. 167), die geheimnisvolle Nostalgie von Richard Hess' Bahnhof (Nr. 178) oder die Streichhölzer von Etienne Delessert (Nr. 208), während Saul Steinbergs Frauenkopf (Nr. 123) immer Anklang fand. Soviel zu einigen Zufallstreffern – der Leser kann sich nun ein eigenes Bild machen.

Die Umschläge bedeuteten mir sehr viel, und es wurde zur Regel, dass ich jeweils einen kurzen Kommentar dazu schrieb. Gewöhnlich war nur wenig Information vorhanden. Ich zog mich also in mein Büro zurück und traf mich zu einem innigen Tête-à-Tête mit dem Bild des Künstlers. Hier war ein Winkel, in dem ich meine eigene Phantasie entfalten und mir mein eigenes Urteil über das Graphik-Design bilden konnte. Zweifellos projizierte ich gelegentlich Gedanken in die Bilder, die dem Künstler nie eingefallen wären; aber ich genoss beispielsweise die philosophische Ambivalenz von André François oder die schalkhaften Implikationen von Roland Topor oder Eugène Mihaesco. Und diese Sitzungen lehrten mich etwas: dass jeder dieser Umschläge mehr enthielt, als auf Anhieb zu sehen war.

Man würde erwarten, dass es eine Menge Anekdoten zu den Entstehungsgeschichten dieser Umschläge zu erzählen gibt. Wie die des polnischen Plakatkünstlers Franek Starowieyski etwa, der anlässlich eines Besuches in Zürich gebeten wurde, einen Umschlag zu gestalten: er ging hin, kaufte Papier und Farben, zog sich in sein Hotel zurück und tauchte am nächsten Morgen mit dem fertigen Bild auf (Nr. 157). Doch will man mehr erfahren, so sind die früheren Mitarbeiter ratlos. Legenden konnten sich nie verbreiten, weil jeder in seiner eigenen kleinen Domäne arbeitete. Zweifellos hat Walter Herdeg einige Geschichten auf Lager, aber dieses Buch soll eine Überraschung für ihn sein, und daher können wir ihn nicht befragen.

Ein abschliessendes Wort sei noch über den Mann gesagt, der all diese Umschläge ausgewählt und in gewissem Sinne auch ins Leben gerufen hat. Sie eignen sich hervorragend, um sein Lebenswerk zu veranschaulichen: dieses gewaltige Potential an Erfahrung, Stilgefühl, Urteilsvermögen und harter Arbeit, das er in seinen Beruf einbrachte, die gleichbleibend hohen ästhetischen Ansprüche, die er stellte, den stimulierenden und inspirierenden Einfluss, den er auf das Graphik-Design des 20. Jahrhunderts ausübte. Er war in der Tat ein Alleingänger und seine Arbeitsweise recht zurückgezogen. Vieles, was ich oben über die Umschläge gesagt habe, vermittelt sich uns aus einer Welt der Stille. Doch keine Stille war für mich je so beredt.

Stanley Mason, der Autor dieses Vorwortes, wurde 1917 in Kanada geboren. Er ist britischer Staatsbürger und lebt seit vielen Jahren in der Schweiz. Von 1963-1983 war er Assistant Editor beim Graphis Verlag. Heute arbeitet er als Schriftsteller und freier Übersetzer.

1966

In his office
In seinem Büro
Dans son bureau

1975

At the AGI meeting in Greece

Am AGI Treffen in Griechenland

Au congrès de l'AGI en Grèce

Il se trouve qu'au moment où j'ai été informé de la mise en chantier du présent ouvrage, je m'occupais de peinture indienne ancienne. Je venais de prendre connaissance de ce qu'écrivait B.N. Goswamy, professeur d'histoire de l'art à l'Université du Pendjab à Chandigarh: «Il semblerait qu'au plan des faits la peinture indienne soit un monde du silence où il faut vraiment tendre l'oreille pour percevoir les chuchotements venant du passé.» La peinture indienne et les couvertures des publications GRAPHIS ont beau avoir l'air d'appartenir à deux mondes différents, je n'en ai pas moins été frappé par un certain parallélisme. Les couvertures de GRAPHIS de l'ère Walter Herdeg proviennent également d'un monde du silence, particulièrement depuis que cette ère est révolue. Pendant 42 ans, les couvertures du magazine ont paru au rythme d'une tous les deux mois; elles surprenaient et ravissaient, impressionnaient et intriguaient un bon nombre de ceux qui se trouvaient loin du lieu de leur genèse et ne savaient pratiquement rien des mécanismes inhérents à leur conception et à leur production. Il est vrai que des curieux venaient occasionnellement se renseigner à la source, mais dans l'ensemble les visiteurs ont plutôt été rares. Les Américains étaient les mieux représentés. Ils débarquaient à Zurich pensant trouver une équipe de rédaction importante, des grands studios remplis de créatifs survoltés, et probablement aussi une imprimerie annexe. La réalité les déconcertait: quelques bureaux feutrés occupés sporadiquement par une poignée de maquettistes, de plumitifs et de secrétaires sans prétention. En fait, il s'agissait d'un centre bien silencieux, et maintenant que Walter Herdeg s'en est discrètement retiré, toute personne contemplant les 246 numéros du magazine et les nombreux ouvrages qu'il publia et réalisa – représentés ici par autant de couvertures remarquables – doit nécessairement aboutir à la conclusion que j'ai fait mienne, à savoir que cet œuvre magistral, tout comme la peinture indienne, nous apparaît porté par une vague de puissance, mais n'émane pas moins d'un vaste silence.

Silence qui n'est, il faut bien l'admettre, pas tout à fait celui de la tradition indienne. Les artistes du sous-continent brillent par leur anonymat, n'ayant jamais signé leurs œuvres. Les couvertures reproduites dans cet ouvrage portent toutes le nom de l'artiste et constituent un rôle prestigieux, de Munch à Picasso en passant par Steinberg et Glaser. Le silence n'est pas fonction de l'anonymat, mais de l'obscurité relative qui a présidé à la genèse de cette extraordinaire parade d'art et de design de notre siècle.

Je me sens en droit de l'affirmer après avoir côtoyé le cœur même du mystère pendant une quarantaine d'années. Dès avant la parution du premier numéro de GRAPHIS, le Dr Walter Amstutz prit conseil auprès de moi pour déterminer le nom du nouveau périodique. Celui que je proposai ne fut pas retenu. Pendant les vingt premières années du magazine, je me suis chargé de travaux de traduction et de rédaction pour GRAPHIS, après quoi j'ai quitté le monde de l'ingénierie où j'avais si longtemps joué avec succès le rôle de l'imposteur, pour rejoindre l'équipe rédactionnelle. Désormais j'étais réellement, personnellement admis dans le saint des saints où je percevais les battements du cœur créatif. Pourtant, même alors, j'ai dû tendre l'oreille comme le Pr Goswamy, tant il battait doucement.

Cela a à voir avec le caractère de Walter Herdeg. Cet homme plein de réserve ne dédaigne pas les honneurs, mais fuit comme la peste la lumière des projecteurs et ne redoute rien autant que d'avoir à faire un discours. Cette attitude semble avoir déteint sur son entourage. La plupart de ses proches collaborateurs vivaient repliés sur eux-mêmes, ne

faisaient guère circuler l'information, uniquement préoccupés de leur tâche. Cet environnement n'a jamais été très communicatif. Il fallait bien sûr des auxiliaires pour mener à bien cette formidable entreprise. Certains jouaient le rôle de rédacteurs en chef adjoints. C'était en règle générale de jeunes designers dont les performances m'arrachent encore des vivats d'admiration. Ils ne restaient souvent pas plus de deux ou trois ans, le temps de faire leurs armes, puis repartaient gonflés à bloc pour une carrière à succès. Je n'ai qu'à rappeler le nom de Paul Arthur, qui s'est taillé une belle réputation de rédacteur et designer au Canada, ou celui de Ken Baynes, devenu l'un des meilleurs essayistes britanniques en matière de design graphique. Cette série de succès remarquables s'arrêta net lorsque je pris mes fonctions.

Pourtant, Walter Herdeg restant sincèrement convaincu qu'il lui fallait une main droite, un ou deux autres adjoints suivirent lorsque le jour arriva où je fis partie de l'inventaire. Il serait néanmoins futile de chercher une quelconque trace de leur influence dans le choix des couvertures. Il faut bien dire qu'un tas de gens ont rejoint l'équipe de GRAPHIS fermement convaincus qu'ils allaient jouer un rôle actif dans la mise en œuvre de ce prestigieux magazine, qu'ils participeraient aux décisions une fois admis dans l'intimité du grand chef et qu'ils deviendraient des acteurs importants au sein d'une équipe créative en pleine effervescence. Il n'en fut rien. La symbiose semblait bien fonctionner à petite échelle pendant un certain temps, puis le feu s'éteignait. Les mains droites ne tardaient pas à se rendre compte qu'ils n'avaient pas grand-chose à dire. La frustration s'emparait d'eux, et l'un après l'autre ils décrochaient.

Je suis le seul dont la collaboration a couvert toute la période de 42 ans constellée par ces couvertures, et c'est bien mon unique qualification pour ces commentaires offerts en guise de préface. Si j'ai tenu aussi longtemps, c'est notamment parce que je ne venais pas du design et n'avais donc pas le droit de mettre en cause les verdicts de celui qui m'était bien supérieur en expérience et en connaissances. C'est ce qui m'a fait accentuer l'aspect littéraire de mon travail. Je pense que j'avais aussi en commun avec Walter Herdeg une qualité proche de l'opiniâtreté, une certaine inflexibilité. En 42 années de coopération, et bien que notre relation ait pris une forme amicale, nous ne sommes jamais parvenus à nous appeler par notre prénom. Aujourd'hui, à l'âge où nous sommes, l'échine que nous n'avons pas assouplie nous cause des ennuis, ce qui le fait renoncer à son golf favori et moi à mon violon d'Ingres, le jardinage.

Il est en un sens assez paradoxal que les couvertures de GRAPHIS aient pris une telle importance, car contrairement à la plupart des périodiques, ce magazine n'a jamais vraiment misé sur ses couvertures. Son prix était assez élevé pour ne pas induire à l'achat au kiosque sur une simple impulsion. Ses lecteurs ont donc été avant tout ses abonnés – pendant longtemps, une vingtaine de milliers de personnes. Les qualités tape-à-l'oeil étaient ainsi reléguées au second plan. Et pourtant, ces couvertures ont accroché l'attention et sont devenues l'une des caractéristiques majeures du magazine. L'éditeur s'en est rendu compte: les couloirs de GRAPHIS sont pavés d'une collection de couvertures exposées pour la délectation du visiteur et l'orgueil justifié de l'entreprise.

L'obtention des couvertures ne posait guère de problèmes. Les designs idoines étaient parfois repérés dans les matériaux soumis par tel collaborateur pour un article de fond. L'éditeur était de plus constamment à l'affût de motifs propres à fournir une bonne couverture dans la masse des travaux qui passaient entre ses mains. Il était souvent en mesure de fournir des instructions précises quant à ce qu'il désirait obtenir en s'inspirant d'une facette spécifique de l'œuvre d'un artiste. Une couverture pouvait aussi être sollicitée, et plus d'une fois il y eut des moments pénibles quand, à l'ouverture du paquet tant attendu, le résultat décevait l'espoir de l'éditeur. Pourtant, il n'y a jamais eu pénurie d'illustrations de couverture. Un flot continu les amenait sur la table de Walter Herdeg. Souvent des artistes et designers soumettaient leurs travaux dans le fol espoir de voir leur œuvre couronnée par une parution en couverture de GRAPHIS. Certains d'entre eux étaient même disposés à assumer les frais de la reproduction couleur. En raison même de cette compétition et du fait qu'obtenir une couverture dans GRAPHIS équivalait à un coup de pub brillant, aucun des artistes concernés n'a jamais touché d'honoraires. Cette règle étonnante a même valu pour les Picassos, avec l'aval de Picasso, Daniel-Henry Kahnweiler servant d'intermédiaire. Pour apaiser l'ire de ceux dont la couverture n'avait pas été acceptée, des articles occasionnels regroupaient le meilleur des «rebuts», qui s'avéraient souvent l'égal des couvertures publiées.

Une fois qu'un projet était accepté, un formidable effort était consenti en vue d'une qualité de reproduction optimale. En règle générale, le titre et le numéro de GRAPHIS étaient surajoutés avec les moyens du bord, et un designer pouvait passer des jours entiers à essayer de trouver un lettrage convenable. Dans certains cas, on allait jusqu'à essayer douze couleurs différentes. Lorsque la couverture du no 91 fut achevée, Ben Nicholson se déclara enchanté: il n'aurait pas mieux su insérer le titre. Le no 140 fut également l'objet d'une expérimentation ardue, puisqu'il requérait la présentation du titre au beau milieu d'affiches lacérées. Le no 185 avait déjà été tiré lorsque l'on s'avisa que le lettrage blanc n'était quand même pas la réponse optimale: un designer dut le transformer en rose au moins sur l'exemplaire destiné à l'exposition.

Quiconque parcourt cette kyrielle de couvertures notera la transformation progressive des goûts et des styles publicitaires en l'espace de près d'un demi-siècle. Les transitions se font imperceptiblement; c'est ainsi que les œuvres poétiques, picturales d'antan cohabitent encore un certain temps avec la nouvelle clarté informative des années 60. Certaines compositions commencent évidemment à dater; ce qui est plus surprenant, c'est que certaines autres qui semblent avoir été composées avant leur époque, tel le Tarzan du no 171, rendent un son résolument moderne. Ce qui n'est pas moins impressionnant, c'est que toutes les formes d'art imaginables sont représentées: les dessins à la plume et au pastel, les huiles et les acryliques, les lithos, les eaux-fortes, les aquatintes, les bois et les linos, les photos, les artefacts tridimensionnels – la gamme complète, quoi. Cette universalité des formes d'expression n'a d'égale que celle du goût. C'est que Walter Herdeg n'a pas tardé à reconnaître la qualité là où elle se manifestait. En dépit d'une certaine retenue – il hésita à froisser des sensibilités par le sujet du no 195 –, il était toujours ouvert à tout développement nouveau, voire audacieux à condition qu'il y vît briller l'étincelle de la beauté et du talent.

Les jaquettes des annuaires diffèrent quelque peu des couvertures du magazine. Ainsi, celles qui ont été exécutées pour PHOTOGRAPHIS ou les ouvrages d'emballagisme révèlent une ligne stylistique bien plus stricte. N'empêche qu'elles furent sélectionnées et reproduites selon les mêmes critères esthétiques rigoureux et avec la même recherche inlassable d'une qualité parfaite.

Les couvertures ont fasciné les lecteurs de GRAPHIS comme elles ont fasciné l'équipe qui s'est occupée de leur mise en valeur. Plus d'une fois, nous avons passé un moment dans les couloirs à comparer leurs mérites respectifs, tout comme le lecteur va avoir l'occasion de déterminer son favori. Il est vraiment détestable de devoir limiter l'énumération de toutes ces richesses à quelques titres seulement. Prenons notre courage à deux mains et disons que les lecteurs ont été particulièrement enchantés, entre autres, par la composition originale de Günther Kieser dans le style d'Arcimboldo (no 184), d'autres par la maîtrise technique de Braldt Bralds (les chats du no 215). D'autres encore ont admiré la subtile excellence chromatique du revolver de James McMullan (no 213), le symbolisme de la chaussure ailée de Roger Hane (no 167), la nostalgie teintée de mystère que respire la gare de Richard Hess (no 178) ou les allumettes d'Etienne Delessert (no 208). La tête de femme de Saul Steinberg (no 123) lui a valu l'admiration générale. Vous me pardonnerez ces quelques coups de serpe dans la jungle luxuriante des couvertures où vous vous taillerez aisément des sentiers avenants. Ces couvertures ont beaucoup signifié pour moi du fait que j'ai été appelé à en proposer de brèves interprétations. Sans disposer de beaucoup d'informations, je me retirais quelques heures dans mon bureau, en tête-à-tête avec l'image de l'artiste. Je pouvais alors déployer mon imagination et prendre conscience de mes propres réactions à la composition en question. Inévitablement j'ai parfois projeté dans ces images des pensées qui n'étaient certes pas venues à l'artiste, mais j'ai eu un plaisir inouï à frayer de la sorte avec la philosophie ambivalente d'un André François ou les implications sarcastiques d'un Roland Topor ou d'un Eugène Mihaesco. Ces séances m'ont appris que chacune des couvertures porte en elle un message plus profond que ce qu'elle en révèle à l'œil.

On s'attendrait à découvrir tout un côté anecdotique à ces illustrations de couverture. C'est ainsi que l'on se souvient de l'affichiste polonais Franek Starowieyski: de passage à Zurich, il se vit invité à réaliser une couverture. Il se précipita chez le marchand de couleurs, s'enferma dans sa chambre d'hôtel et réapparut le lendemain matin avec la composition que l'on a pu admirer en couverture du no 157. Autre chose à raconter? Les anciens secouent la tête. Comment voulez-vous que naissent des légendes si chacun s'enferme dans sa petite sphère de travail personnelle? Nul doute que Walter Herdeg en ait des savoureuses à raconter; mais comme cet ouvrage est une surprise que nous lui préparons, nous n'avons pu le consulter.

Pour terminer, braquons un instant le projecteur sur l'homme qui sélectionna toutes ces couvertures et un fut en quelque sorte le père spirituel. Elles symbolisent à merveille ses vertus intrinsèques: l'énorme fonds d'expérience, de goût, de jugement et de labeur assidu dont s'est nourri ce qu'il a parachevé, ses normes esthétiques invariablement exigeantes, l'influence qu'il a exercée sur l'art publicitaire du 20e siècle qui lui doit une forte somme de stimulations et d'inspirations. Il est vrai qu'il a été un réalisateur solitaire, replié sur lui-même, sur ses méthodes de travail particulières. Il y a beaucoup à dire au sujet de ces couvertures qui nous proviennent d'un monde du silence. Mais je ne connais pas de silence plus éloquent que celui-là.

Stanley Mason, l'auteur de cette préface, est né en 1917 au Canada. Il est citoyen anglais et vit depuis de nombreuses années en Suisse. Il était assistant éditeur aux éditions Graphis de 1963 à 1983. Aujourd'hui il travaille comme écrivain et traducteur indépendant.

1976

At the Biennale in Warsaw

An der Biennale in Warschau

A la Biennale de Varsovie

1944—1948

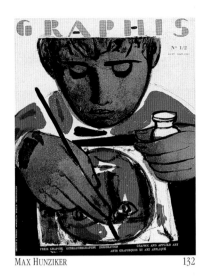

MAX HUNZIKER 132

E. HAEFELFINGER 132

EDVARD MUNCH 132

WERNER BISCHOF 132

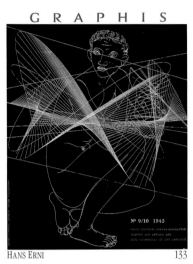

HANS ERNI 133

ANDRÉ DERAIN 133

IMRÉ REINER 133

MILNER GRAY 133

PAUL SOLLBERGER 134

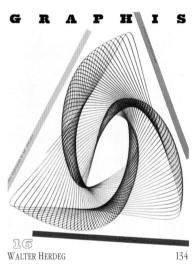

WALTER HERDEG 134

HANS ERNI 134

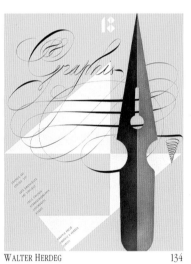

WALTER HERDEG 134

PABLO PICASSO 135

PIERO FORNASCETTI 135

JEAN-DENIS MALCLÈS 135

JACQUES N. GARAMOND 135

1948–1951

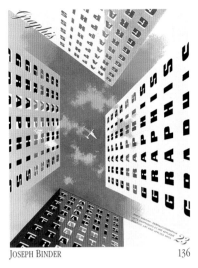

JOSEPH BINDER   136

PABLO PICASSO   136

HANS ERNI   136

GEORGE GIUSTI   136

JEAN PICART LE DOUX   137

HANS HARTMANN   137

JOSEPH BINDER   137

JAN BONS   137

THOMAS ECKERSLEY   138

JACQUES N. GARAMOND   138

CARLO DINELLI   138

ANTONIO CLAVÉ   138

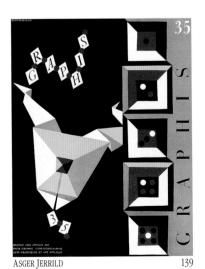

ASGER JERRILD   139

DONALD BRUN   139

F. H. K. HENRION   139

(CHILDREN'S COLLECTIVE PAINTING) 139

1952—1954

OLLE EKSELL   140

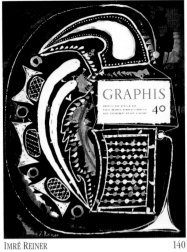

IMRÉ REINER   140

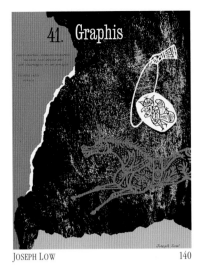

JOSEPH LOW   140

MAX HUNZIKER   140

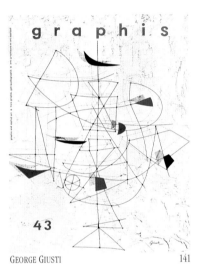

GEORGE GIUSTI   141

ANDRÉ FRANÇOIS   141

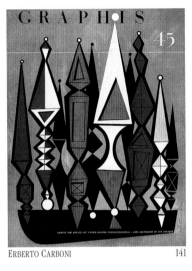

ERBERTO CARBONI   141

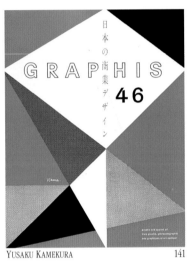

YUSAKU KAMEKURA   141

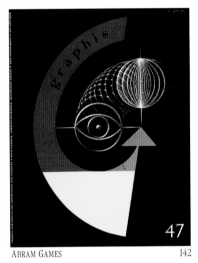

ABRAM GAMES   142

ARNE UNGERMANN   142

HANS HARTMANN   142

GOTTFRIED HONEGGER   142

MARCEL VERTÈS   143

PABLO PICASSO   143

HANS ERNI   143

BERTRAM A. TH. WEIHS   143

1954–1957

GRAPHIS 55

HANS FISCHER 144

GRAPHIS 56

PABLO PICASSO 144

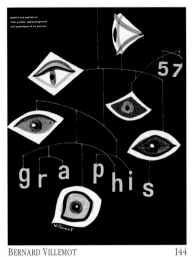

57

graphis

BERNARD VILLEMOT 144

58 graphis

ANDRÉ FRANÇOIS 144

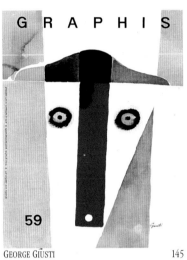

GRAPHIS

59

GEORGE GIUSTI 145

graphis

60

MICHAEL WOLGENSINGER 145

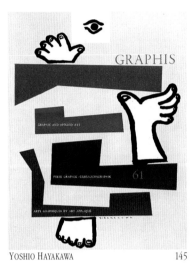

GRAPHIS

61

YOSHIO HAYAKAWA 145

GRAPHIS 62

BEN SHAHN 145

graphis 63

ANTONIO CLAVÉ 146

GRAPHIS 64

LEO LONGANESI 146

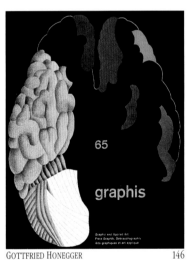

65

graphis

GOTTFRIED HONEGGER 146

GRAPHIS 66

CELESTINO PIATTI 146

67 graphis

UMETARO AZECHI 147

graphis 68

JOAN JORDAN 147

69 graphis

HERBERT AUCHLI 147

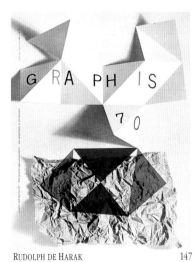

GRAPHIS 70

RUDOLPH DE HARAK 147

1957–1959

PHILIPPE DELESSERT   148

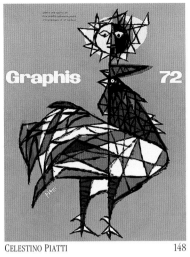

CELESTINO PIATTI   148

LE CORBUSIER   148

BERT STERN   148

JEAN LURÇAT   149

ANDRÉ FRANÇOIS   149

(CHILD'S PAINTING)   149

GEORGE GIUSTI   149

SINÉ   150

RONALD SEARLE   150

JACK WOLFGANG BECK   150

KURT WIRTH   150

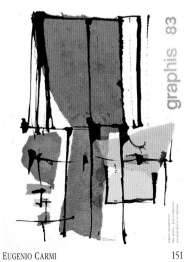

EUGENIO CARMI   151

STIG LINDBERG   151

HANS HARTMANN   151

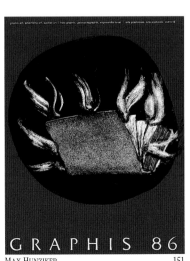

MAX HUNZIKER   151

1960—1962

87 GRAPHIS

GEORGE GIUSTI 152

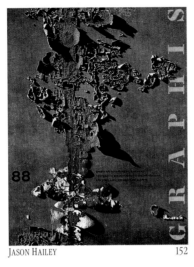

88

JASON HAILEY 152

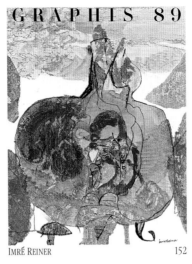

GRAPHIS 89

IMRÉ REINER 152

GRAPHIS 90

COLL. E. ERICKSON 152

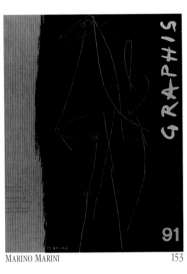

91

MARINO MARINI 153

92

ALAN FLECHTER 153

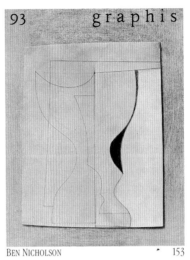

93 graphis

BEN NICHOLSON 153

Graphis 94

FRANCO GENTILINI 153

95 graphis

JAN LENICA 154

GRAPHIS 96

WILLY EIDENBENZ 154

GRAPHIS 97

HOOT VON ZITZEWITZ 154

GRAPHIS 98

HEIRI STEINER 154

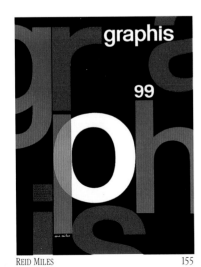

graphis 99

REID MILES 155

100 GRAPHIS

ANTONIO FRASCONI 155

GRAPHIS 1o1

FELIX MÜLLER 155

GRAPHIS 102

SEYMOUR CHWAST 155

1962–1965

PINO TOVAGLIA 156

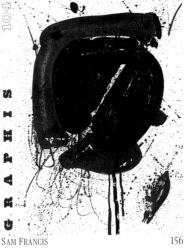

SAM FRANCIS 156

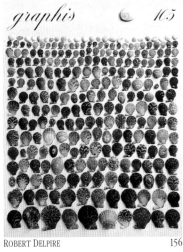

ROBERT DELPIRE 156

ANDRÉ FRANÇOIS 156

RICCARDO MANZI 157

FRANCO GRIGNANI 157

RAYMOND SAVIGNAC 157

WALTER GRIEDER 157

RITVA PUOTILA 158

PABLO PICASSO 158

HEINZ EDELMANN 158

ANDRÉ FRANÇOIS 158

CELESTINO PIATTI 159

EDUARD PRÜSSEN 159

FLAVIO COSTANTINI 159

HERBERT LEUPIN 159

1965–1967

FLETCHER, FORBES, GILL 160

TOMI UNGERER 160

EBERHARD G. RENSCH 160

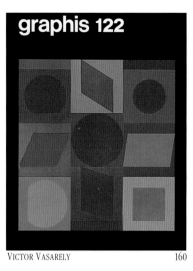

VICTOR VASARELY 160

SAUL STEINBERG 161

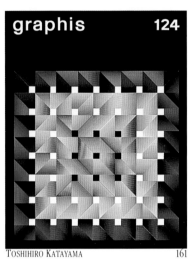

TOSHIHIRO KATAYAMA 161

EUGENE HOFFMAN 161

WALTER GRIEDER 161

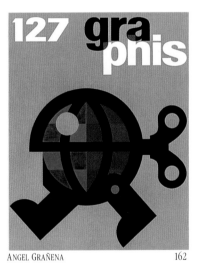

ANGEL GRAÑENA 162

ETIENNE DELESSERT 162

RONALD SEARLE 162

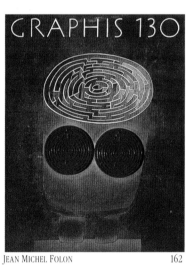

JEAN MICHEL FOLON 162

ELEONORE SCHMID 163

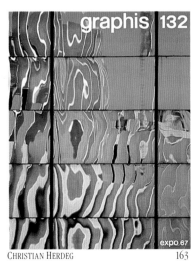

CHRISTIAN HERDEG 163

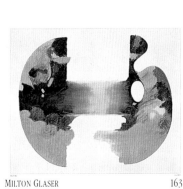

MILTON GLASER 163

ANTONIO FRASCONI 163

1968—1970

PETER MAX   164

GRAPHICTEAM   164

TOMI UNGERER   164

SOFU TESHIGAHARA   164

GENE LAURENTS   165

OLAF LEU   165

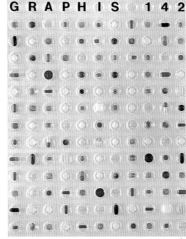

KEITH GODARD   165

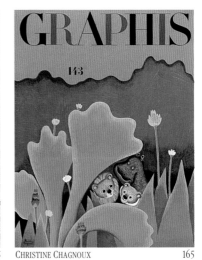

CHRISTINE CHAGNOUX   165

JOSSE GOFFIN   166

JAN LENICA   166

RICHARD GUYATT   166

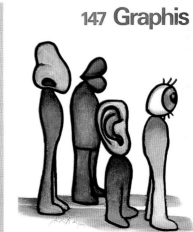

ANDRÉ FRANÇOIS   166

FRITZ GOTTSCHALK   167

F. G. BOES   167

TAKEJI IWAMIYA   167

ROLAND TOPOR   167

1970—1973

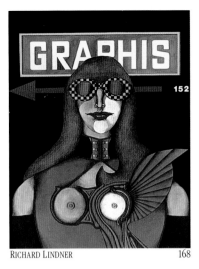

RICHARD LINDNER   168

VICTOR VASARELY   168

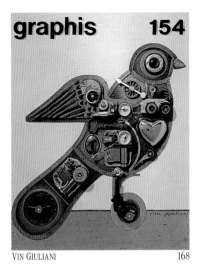

VIN GIULIANI   168

WALTER GRIEDER   168

JEAN MICHEL FOLON   169

FRANCISZEK STAROWIEYSKI   169

MERVYN KURLANSKY   169

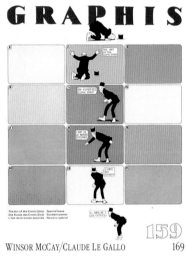

WINSOR MCCAY/CLAUDE LE GALLO   169

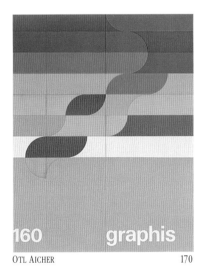

OTL AICHER   170

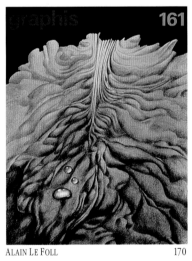

ALAIN LE FOLL   170

OLGA SIEMASZKO   170

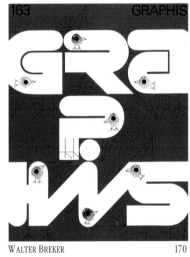

WALTER BREKER   170

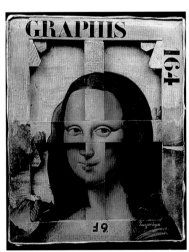

JEAN LAGARRIGUE   171

HANS ERNI   171

HEINZ EDELMANN   171

ROGER HANE   171

1973–1976

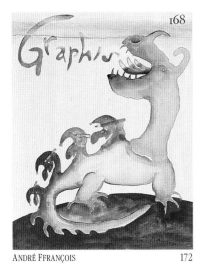

ANDRÉ FFRANÇOIS   172

RONALD SEARLE   172

HANS-GEORG RAUCH   172

TADANORI YOKOO   172

CHRISTIAN PIPER   173

JEAN MAZENOD   173

LES MASON   173

SEYMOUR CHWAST   173

EUGÈNE MIHAESCO   174

ÉTIENNE DELESSERT   174

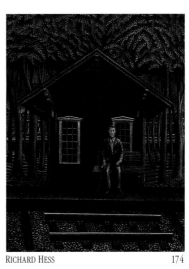

RICHARD HESS   174

ROLAND TOPOR   174

FRANCO GRIGNANI   175

ROY CARRUTHERS   175

PAUL DAVIS   175

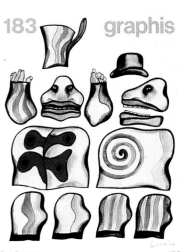

JAN LENICA   175

1976—1978

GÜNTHER KIESER 176

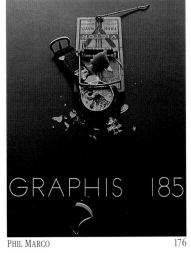

PHIL MARCO 176

HENRYK TOMASZEWSKI 176

ZÉLIO ALVES PINTO 176

TADANORI YOKOO 177

GÉRARD MIEDINGER 177

BARRIE TUCKER 177

RICHARD HESS 177

ALAIN LE FOLL 178

SOPHIE GRANDVAL 178

ALAIN GAUTHIER 178

ROLAND TOPOR 178

JACQUI MORGAN 179

SEYMOUR CHWAST 179

KAZUMASA NAGAI 179

JAMES MARSH 179

1978–1981

ANNEGERT FUCHSHUBER 180

TOMI UNGERER 180

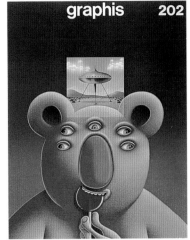

ROBERT GIUSTI 180

KIYOSHI AWAZU 180

WALTER BALLMER 181

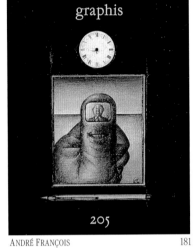

ANDRÉ FRANÇOIS 181

JAY MAISEL 181

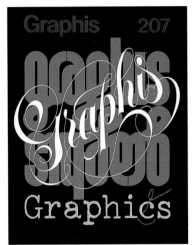

ALAN PECKOLICK, ERNIE SMITH, TONY DiSPIGNA 181

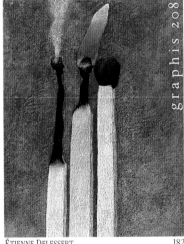

ÉTIENNE DELESSERT 182

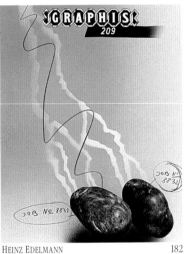

HEINZ EDELMANN 182

JAN SAWKA 182

FRANÇOIS ROBERT 182

HERBERT MATTER 183

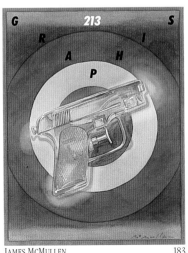

JAMES McMULLEN 183

GILBERT STONE 183

BRALDT BRALDS 183

1981—1984

216 graphis

ANDRÉ FRANÇOIS 184

Graphis 217

MILTON GLASER 184

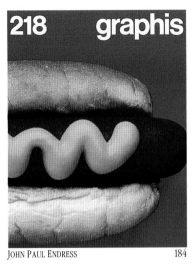

218 graphis

JOHN PAUL ENDRESS 184

219 graphis

JOSSE GOFFIN 184

LEO LIONNI 185

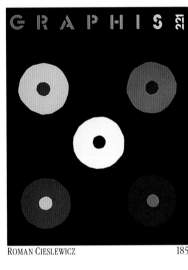

GRAPHIS 221

ROMAN CIESLEWICZ 185

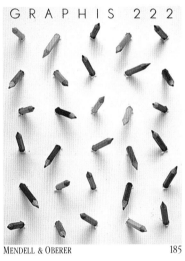

GRAPHIS 222

MENDELL & OBERER 185

GRAPHIS

223

HEINZ EDELMANN 185

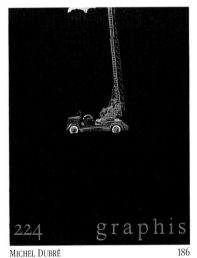

224 graphis

MICHEL DUBRÉ 186

225 graphis

MARVIN RUBIN 186

graphis 226

ZENJI FUNABASHI 186

graphis

227

EUGENE HOFFMAN 186

graphis 228

JACQUES N. GARAMOND 187

229 GRAPHIS

HOLGER MATTHIES 187

graphis 230

YUSAKU KAMEKURA 187

231

PAUL BRÜHWILEi 187

1984—1986

232 graphis

HANS HILLMANN 188

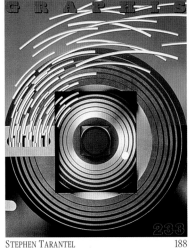

GRAPHIS

STEPHEN TARANTEL 188

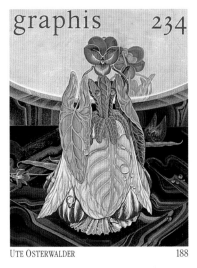

graphis 234

UTE OSTERWALDER 188

graphis 235

BRAD HOLLAND 188

GRAPHIS

JAN MLODOZENIEC 189

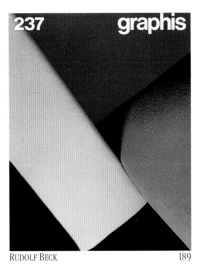

237 graphis

RUDOLF BECK 189

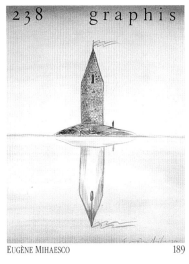

238 graphis

EUGÈNE MIHAESCO 189

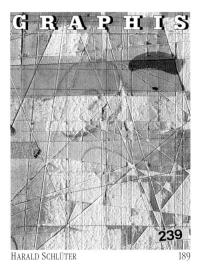

GRAPHIS

HARALD SCHLÜTER 189

GRAPHIS 240

Hiroshima 1945/1985
MINORU MORITA 190

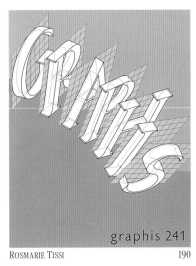

graphis 241

ROSMARIE TISSI 190

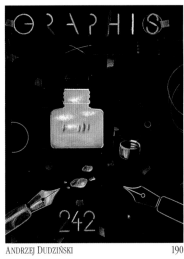

GRAPHIS

242
ANDRZEJ DUDZIŃSKI 190

graphis 243

MARSHALL ARISMAN 190

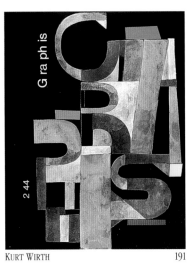

Graphis

2 44
KURT WIRTH 191

GRAPHIS 245

TAKENOBU IGARASHI 191

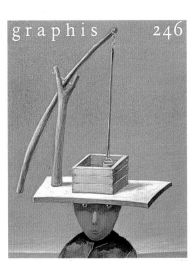

graphis 246

STASYS EIDRIGEVIČIUS 191

MAX HUNZIKER ▶

GRAPHIS

N° 1/2

SEPT./OKT. 1944

FREIE GRAPHIK   GEBRAUCHSGRAPHIK   DEKORATION   GRAPHIC AND APPLIED ART

ARTS GRAPHIQUES ET ART APPLIQUÉ

EDVARD MUNCH ▶

GRAPHIS

№ 5/6

AMSTUTZ & HERDEG
«GRAPHIS» ZURICH

PABLO PICASSO ▶

GRAPHIS

FREIE GRAPHIK UND GEBRAUCHSGRAPHIK
ARTS GRAPHIQUES ET ART APPLIQUÉ
GRAPHIS PRESS. ZÜRICH

Picasso

MAX HUNZIKER ▶

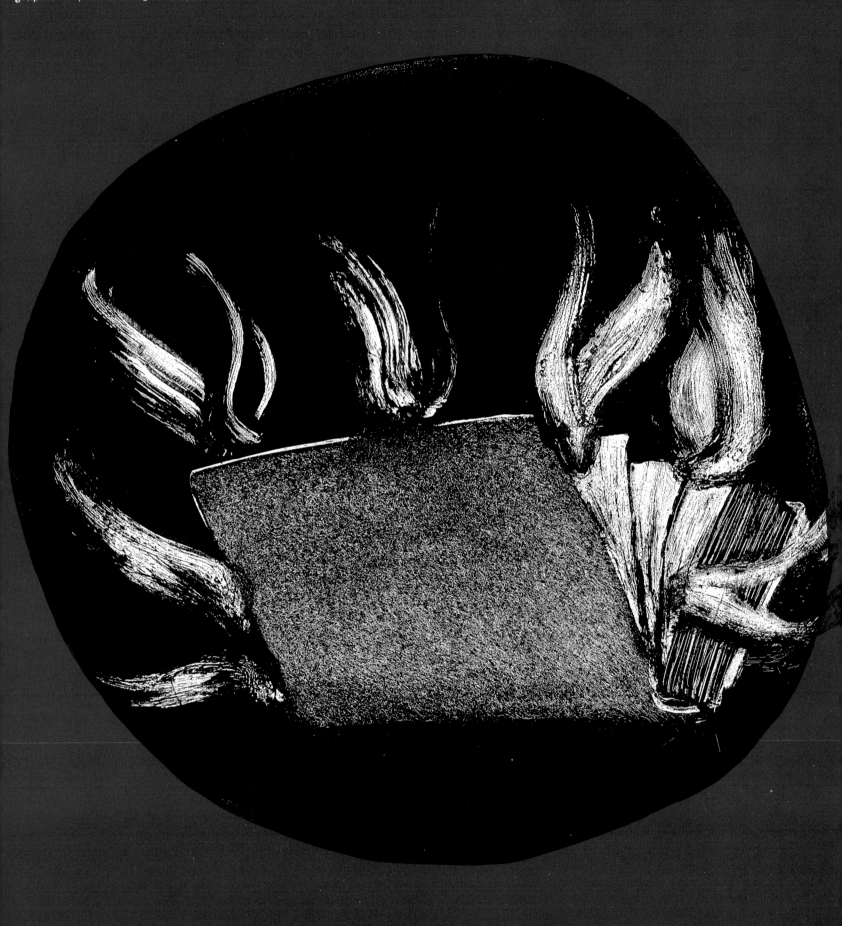

GRAPHIS 86

PABLO PICASSO ▶

FLETCHER, FORBES, GILL ▶

graphic and applied art
freie graphik, gebrauchsgraphik
art graphique et art appliqué

Graphis 119

R LONDON, W.C.1
No 7521

Eilsendung
Express - Espresso

LUFTPOST
PAR AVION VIA AEREA

DOUANE C.
(peut être ouvert d'office)

Part to be detached if the item is ac

Designation du contenu
Description of contents

Valeur
Value } N.C.V
Poids net
Net weight

BASEL2 E I ZUST
22. 1 65

DON'T CRUSH

Fletcher|Forbes|Gill Ltd 2 Irongate Wharf, London W2 Telephone Paddington 4041

Walter Herdeg
Graphis Press
Nuschelerstr. 45
Zurich
Switzerland

URGENT

TOMI UNGERER ▶

VICTOR VASARELY ▶

graphis 122

SAUL STEINBERG ▶

CHRISTIAN HERDEG ▶

graphis 132

expo 67

MILTON GLASER ▶

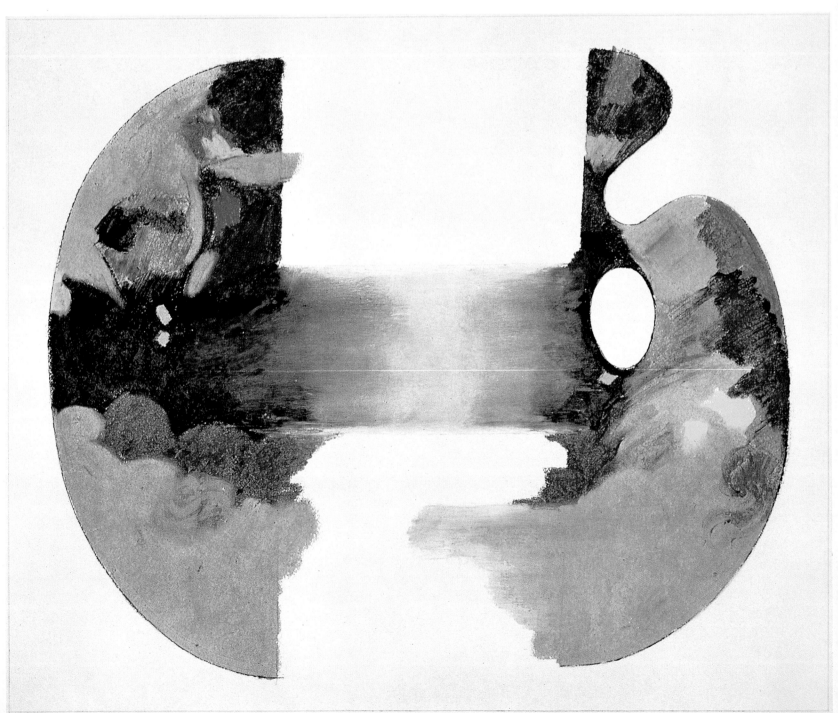

PETER MAX ▶

GRAPHIS

GRAPHIK UND ANGEWANDTE KUNST
ARTS GRAPHIQUES ET ARTS APPLIQUÉS
GRAPHIC ART AND APPLIED ART
GRAPHIS PRESS

135

peter max

MERVYN KURLANSKY ▶

GRAPHIS 158

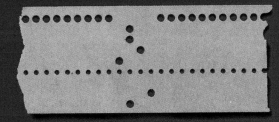

JEAN MAZENOD ▶

173 graphis

SEYMOUR CHWAST ▶

GRAPHIS 175

RICHARD HESS ▶

PAUL DAVIS ▶

Paul Davis

PHIL MARCO ▶

GRAPHIS 185

RICHARD HESS ▶

PECKOLICK, SMITH, DI SPIGNA ▶

Graphis   207

graphis

Graphis

Graphics

ÉTIENNE DELESSERT ▶

graphis 208

JAMES MC MULLEN ▶

213

BRALDT BRALDS ▶

ROMAN CIESLEWICZ ▶

GRAPHIS 221

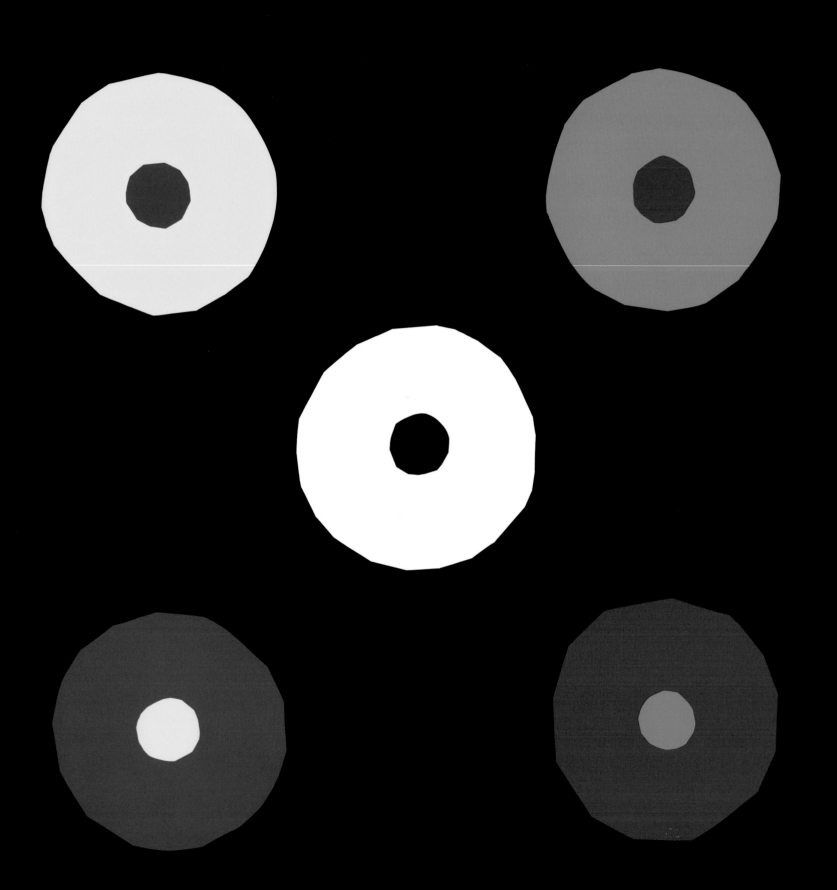

MENDELL & OBERER ▶

STEPHEN TARANTEL ▶

BRAD HOLLAND ▶

EUGÈNE MIHAESCO ▶

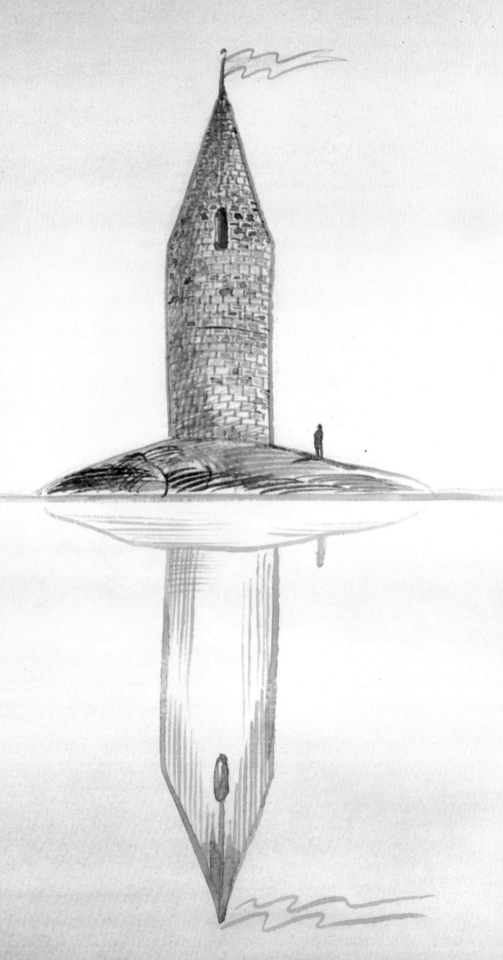

MINORU MORITA ▶

Hiroshima 1945/1985

ANDRZEJ DUDZINSKI ▶

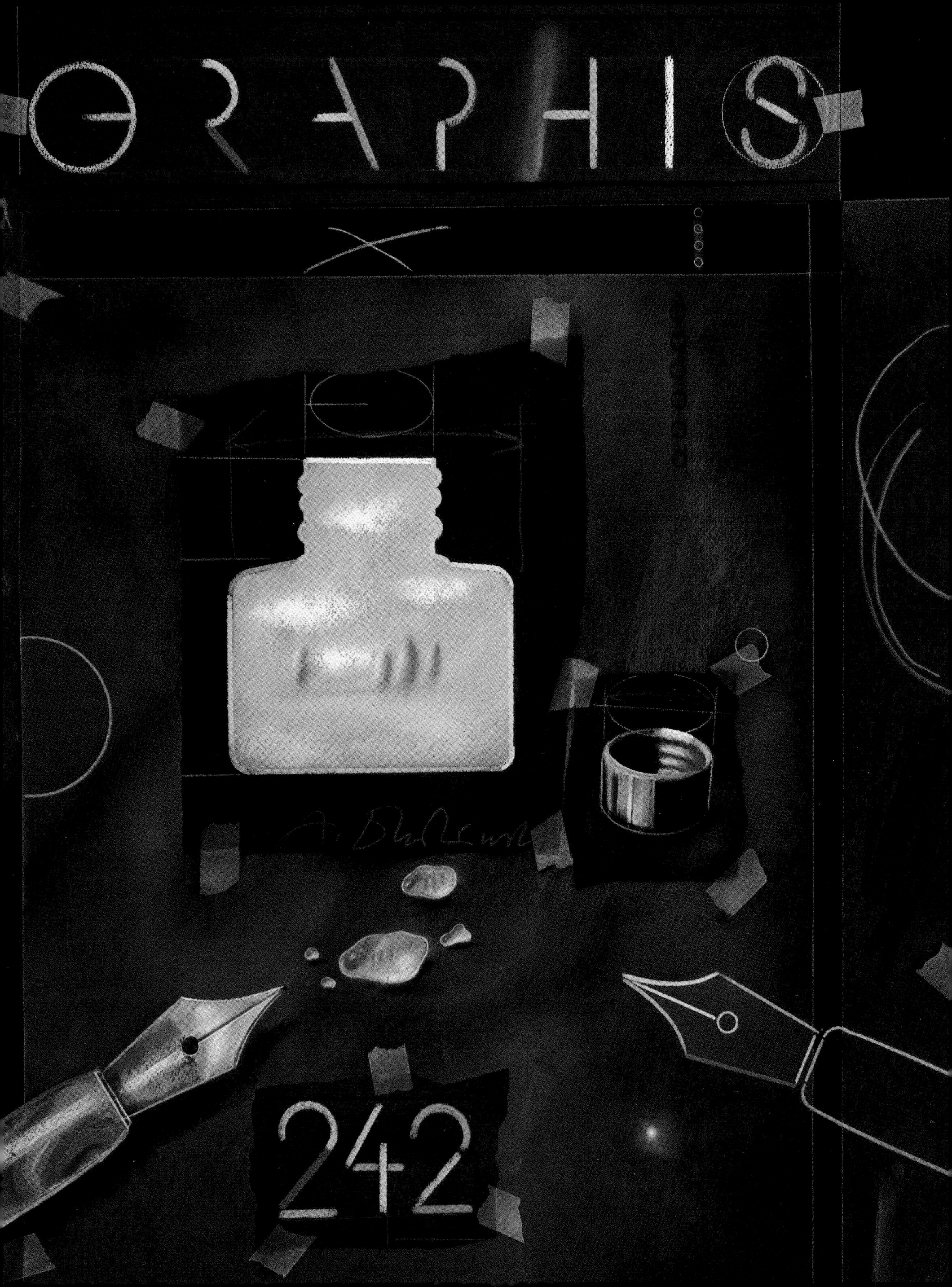
GRAPHIS
242

MARSHALL ARISMAN ▶

graphis

243

TAKENOBU IGARASHI ▶

1952–1963

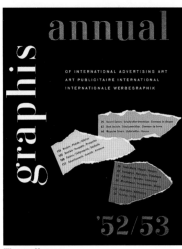

WALTER HERDEG

RAYMOND SAVIGNAC

ZERO

JACQUES N. GARAMOND

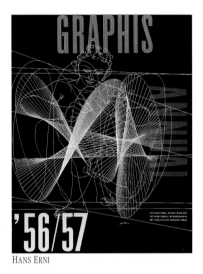

HANS ERNI

ADOLF FLÜCKIGER

CELESTINO PIATTI

GEORGE GIUSTI

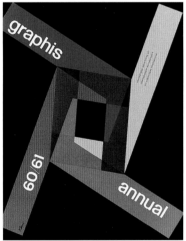

YUSAKU KAMEKURA

ARNO HAMMACHER

CELESTINO PIATTI

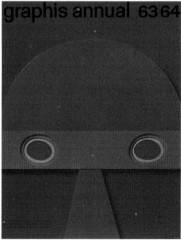

GEORGE GIUSTI

1964—1975

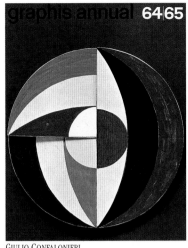

GIULIO CONFALONIERI

PINO TOVAGLIA

ROGER EXCOFFON

FRANCO GRIGNANI

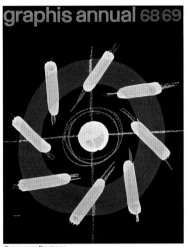

GIOVANNI PINTORI

RAYMOND SAVIGNAC

TOMI UNGERER

JEAN MICHEL FOLON

MASSIMO VIGNELLI

FRIEL

ANDRÉ FRANÇOIS

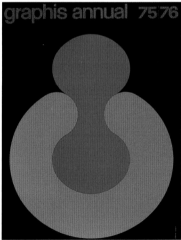

ERBERTO CARBONI

1976–1986

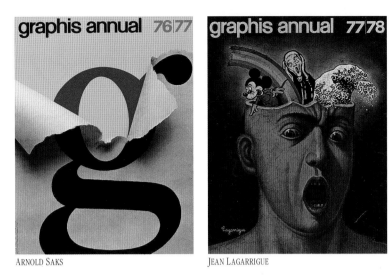

ARNOLD SAKS

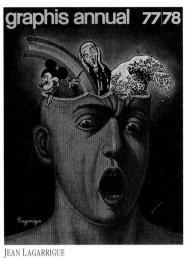

JEAN LAGARRIGUE

PAUL DAVIS

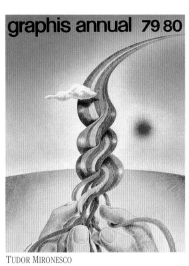

TUDOR MIRONESCO

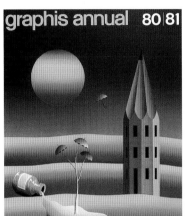

YOSHI KURI

SHIGEO FUKUDA

ANDRÉ FRANÇOIS

JEAN MICHEL FOLON

MILTON GLASER

IKKO TANAKA

ARNOLD SAKS

1966–1972

HANS-JÜRGEN RAU

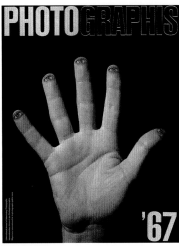

JOHN MASSEY

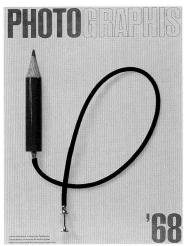

JACQUES DUBOIS

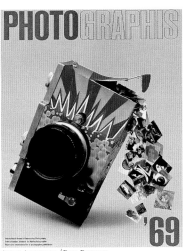

ALAN ALDRIDGE / BOB BROOKS

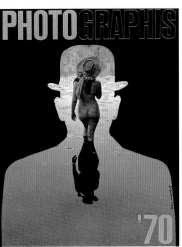

HENRY WOLF

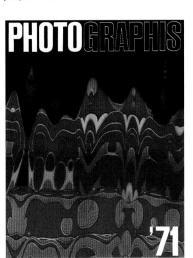

MASANOBU FUKUDA

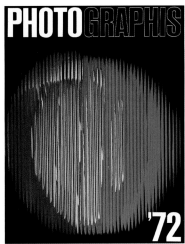

HUMBERT + VOGT

1973–1979

PHIL MARCO

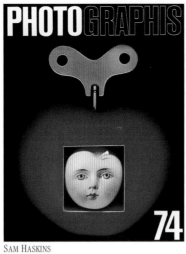

SAM HASKINS

HOLGER MATTHIES

HENRY WOLF

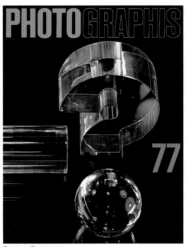

SYLVIA GOESCHKE

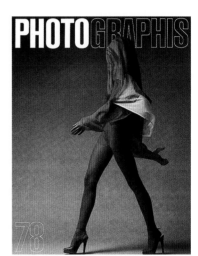

JACQUES SCHUMACHER

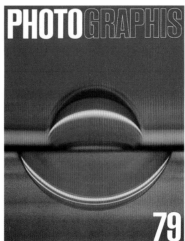

HUMBERT + VOGT

1980–1986

JAN LENICA

JIM LEWIS

TOMI UNGERER

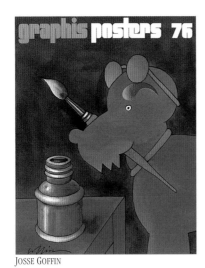

JOSSE GOFFIN

RAYMOND SAVIGNAC

HEINZ EDELMANN

ALAIN LE QUERNEC

1980–1986

RON BENVENISTI

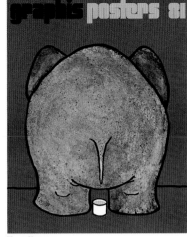

TOMI UNGERER

ROMAN CIEŚLEWICZ

SEYMOUR CHWAST

HOLGER MATTHIES

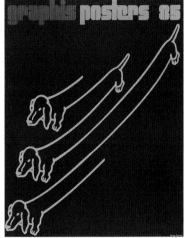

SHIGEO FUKUDA

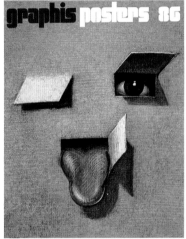

MIECZYSLAW GOROWSKI

ERBERTO GARBONI

SIEGFRIED ODERMATT / WERNER ZRYD

WALTER BALLMER

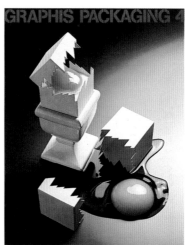

KATSU KIMURA

1959

1970

1977

1984

1974   **1980**

1978   **1974**

graphis diagrams

DIETMAR R. WINKLER

graphis ephemera

Artists' Self-Promotion
Künstler-Eigenwerbung
Auto-promotion des artistes

WALTER HERDEG

archigraphia

graphis

JEAN MICHEL FOLON

GRAPHIS

RECORD COVERS
CHEMISES DE DISQUES
PLATTENHÜLLEN

WALTER HERDEG/ULRICH KEMMNER

MAX HUNZIKER, born in Zürich, 1901. After spending five years working in Italy and a further fourteen years working in France, he returned to Zürich in 1939. He specializes in tempera technique and etchings for book illustrations, various graphic art work and also stained glass.

MAX HUNZIKER, 1901 in Zürich geboren, arbeitete während fünf Jahren in Italien und weitere 14 Jahre in Frankreich. 1939 kehrte er nach Zürich zurück. Er hat sich auf die Temperatechnik spezialisiert und auf Radierungen für Buchillustrationen sowie auf verschiedene Graphiken und Glaskunst.

MAX HUNZIKER, né à Zurich en 1901. Au terme de 19 années de travail à l'étranger – cinq en Italie, quatorze en France –, il rentre à Zurich en 1939. Spécialiste de la détrempe, il a aussi réalisé des eaux-fortes pour l'illustration de livres, divers travaux graphiques et des vitraux d'églises.

EUGEN HÄFELFINGER, 1898–1979, Swiss painter and designer. After craftsman training in Switzerland, he studied at the Applied Arts Academy in Dresden under Baranowsky and Guhr. After his return to Switzerland he became a portrait painter in Sissach, then changed in Zurich to wall painting and received commissions for room design at exhibitions (Swiss Fair) and festival events. Graffiti at the gymnasium of the Zürich High School, wall painting at the Engematthof.

EUGEN HÄFELFINGER, 1898–1979, Schweizer Maler und Raumkünstler. Nach handwerklicher Ausbildung in der Schweiz Studium an der Kunstgewerbeakademie in Dresden bei Baranowsky und Guhr. Nach seiner Rückkehr in die Schweiz wurde er Porträtmaler in Sissach, ging dann in Zürich zur Wandmalerei über und bekam Aufträge für Raumgestaltung bei Ausstellungs- (Schweizerische Messe) und Festanlässen. Sgraffiti an der Turnhalle der Kantonsschule in Zürich, Wandgemälde im Engematthof.

EUGEN HÄFELFINGER (1898–1979), peintre et designer d'intérieurs. Après une formation artisanale en Suisse, il s'en va étudier à l'Académie des arts décoratifs de Dresde sous la direction de Baranowsky et Guhr. A son retour en Suisse, il s'établit peintre de portraits à Sissach, puis part pour Zurich se consacrer à la peinture murale. Il exécute des décorations intérieures pour des expositions (la Foire suisse des échantillons, par exemple) et des festivals. Graffiti décorant la salle de gymnastique du Lycée cantonal de Zurich; peinture murale pour l'Engematthof.

EDVARD MUNCH, Norwegian, 1863–1944. Printmaker, lithographer, painter. Famous for his woodcuts using many colors and his highly expressionistic paintings showing basic human emotions such as fear, the best known being "The Cry".

EDVARD MUNCH, Norweger, 1863–1944. Graphiker, Lithograph, Maler. Berühmt für seine farbigen Holzschnitte und seine sehr ausdrucksstarken Gemälde, die meistens menschliche Emotionen darstellten, wie z. B. Angst. Sein wohl bekanntestes Bild ist «Der Schrei».

EDVARD MUNCH (1863–1944), graveur, lithographe et peintre norvégien. Célèbre pour ses bois polychromes et ses peintures très expressives qui mettent en scène les émotions fondamentales de l'être humain telles que l'angoisse. Son tableau le plus connu s'intitule «Le Cri».

WERNER BISCHOF 1916–1957. Photographer. He was born in Switzerland and studied in Zurich. After the war he turned to photo-journalism and reportage and gained world recognition from his features on Europe, India and later, Japan and Korea which were commissioned by several leading magazines. He suffered a fatal accident in the Andes in Peru at the age of forty-one.

WERNER BISCHOF 1916–1957. Photograph. Er wurde in der Schweiz geboren, war Schüler von Hans Finsler an der Kunstgewerbeschule in Zürich und zuerst der Sachphotographie zugetan. Seine Studien aus dieser Zeit beweisen ein ungewöhnliches künstlerisches Feingefühl für die Komposition und das Spiel von Licht und Schatten. Nach dem Zweiten Weltkrieg wandte er sich der Reportage zu. Im Auftrag verschiedener Zeitschriften bereiste er das blutende Europa, das hungernde Indien und später auch Japan. Er ist 1957 in den peruanischen Anden tödlich verunglückt.

WERNER BISCHOF (1916–1957). Photographe. Né en Suisse, il fut l'élève de Hans Finsler à l'Ecole des arts décoratifs de Zurich et se voua tout d'abord à la photographie d'objets. Il s'y distingua par son extrême sensibilité artistique, qui lui inspira des merveilles de composition et un jeu subtil des ombres et de la lumière. Au lendemain de la Seconde Guerre mondiale, il se fait reporter-photographe et acquiert une stature internationale. Il parcourt l'Europe en ruines, l'Inde affamée, par la suite aussi le Japon et la Corée pour le compte de divers grands magazines. En 1957, il meurt dans un accident dans les Andes péruviennes.

HANS ERNI, born in Switzerland, 1909. He was apprenticed as an architectural draftsman. Art studies in Paris and Berlin. He turned to lithography - and developed a new wash technique. His wide scope includes: paintings, drawings, murals, graphics, theater sets, and costumes, illustrations, ceramics, and posters for international institutions. The Hans Erni Foundation was established in 1977, the Hans Erni Museum was opened in Lucerne in 1979. His work has been shown in worldwide exhibitions and many awards and distinctions have been conferred on him.

HANS ERNI, 1909 in der Schweiz geboren. Kunststudien in Paris und Berlin. Beschäftigte sich dann hauptsächlich mit Lithographien und entwickelte dabei eine neue Waschtechnik. Zu seinem immensen Arbeitsbereich gehören Bilder, Zeichnungen, Wandgemälde, Graphik, Bühnenbilder und Kostüme, Illustrationen, keramische Arbeiten und Plakate für internationale Institutionen. 1977 Gründung der Hans-Erni-Stiftung, 1979 Eröffnung des Hans-Erni-Museums in Luzern. Seine Arbeiten wurden in Ausstellungen auf der ganzen Welt gezeigt und mit zahlreichen Preisen ausgezeichnet.

HANS ERNI, né en Suisse en 1909. Il fait un apprentissage de dessinateur-architecte, puis des études artistiques à Paris et à Berlin. S'intéressant à la lithographie, il met au point une nouvelle technique de lavage. Son vaste répertoire comprend des peintures, des dessins, des murals, des gravures, des décors et costumes de théâtre, des illustrations, des céramiques, des affiches pour des organisations internationales. La Fondation Erni date de 1977, le Musée Hans Erni à Lucerne de 1979. Ses œuvres ont été exposées de nombreuses fois à travers le monde et récompensées d'une série impressionnante de prix et de médailles.

ANDRÉ DERAIN, 1880-1954. French painter and one of the founders of Fauvism. He was befriended by Matisse and worked with the most famous artists of his time: Matisse in 1905, Picasso in 1907, Braque in 1913 and also with Vlaminck. His pre-war works are divided in three periods: Fauvism (the "Thames" series, 1905-6), African art and Cubism. His paintings are held in famous museums, including the Tate Gallery in London.

ANDRÉ DERAIN, 1880-1954. Französischer Maler und Mitbegründer des Fauvismus. Er war mit Matisse befreundet und arbeitete mit den berühmtesten Künstlern seiner Zeit zusammen: mit Matisse 1905, mit Picasso 1907, mit Braque 1913 sowie mit Vlaminck. Seine Arbeit wird in drei Perioden aufgeteilt: Fauvismus (die «Thames»-Serie, 1905-6), Afrikanische Kunst und Kubismus. Seine Bilder befinden sich in berühmten Museen, u. a. in der Tate Gallery, London.

ANDRÉ DERAIN (1880-1954). Peintre français, un des créateurs du fauvisme. Ami de Matisse, il travailla avec les génies de son epoque: Matisse en 1905, Picasso en 1907, Braque en 1913, Vlaminck. Dans son œuvre d'avant-guerre, on distingue trois périodes: celle du fauvisme (la série des «Tamise», 1905-6), la période «nègre» et la gothique proche du cubisme. Ses peintures se trouvent dans les grands musées du monde, notamment à la Tate Gallery de Londres.

IMRE REINER, born in Hungary, 1900. Typographer, painter, engraver, lithographer. He trained as a sculptor in Hungary. In 1920 he moved to Germany and studied graphic art in Stuttgart. After two years in the USA and Europe he settled in Switzerland in 1932 and became a Swiss citizen. He illustrated some 40 books, mostly with wood engravings, etchings and lithos for classical authors' works: Homer, Cervantes, Goethe, Voltaire, etc. From 1950 he worked with UNESCO in Paris. He has been exhibited widely in USA and Europe and his work has claimed numerous Gold Medals and awards.

IMRE REINER, 1900 in Ungarn geboren. Typograph, Maler, Graveur, Lithograph. In Ungarn erhielt er eine Ausbildung als Bildhauer. 1920 übersiedelte er nach Deutschland, wo er in Stuttgart Graphik studierte. Nach weiteren zwei Jahren in den USA und in Europa liess er sich 1932 in der Schweiz nieder und erhielt das Schweizer Bürgerrecht. Er hat rund 40 Bücher illustriert, meistens mit Holzschnitten, Radierungen und Lithographien, für Klassiker wie Homer, Cervantes, Goethe, Voltaire usw. Auch hat er verschiedene Arbeiten für die UNESCO gemacht. Er hatte zahlreiche Ausstellungen in den USA und Europa und erhielt diverse Goldmedaillen und Auszeichnungen.

IMRE REINER, né en Hongrie en 1900. Typographe, peintre, graveur, lithographe. Il suit une formation de sculpteur dans son pays natal, puis part en 1920 pour l'Allemagne, où il étudiera l'art graphique à Stuttgart. Il passe deux années aux Etats-Unis et en Europe, s'installe en Suisse en 1932 et prend la nationalité suisse. Il a illustré de ses bois, eaux-fortes et lithos une quarantaine d'ouvrages classiques - Homère, Cervantès, Goethe, Voltaire, etc. Dès 1950, il se met au service de l'Unesco. Ses travaux ont eu les honneurs de nombreuses expositions aux Etats-Unis et en Europe et lui ont valu force prix et médailles d'or.

MILNER GRAY, born in London, 1899. Studied painting and design in Great Britain. Exhibition designer, industrial designer, graphic arists. Founder, partner of the Design Research Unit in London. British President of AGI 1963-1971. Past master of the Faculty of Royal Designers for Industry.

MILNER GRAY, 1899 in London geboren. Studium der Malerei und Graphik in England. Graphik, Ausstellungs- und Industrie-Design. Gründer und Partner des «Design Research Unit» in London, britischer AGI-Präsident von 1963-71 und ehemaliger Leiter der Fakultät für Industrie-Design (Faculty of Royal Designers for Industry).

MILNER GRAY, né à Londres en 1899, a étudié la peinture et le design en Grande-Bretagne. Spécialiste du design d'expositions, esthéticien industriel, artiste graphique. Associé-fondateur de Design Research Unit à Londres. Président de la section britannique de l'AGI de 1963 à 1971. Ancien doyen de la Faculty of Royal Designers for Industry.

PAUL SOLLBERGER, born in Switzerland, 1913. Apprenticeship in a big graphic studio. Student at the Applied Arts School in Vienna 1933–34. Works as a freelance graphic artist since 1934.

■

PAUL SOLLBERGER, 1913 in der Schweiz geboren. Lehrzeit im Atelier eines graphischen Grossbetriebes. 1933–34 Schüler an der Kunstgewerbeschule in Wien. Arbeitet seit 1934 als freischaffender Graphiker.

■

PAUL SOLLBERGER, né en Suisse en 1913. Apprentissage des arts graphiques. Etudiant à l'Ecole des arts décoratifs de Vienne, 1933–34. Depuis 1934, artiste indépendant.

■

WALTER HERDEG, born in Zurich, 1908. He studied at the Kunstgewerbeschule in Zurich and with Prof. Hadank in Berlin. Further studies in Paris, London and New York. Initiator, designer, art director, editor of *Graphis*. (Formed partnership with Dr. W. Amstutz in 1938: Amstutz & Herdeg. First *Graphis* issue in 1944. In 1963 he founded Graphis Press) Annuals published: *Graphis Annual, Photographis, Graphis Posters* and books on special subjects. He retired from Graphis Press in 1986. In 1987 honored by the presentation of the "Walter" – an award of the Parson's School of Design, N.Y., named after him for graphic excellence – and by the "Medalist Award" of the AIGA.

■

WALTER HERDEG, 1908 in Zürich geboren. Studierte an der Kunstgewerbeschule in Zürich und bei Prof. Hadank in Berlin. Weitere Studien in Paris, London und New York. Initiator, Designer, Art Direktor und Herausgeber der Zeitschrift *Graphis* (Verlag Amstutz & Herdeg, 1938 gegründet. Erste *Graphis*-Ausgabe 1944. 1963 Gründung des Graphis-Verlags). Jahrbücher: *Graphis Annual, Photographis, Graphis Posters* sowie Bücher über Spezialgebiete. 1986 Rückzug aus dem Verlagsgeschäft. 1987 wurde er in New York mit dem «Walter», ein nach ihm benannter Graphikpreis der Parson's School of Design, und mit dem «Medalist Award» der AIGA ausgezeichnet.

■

WALTER HERDEG, né à Zurich en 1908. Ancien élève de l'Ecole des arts décoratifs de Zurich et du Pr Hadank à Berlin. Etudes à Paris, Londres, New York. Initiateur, designer, directeur artistique et éditeur de *Graphis* – d'abord en association avec le Dr. W. Amstutz dès 1938, sous la raison sociale Amstutz & Herdeg. Premier numéro de *Graphis* en 1944. Fonde en 1963 les Ed. Graphis. Annuels publiés: *Graphis Annual, Photographis, Graphis Posters*, ouvrages spéciaux. S'est retiré des Ed. Graphis en 1986. Honoré en 1987 par le prix «Walter» d'art graphique de la Parson's School of Design (New York), qui porte son nom, et par le «Medalist Award» de l'AIGA.

■

For short biography, see page 133.
HANS ERNI worked at first almost exclusively for public institutions. He began his career by studying architecture but stopped in order to better absorb the influence of the great exponents of abstract art: Mondrian, Calder, Kandinsky and the group "Blauer Reiter". He also studied the painters of the Renaissance – and Picasso – who was his greatest master.

■

Kurzbiographie Seite 133.
HANS ERNI hat seine Arbeit ursprünglich fast ausschliesslich in den Dienst der Öffentlichkeit gestellt. Die grossen Meister der abstrakten Kunst wie Mondrian, Calder, Kandinsky und die Gruppe «Blauer Reiter» haben ihn inspiriert. Aber auch die Maler der Renaissance hat er studiert und vor allem Picasso, der für ihn der grosse Lehrer war und bleibt.

■

Voir la notice biographique en p. 133.
HANS ERNI a travaillé à ses débuts presque exclusivement pour des collectivités. Il interrompit ses études d'architecture pour s'inféoder aux grands ténors de l'art abstrait – Mondrian, Calder, Kandinsky, les membres du «Blauer Reiter». Il a aussi beaucoup étudié les peintres de la Renaissance, ainsi que Picasso, qui reste pour lui le maître des maîtres.

■

For short biography, see page 134.
The quill – and its beautiful result – form the motif for this cover-design by WALTER HERDEG. The art of calligraphy through the centuries has always held a continual fascination for Herdeg. Inspired by masters of calligraphy of the 16th and 17th century, he drew lettering which had an everlasting elegance. The most famous of his handwritten pieces have lasted until the present time: the logotype used today by St. Moritz and also the logotype for the Café Littéraire in Zurich.

■

Kurzbiographie Seite 134.
Die Schreibfeder und ihr Ergebnis bilden das Motiv dieses Umschlagentwurfs von WALTER HERDEG. Die Kunst der Schönschrift durch die Jahrhunderte übte auf Herdeg bis heute eine ungebrochene Faszination aus. Inspiriert von Vorbildern des 16. und 17. Jahrhunderts (Barbedor-Stil) fertigte er Schriften von unvergänglicher Eleganz. Die berühmtesten von seiner Handschrift geprägten Entwürfe überdauerten bis heute: der Schriftzug von St. Moritz und des Café Littéraire in Zürich.

■

Voir la notice biographique en p. 134.
La plume et son tracé de toute beauté constituent le motif de cette couverture réalisée par WALTER HERDEG. L'art de la calligraphie tel qu'il a évolué au fil des siècles a toujours fasciné Herdeg. En s'inspirant des maîtres des XVIe et XVIIe siècles, il a calligraphié des caractères d'une rare élégance. Deux de ses créations impérissables sont encore sous tous les yeux: le logo de Saint-Moritz et celui dont s'enorgueillit le Café Littéraire de Zurich.

■

PABLO PICASSO (real name Pablo Ruiz y Picasso), 1881–1973. Painter, graphic designer, sculptor, potter and author. Art studies in Barcelona and Madrid. In 1904 he settled in Paris. The style of his early works: melancholy figure paintings ("blue" and "pink" periods). He paved the way for cubism with, among other paintings, "The Girls of Avignon", 1907 (with G. Braque). Since 1917 he also worked in neoclassic style. In the mid twenties he began surrealistic distortion as expression of a time of disturbance (wall painting "Guernica", 1937). Remarkable for his constantly changing diversity and his lead in styles.

PABLO PICASSO (Eigtl. Pablo Ruiz y Picasso). 1881–1973. Maler, Graphiker, Bildhauer, Keramiker und Dichter. Kunststudium in Barcelona und Madrid, 1904 Übersiedlung nach Paris. Stil der frühen Werke: schwermütige Figurenbilder («Blaue –» und «Rosa Periode»). Wegbereitend waren u. a. «Die Mädchen von Avignon». 1907 (mit G. Braque) erste Bilder des Kubismus; seit 1917 auch Werke eines neuen klassizistischen Stils. Mitte der 20er Jahre Beginn der surrealistischen Verzerrungen als Ausdruck einer zerrütteten Zeit (Wandbild «Guernica» 1937). Kennzeichnend sind die sich ständig wandelnde Vielfalt und das Nebeneinander der Stilrichtungen.

PABLO PICASSO (de son vrai nom Pablo Ruiz y Picasso), 1881–1973. Peintre, graphiste, sculpteur, céramiste et poète. Etudes artistiques à Barcelone et à Madrid. S'installe à Paris en 1904. Premières œuvres figuratives mélancoliques (périodes bleue et rose). Fait figure de précurseur avec ses «Demoiselles d'Avignon», etc. En 1907, premières œuvres cubistes avec Georges Braque; dès 1917 verse dans le néoclassicisme. Vers le milieu des années 1920, se met à déformer le réel de manière surréaliste, symbolisant ainsi un monde qui part à la dérive (mural «Guernica», 1937). Ce qui le caractérise, c'est la multiplicité des styles qui se chevauchent et se transforment inlassablement.

PIERO FORNASETTI, born in Milan, 1913. He studied painting, sculpture, gravure, and lithography in his native city. He designed in a wide range of media: fashion, interiors, stage sets, mosaics, ceramics, etc.

PIERO FORNASETTI, 1913 in Mailand geboren, wo er Malerei, Bildhauerei und graphische Reproduktionstechniken studierte. Zu seinem umfassenden Arbeitsbereich gehören Keramikmalerei, Mode, Innenausstattungen, Bühnenbilder etc.

PIERO FORNASETTI, né à Milan en 1913. Poursuit dans sa ville natale des études de peinture, de sculpture, de gravure et de lithographie. Ses œuvres recouvrent une vaste palette: créations de mode, décorations intérieures, décors de théâtre, mosaïques, céramiques, etc.

JEAN-DENIS MALCLÈS, born in Paris, 1912. He studied in Paris and specialized mainly in painting and theater decor. He executed stage sets for the Comédie-Française, le Théâtre de l'Œuvre, l'Opéra National, l'Opéra Comique, La Scala (Milan), Covent Garden (London), the Renaissance Theater of Berlin, the Hamburg Opernhaus - and many more famous theaters. He was awarded the Legion of Honor distinction, and among his numerous prizes is the Grand Prix National du Théâtre (1973).

JEAN-DENIS MALCLÈS, 1912 in Paris geboren. Er studierte in Paris und beschäftigte sich hauptsächlich mit Malerei und Bühnenbildern. Unter den vielen berühmten Theatern, für die er Bühnenbilder entwarf, sind die Comédie-Française, le Théâtre de l'Œuvre, l'Opéra National, l'Opéra Comique, La Scala (Mailand), Covent Garden (London) das Renaissance-Theater Berlin und die Hamburger Staatsoper. Er ist Mitglied der Akademie der Ehrenlegion und unter den vielen Preisen, die er erhielt, ist der Grand Prix National du Théâtre (1973).

JEAN-DENIS MALCLÈS, né en 1912 à Paris, où il fait ses études. Peintre et décorateur de théâtre. A ce titre, il a réalisé des décors pour la Comédie-Française, le théâtre de l'Œuvre, le théâtre national de l'Opéra, l'Opéra-Comique, la Scala de Milan, le Covent-Garden de Londres, le Renaissance Theater de Berlin, l'Opéra de Hambourg – et bien d'autres scènes prestigieuses. Chevalier de la Légion d'honneur, il est entre autres lauréat du Grand Prix national du théâtre 1973.

JACQUES N. GARAMOND born in Paris, 1910. He began his career in 1930 and shortly afterwards set up his own studio. His range of design work is wide and includes exhibition design, posters, advertising art, typography etc. He executed the decorative panels in the Paris Pavilion at the World Fair in Brussels (1958). Winner of numerous awards including a Gold Medal, he is a founder-member of AGI.

JACQUES N. GARAMOND 1910 in Paris geboren. Seine Karriere begann 1930, bald darauf gründete er sein eigenes Studio. Seine umfangreichen Arbeiten als Designer beinhalten Ausstellungsgraphik, Plakate, Werbung, typographische Arbeiten etc. Ausstellungsgraphik für die Weltausstellung in Brüssel (1958). Er erhielt verschiedene Auszeichnungen, unter anderem eine Goldmedaille. Er ist eines der Gründungsmitglieder der AGI.

JACQUES N. GARAMOND né à Paris en 1910. Sa carrière débute en 1930. Peu de temps après, il s'établit à son compte. Designer polyvalent, il réalise des stands d'exposition, des affiches, des illustrations publicitaires, des créations typographiques, etc. C'est à lui que l'on doit les panneaux décoratifs du Pavillon de Paris à l'Expo de Bruxelles en 1958. Lauréat de nombreux prix, y compris une médaille d'or. Membre fondateur de l'AGI.

JOSEPH BINDER, Austria, 1898–1972. He established his own studio in Vienna in 1924 and emigrated to the USA in 1935. He became a naturalized American citizen in 1944. Until his death he worked as a freelance graphic designer in New York and was awarded numerous awards. His scope encompassed graphics, typography and poster creation. Past member of AGI and AIGA.

JOSEPH BINDER, Österreich, 1898–1972. 1924 eigenes Studio in Wien, 1935 Emigration in die USA, wo er 1944 amerikanischer Staatsbürger wurde. Bis zu seinem Tode arbeitete er als freischaffender Graphiker in New York. Er erhielt diverse Auszeichnungen für seine Graphiken, Typographie und Plakate. Ehemaliges Mitglied der AGI und des AIGA.

JOSEPH BINDER, 1898–1972. Cet Autrichien ouvre son premier studio à Vienne en 1924, émigre aux Etats-Unis en 1935 et obtient la nationalité américaine en 1944. A travaillé jusqu'à sa mort comme graphiste indépendant à New York. Lauréat de nombreux prix pour ses travaux graphiques et typographiques et ses affiches. Membre de l'AGI et de l'AIGA.

For short biography, see page 135.
This illustration by PABLO PICASSO related to a feature on his "Illustrations to the Sonnets of Gongora" in this issue. The technique he used was the sugar process or sugar aquatint. It was used in the previous century by artists, but was neglected. It was shown to Picasso by masterprinter Roger Lacourière; Picasso was quick to see the possibilities and at once used it in his plates for the *Buffon*. He also developed the technique further.

Kurzbiographie Seite 135.
Diese Illustration von PABLO PICASSO bezieht sich auf einen Artikel in dieser Ausgabe über seine Illustrationen zu den Sonetten von Gongora. Die Technik, die Picasso für diese Illustration anwendete, ist unter dem Namen «Aquatinte au Sucre» (Aussprengverfahren) bekannt. Sie war im vergangenen Jahrhundert bei Künstlern gebräuchlich, geriet inzwischen aber in Vergessenheit. Es war der Meisterdrucker Roger Lacourière, der sie Picasso zeigte. Picasso erkannte sofort ihre Möglichkeiten und wandte sie bei seinen Platten für den *Buffon* an. Er hat diese Technik noch weiterentwickelt.

Voir la notice biographique en p. 135.
Cette illustration de PABLO PICASSO se rapporte à une présentation de ses «Illustrations des sonnets de Góngora» dans le même numéro. La technique employée est celle de l'aquatinte au sucre. Des artistes du XIXe siècle y avaient eu recours, puis elle était tombée dans l'oubli. C'est le maître-imprimeur Roger Lacourière qui la lui apprit; Picasso en vit rapidement les avantages et l'utilisa immédiatement dans ses planches pour le *Buffon*. Par la suite, il devait encore améliorer cette technique.

For short biography, see page 133.
HANS ERNI is as versatile in his culture as he is in lithography, frescoes, engravings, murals, poster art, book illustrations, oils, pastels... all are within his wide scope of craftsmanship. He is a man who has achieved in himself and in his work something very like a modern humanism.

Kurzbiographie Seite 133.
So vielseitig wie in der technischen Beherrschung - HANS ERNI ist gleich gewandt in der Lithographie wie im Fresko, in der Radierung wie in der Plakatkunst, im Wandbild wie in der Buchillustration, im Ölbild wie im Pastell – ist Erni auch in kulturellen Belangen. Er ist einer jener, die mit Begeisterung und Methodik in sich und ihren Werken einen eigentlichen modernen Humanismus verfechten.

Voir la notice biographique en p. 133.
HANS ERNI, artiste aux talents multiples, excelle dans la lithographie, la fresque, l'eauforte, l'affiche, le mural, l'illustration de livres, la peinture à l'huile et le pastel. Appliquant la même curiosité insatiable aux faits de civilisation, il compte parmi les représentants enthousiastes autant que méthodiques d'un humanisme résolument moderne.

GEORGE GIUSTI, born in Milan, 1908. He studied at the Reale Accademia di Belle Arti in his native city. Founded his own studio in Zürich in 1930 and emigrated to the USA in 1938. He was engaged on projects for the US government buildings in Washington and was design consultant for *Geigy Pharmaceuticals* for twelve years. His works have been widely exhibited and he was awarded gold and silver medals among numerous other prizes. In 1979 he was admitted to the New York Art Directors Hall of Fame.

GEORGE GIUSTI, 1908 in Mailand geboren, wo er an der Reale Accademia di Belle Arti studierte. Ab 1930 eigenes Graphik-Atelier in Zürich, 1938 Emigration in die USA. Arbeitete an verschiedenen Projekten an den Regierungsgebäuden in Washington. War 12 Jahre Werbeberater für *Geigy Pharmaceuticals*. Gewann mehrere Gold- und Silbermedaillen; 1979 Art Directors' «Hall of Fame», New York.

GEORGE GIUSTI, né à Milan en 1908. Etudes à l'Académie Royale des Beaux-Arts de sa ville natale. Fonde son propre studio à Zurich en 1930, émigre aux Etats-Unis en 1938. Collabore à divers projets immobiliers du gouvernement américain à Washington et conseille pendant douze ans *Geigy Pharmaceuticals* en matière de design. Ses travaux, exposés dans divers pays, lui ont rapporté une riche moisson de prix, de médailles d'or et d'argent. Depuis 1979, son nom figure dans le registre du New York Art Directors Hall of Fame.

JEAN PICART LE DOUX, France, 1902–1982. He began his career as bookbinder and publisher and later turned to graphic art, experimenting in the media of tapestry, mosaic and ceramics. His tapestries bore the disciplines of graphic art and were highly prized masterpieces sought out by governments, embassies and cultural institutions: for example the Paris Chamber of Commerce, the Frankfurt Opera and the NATO building. His works have been widely exhibited throughout Europe, the USA and Japan. He was the recipient of numerous international prizes and was one time president of AGI.

JEAN PICART LE DOUX, Frankreich, 1902–1982. Er begann seine Karriere als Buchbinder und Verleger und wendete sich später der Graphik zu. Er entwarf Wandteppiche, Mosaike und keramische Gegenstände. Seine Wandteppiche, die viele graphische Elemente aufweisen, sind hochgeschätzte Meisterstücke und wurden von verschiedenen Regierungen, Botschaften und kulturellen Institutionen erworben, z. B. von der Pariser Handelskammer, der Frankfurter Oper und der NATO. Seine Werke wurden in Europa, den USA und Japan ausgestellt. Er hat verschiedene internationale Preise erhalten und war Präsident (später Ehrenpräsident) der AGI.

JEAN PICART LE DOUX, France, 1902–1982. Relieur et éditeur au début de sa carrière, il s'oriente par la suite vers l'art graphique. Travaux expérimentaux dans le domaine de la tapisserie, de la mosaïque et de la céramique. Ses tapisseries, qui incorporent bon nombre d'éléments graphiques, constituent de véritables chefs-d'œuvre fort prisés des gouvernements, ambassades et institutions culturelles - Chambre de Commerce de Paris, Opéra de Francfort, bâtiment de l'O.T.A.N., etc. Il a eu de nombreuses expositions en Europe, aux USA et au Japon. Lauréat d'une série impressionnante de prix internationaux, il a été président (et par la suite président d'honneur) de l'AGI.

HANS HARTMANN, born in Switzerland, 1913. He started his career in the advertising department of the *Bally Shoe Company* before studying at the Kunstgewerbeschule, Zürich. In 1938 he founded his own studio in Berne which he transferred to Köniz in 1964. He won the Philatec Medal in Paris in 1964 and has been awarded numerous other prizes for his posters as well as first prize in a UN sponsored postage stamp competition. His scope of work encompasses advertising art, book design, exhibition display, lettering, postage stamps and trademarks, symbols etc.

HANS HARTMANN, 1913 in der Schweiz geboren. Seine Karriere begann in der Werbeabteilung der *Bally Schuhfabriken.* Anschliessend Studium an der Kunstgewerbeschule Zürich. 1938 eigenes Studio in Bern, 1964 Umzug nach Köniz. Im gleichen Jahr erhielt er die Philatec-Medaille in Paris. Es folgten zahlreiche andere Auszeichnungen, unter anderem der erste Preis in einem UNO-Wettbewerb für Briefmarkengestaltung. Seine Arbeiten umfassen Werbung, Buchentwürfe, Ausstellungsmaterial, Beschriftungen, Briefmarken, Schutzmarken, Symbole etc.

HANS HARTMANN, né en Suisse en 1913. Sa carrière débute au département publicité de *Bally Schuhfabriken,* le chausseur suisse. Il retourne étudier à l'Ecole des arts décoratifs de Zurich, fonde son propre studio à Berne en 1938, s'installe à Köniz près de Berne en 1964, l'année où il obtient la médaille Philatec à Paris. Lauréat de nombreux prix pour ses affiches, il est aussi premier prix d'un concours de création de timbresposte pour l'O.N.U. Son domaine créatif comprend l'art publicitaire, la conception de livres, le design d'expositions, le lettrage, la création de timbres, marques déposées, emblèmes, etc.

For short biography, see page 136.
Hans Hartmann had taken up the motif of the cockerel for *Graphis* 28 certainly not knowing that JOSEPH BINDER at almost the same time was working on the same theme in New York. It is impressive how different the two covers are - not only in form, but also in content. Binder's cockerel shown here is a showman who, with the palette of his feathers, calls for instant attention. The cockerel as advertising symbol?

Kurzbiographie Seite 136.
Hans Hartmann hatte für *Graphis* Nr. 28 das Motiv des Hahns aufgegriffen, sicherlich nicht ahnend, dass JOSEPH BINDER fast zur gleichen Zeit in New York das selbe Thema behandelte. Eindrucksvoll, wie verschieden die zwei Titelblätter ausgefallen sind. Nicht nur formal völlig unterschiedlich, sondern auch inhaltlich. Bei Binder der Hahn als Marktschreier, der mit der Palette seines Gefieders die ganze Aufmerksamkeit auf sich zieht. Der Hahn als Sinnbild des Werbens?

Voir la notice biographique en p. 136.
Pour *Graphis* 28, Hans Hartmann avait choisi l'emblème du coq sans savoir que JOSEPH BINDER, à New York, optait au même moment pour le même symbole. Il est d'autant plus impressionnant de constater qu'un sujet identique a été traité différemment, tant sur le plan formel que sur celui du message. Chez Binder, le coq devient le bonimenteur de foire qui attire l'attention en vertu de la palette criarde de son plumage. Le coq symbole de l'art publicitaire?

JAN BONS, born in Rotterdam, 1918. He is best known for his murals, mosaics, sculptures and book design, but he also works in advertising art and has designed exhibitions for many national fairs and for Dutch pavilions at the World Fair in Brussels (1958). He was awarded the Werkman Prize for typography in 1968 by the city of Amsterdam.

JAN BONS, 1918 in Rotterdam geboren. Wurde bekannt durch seine Wandgemälde, Mosaike, Skulpturen und Buchentwürfe. Ausstellungsgestaltung für verschiedene nationale Ausstellungen und für den holländischen Pavillon an der Weltausstellung in Brüssel (1958). 1968 erhielt er von der Stadt Amsterdam den Werkman-Preis für Typographie.

JAN BONS, né à Rotterdam en 1918. S'est fait connaître par ses murals, ses mosaïques, ses sculptures et ses maquettes de livres. Il est aussi artiste publicitaire, a réalisé les stands de diverses expositions nationales et les pavillons hollandais de l'Exposition universelle à Bruxelles (1958). A reçu en 1968 le prix Werkman de typographie décerné par la ville d'Amsterdam.

THOMAS ECKERSLEY, born in England, 1914. During the second world war he was engaged on government information publications and posters for the Royal Airforce and the GPO. He was appointed Royal Designer for Industry in 1963. In 1977 he designed the murals for the new Heathrow Airport underground railway station. Collections of his work are held in major museums, including the Victoria and Albert Museum, MOMA, etc.

THOMAS ECKERSLEY, 1914 in England geboren. Gestaltete während des Zweiten Weltkriegs Informationsbroschüren und Plakate für die Royal Airforce und das GPO. 1963 wurde er zum Royal Industrie-Designer ernannt. 1977 gestaltete er ein Wandgemälde für die Untergrundstation am Flughafen Heathrow. Sammlungen seiner Arbeiten sind in wichtigen Museen ausgestellt, z. B. im Victoria and Albert Museum, MOMA etc.

THOMAS ECKERSLEY, né en Angleterre en 1914. Durant la Seconde guerre mondiale, il crée des brochures d'information pour le gouvernement, des affiches pour la Royal Airforce et les PTT britanniques. Nommé Royal Designer for Industry (esthéticien industriel) en 1963. Réalise en 1977 les murals de la nouvelle gare souterraine de l'aéroport de Heathrow. Ses œuvres figurent dans les collections des grands musées, y compris le Victoria and Albert Museum, le MOMA, etc.

For short biography, see page 135.
The works of JACQUES N. GARAMOND can be placed under two major cultural influences which appear to be in opposition: Bauhaus and Surrealism. On the one hand the technique, severe style, and purpose of form; on the other imaginative or obscure design. Almost always Garamond was successful in carrying out the task entrusted to him and expressing on a second and almost furtive level his own personal message.

Kurzbiographie Seite 135.
Das Werk von JACQUES N. GARAMOND steht unter zwei beherrschenden kulturellen Einflüssen, die sich scheinbar widersprechen: Bauhaus und Surrealismus. Einerseits Technik, strenger Stil, Formwille, anderseits die imaginäre oder verborgene Gestalt der Dinge. Fast immer hat es Garamond geschafft, über die ihm aufgetragene Botschaft hinaus, auf einer zweiten Ebene und fast verstohlen, seine persönliche Botschaft auszudrücken.

Voir la notice biographique en p. 135.
L'œuvre de JACQUES N. GARAMOND est dominé par deux grands courants culturels en apparence contradictoires: le Bauhaus et le surréalisme. D'un côté, la technique, le style dépouillé, la primauté de la forme; de l'autre, l'aspect imaginaire ou secret des choses. Garamond a presque toujours su investir ses travaux de commande d'un message personnel en filigrane, satisfaisant ainsi à ses aspirations profondes.

CARLO DINELLI, Milan, belongs to a small "club" of cover artists who in addition were the authors of articles within the magazine. As an expert on Italian advertising art, his 1950 article gives a superb overview over the status of commercial graphic design in post-war Italy.

CARLO DINELLI, Mailand, gehört zu den wenigen Gestaltern eines Umschlags, die auch gleichzeitig Autoren eines Artikels waren. Als Kenner der italienischen Werbekunst war es ihm möglich, in seinem Artikel von 1950 einen einzigartigen Überblick über die Gebrauchsgraphik der Nachkriegszeit in Italien zu geben.

Le Milanais CARLO DINELLI fait partie du petit groupe d'artistes qui n'ont pas seulement réalisé une couverture de *Graphis,* mais ont également assumé la rédaction d'un article du magazine. Cet expert de l'art publicitaire italien dresse dans son survol de 1950 un précieux tableau de la scène graphique commerciale italienne au lendemain de la guerre.

ANTONI CLAVÉ, born in Barcelona, 1913. He started his career as illustrator of children's magazines before turning to poster design and graphic art. In 1939 he went to France, eventually settling in Paris. He designed stage sets (including Roland Petit's ballet production *Carmen)* and illustrated several books. He spent 3 years in drawing 58 lithographs directly on stone for colored initial letters commissioned by the Comité des Bibliophiles de Provence. He has also worked as a sculptor. He is the recipient of many prizes, including a UNESCO award for engraving.

ANTONI CLAVÉ, 1913 in Barcelona geboren, begann seine Karriere als Illustrator von Kinderzeitungen. Es folgten Plakate und Graphiken. 1939 Übersiedlung nach Frankreich, wo er Bühnenbilder entwarf (unter anderen für Roland Petits Ballett-Produktion *Carmen)* und verschiedene Bücher illustrierte. Er brauchte drei Jahre, um 58 Lithographien, die er direkt auf den Stein malte, herzustellen. Es handelte sich um farbige Anfangsbuchstaben, die vom Comité des Bibliophiles de Provence in Auftrag gegeben wurden. Daneben arbeitete er auch als Bildhauer. Ihm wurden verschiedene Preise verliehen, z. B. ein Preis der UNESCO für Radierungen.

ANTONI CLAVÉ, né à Barcelone en 1913. A débuté comme illustrateur de magazines pour enfants avant de s'orienter vers l'affiche et la création graphique. Passe en France en 1939, s'installe finalement à Paris. Réalise des décors de théâtre, notamment pour le ballet *Carmen* de Roland Petit, et illustre divers ouvrages. Il passe trois longues années à dessiner 58 lithos à même la pierre pour des initiales en couleur que lui commande le Comité des bibliophiles de Provence. On lui doit aussi des sculptures. De nombreux prix sont venus récompenser ses œuvres, entre autres un prix de gravure de l'UNESCO.

■

ASGER JERRILD, Denmark. One of Copenhagen's better-known graphic designers of the immediate post-war era, Mr. Jerrild's trademark was his interesting use of colors. His work included a 16-color poster for the Danish paint manufacturer *Sadolin & Holmblad.*

■

ASGER JERRILD, Dänemark, war einer der bekannteren Graphik-Designer der Nachkriegszeit, dessen Kennzeichen die spezielle Verwendung der Farben war. Unter anderem hat er ein Plakat in 16 Farben für die dänische Farbenfabrik *Sadolin & Holmblad gestaltet.*

■

ASGER JERRILD. Ce Danois est l'un des graphistes les plus en vue de l'immédiat aprèsguerre à Copenhague. Son œuvre est caractérisé par un emploi suggestif de la couleur. Il s'est notamment fait connaître par l'affiche en 16 couleurs qu'il réalisa pour le fabricant de peintures danois *Sadolin & Holmblad.*

■

DONALD BRUN, born in Switzerland, 1909. After his studies, he set up his own studio in Basle in 1933. His scope includes advertising art, exhibition display, industrial design, packaging, photography and poster design, the latter which brought him many awards. Founder member of AGI.

■

DONALD BRUN, 1909 in der Schweiz geboren. Nach seinen Studien begann er 1933 als selbständiger Graphiker in Basel. Seine Arbeiten umfassen Werbung, Ausstellungsmaterial, Industrie-Design, Verpackungen, Photographien und Plakate. Als Plakatkünstler besonders erfolgreich und vielfach ausgezeichnet. Gründungsmitglied der AGI.

■

DONALD BRUN, né en Suisse en 1909. Ses études terminées, il s'installe à son compte à Bâle en 1933. Sa créativité s'exprime dans l'art publicitaire, le design d'expositions, l'esthétique industrielle, l'emballagisme, la photo et l'affiche. C'est surtout comme affichiste qu'il s'est fait connaître, remportant de nombreux prix. Membre fondateur de l'AGI.

■

F. H. K. HENRION, born in Germany, 1914. He studied and worked in Paris and London. During the second world war he was exhibition adviser to the Ministry of Information, London. He designed two pavilions for the Festival of Britain (1951). His scope embraces corporate design, book design, exhibition display, typography and packaging etc. He was awarded the British MBE in 1951 and has won numerous other prizes.

■

F. H. K. HENRION, 1914 in Deutschland geboren. Studierte und arbeitete in Paris und London. Während des Zweiten Weltkriegs war er Ausstellungsberater des britischen Informationsministeriums. Er gestaltete zwei Pavillons für das Festival of Britain (1951). Seine Arbeiten umfassen Corporate Design, Buchgestaltung, Ausstellungsmaterial, Typographie und Verpackungen. Er erhielt den British MBE (1951) sowie zahlreiche andere Preise.

■

F. H. K. HENRION, né en Allemagne en 1914. Etudes et activité professionnelle à Paris et à Londres. Durant la Seconde Guerre mondiale, il conseille le ministère britannique de l'Information en matière d'expositions. On lui doit deux pavillons du Festival of Britain 1951. Ses travaux comprennent des campagnes d'identité globale de marque, des maquettes de livres, des stands d'exposition, des créations typo, des emballages, etc. Lauréat de nombreux prix, il s'est vu décerner le British MBE en 1951.

■

CHILDREN'S COLLECTIVE PAINTING. This illustration related to a feature inside the magazine with the same title. It is a painting showing the famous cathedral in Paris and is the work of 24 boys, 11 and 12 years of age, each of whom contributed a small section of the picture. Collective painting by Parisian schoolchildren was an experiment initiated by 2 schoolteachers and the groups of children chose a subject which was then drafted into squares, each child taking a square to paint. The sections were then stuck together. The paintings were done in their leisure time.

■

KOLLEKTIVZEICHNUNGEN VON KINDERN. Diese Illustration bezieht sich auf einen Artikel mit dem gleichen Titel in dieser Ausgabe. Sie zeigt ein Bild der berühmten Pariser Kathedrale und wurde von 24 Jungen im Alter von 11 und 12 Jahren gemalt. Kollektivzeichnungen von Pariser Schulkindern war ein Experiment, welches von zwei Lehrern initiiert wurde. Die ausgewählten Gegenstände wurden in Vierecke aufgeteilt, und jedes Kind bemalte eines der Vierecke. Zum Schluss wurden alle Vierecke zusammengeklebt. Alle Bilder wurden von den Kindern in ihrer Freizeit ausgeführt.

■

PEINTURES COLLECTIVES DE MAIN D'ENFANTS. Cette illlustration se rapporte à un article du même titre paru dans ce numéro. Il s'agit d'un tableau de Notre-Dame de Paris peint par 24 garçons de 11 et 12 ans, chacun réalisant une petite portion de l'œuvre collective. Ce projet est dû à l'initiative de deux professeurs parisiens. Les enfants étaient libres de choisir un sujet qui était ensuite décomposé en carrés confiés à chacun d'entre eux. Une fois terminés, ces carrés étaient assemblés par collage. Les jeunes artistes ont fourni cet effort créatif pendant leurs heures de loisirs.

■

OLLE EKSELL, born in Sweden, 1918. He studied engineering before turning to graphic art and his scope includes book design, exhibition display, advertising art and packaging etc. He founded his own studio and he has won first prizes in numerous design contests. In 1974 he was awarded the largest Swedish State Grant for artists.

OLLE EKSELL, 1918 in Schweden geboren. Er studierte Maschinenbau, bevor er sich der graphischen Kunst zuwandte. Sein Arbeitsbereich umfasst Buchentwürfe, Ausstellungsgestaltung, Werbung, Pakkungsmaterial etc. Er ist als freier Graphiker tätig und hat für seine Arbeiten viele Preise gewonnen. 1974 Verleihung des höchsten staatlichen Kunststipendiums.

OLLE EKSELL, né en Suède en 1918. Etudie les sciences de l'ingénieur avant de se convertir à l'art graphique, notamment à la création de livres, au design d'expositions, à l'art publicitaire et à l'emballagisme. A la tête de son propre studio, il remporte des premiers prix dans de nombreux concours de design. Reçoit en 1974 la Bourse d'etat la plus importante que la Suède ait à accorder à ses artistes méritants.

For short biography, see page 133.
IMRE REINER loved the small format, the compression of a wealth of observation and vision into the smallest space. He respected the synthesis of great simplicity and great refinement – and managed to fill the most modest and unprepossessing of forms with the richest of contents, often giving the carefully thought out composition the form of something apparently unfinished.

Kurzbiographie Seite 133.
IMRE REINER hat eine Vorliebe für das zugleich sehr kostbare und ganz Unauffällige, für eine Synthese aus höchster Schlichtheit und höchstem Raffinement. Er liebt das kleine Format, die Verdichtung einer Fülle von Beobachtungen und Visionen auf engstem Raum, und er liebt es, dem bis ins letzte Durchdachten die Gestalt des scheinbar Unfertigen, der Skizze zu geben.

Voir la notice biographique en p. 133.
IMRE REINER affectionne le précieux dans la mesure où il ne s'impose pas à l'attention, cherche à marier l'extrême simplicité et l'extrême raffinement, préfère le format réduit où condenser une foule d'observations et de visions. Il excelle à donner à des compositions étudiées dans leurs moindres détails l'apparence de l'inachevé, d'une esquisse hâtive.

JOSEPH LOW, born in the USA, 1911. After studying at the University of Illinois and in New York (under George Grosz) he founded his own printing studio in 1933. In 1941 he founded his own design studio and also taught design and graphic art at Indiana University. He produced his own broadsheets (printed from linocuts and type on handmade paper in limited runs). In 1959 he founded the *Eden Hill Press*. He specializes in linocuts and typographic design for record covers, book illustrations, and advertising.

JOSEPH LOW, 1911 in den USA geboren. Nach Studien bei George Grosz an den Universitäten von Illinois und New York, gründete er 1933 seine eigene Druckerei. 1941 machte er sich als Graphiker selbständig und unterrichtete gleichzeitig an der Universität von Indiana. Er stellte eigene Flugblätter her, Linolschnitte auf handgemachtes Papier gedruckt, in limitierter Auflage. 1959 gründete er die *Eden Hill Press.* Er hat sich auf Linolschnitte und typographische Gestaltung für Plattenhüllen, Buchillustrationen und Werbung spezialisiert.

JOSEPH LOW, né aux Etats-Unis en 1911. Etudes à l'Université de l'Illinois et à New York (sous la direction de George Grosz). Fonde en 1933 son propre atelier d'imprimerie. En 1941, il s'établit à son compte comme designer, enseigne le design et l'art graphique à l'Université de l'Indiana, produit des dépliants au grand format tirés sur papier à la cuve, en tirage limité, à partir de ses linogravures. Fondateur des Editions *Eden Hill Press* en 1959, il se spécialise dans les linos et la création typographique appliqués aux pochettes de disques, à l'illustration de livres, à l'art publicitaire.

For short biography, see page 132.
This illustration shows a detail from the window designed by MAX HUNZIKER in the vestibule of the auditorium wing of the Cantonal Hospital in Zurich. The whole window measures 18 ft $7\frac{1}{4}$ ins. by 11 ft $4\frac{1}{2}$ ins. Hunziker created his first stained-glass design long before he ever took a piece of glass in his hands. It was when he met Karl Ganz and his associates that he found the bale craftsmen to collaborate in his stained-glass workmanship.

Kurzbiographie Seite 132.
Das Umschlagbild ist ein Ausschnitt aus dem von HAX HUNZIKER vollendeten 5,67 m hohen Fenster im Vestibül des Hörsaaltraktes im Kantonsspital Zürich. Seine ersten Glasbildentwürfe schuf Hunziker lange bevor er ein Glas in die Hand nahm. Er besann sich der ursprünglichen Formen im Umgang mit dem Werkstoff und verhalf diesem zu neuer Leuchtkraft.

Voir la notice biographique en p. 132.
L'illustration de couverture représente un fragment du vitrail de 5,67 m de haut et de 4,47 m de large que MAX HUNZIKER réalisa pour le vestibule des salles de cours de l'Hôpital cantonal de Zurich. Ses premiers projets de vitraux datent d'une époque où il ne s'était pas encore intéressé au verre en tant que matériau. Ce n'est qu'au contact de Karl Ganz et de son équipe d'artisans du verre qu'il réalisa le potentiel créatif du vitrail et le hissa à de nouveaux sommets d'expressivité lumineuse.

For short biography, see page 136.
GEORGE GIUSTI's works frequently featured concepts of space, as on this cover – a suspended geometric omnipresence in the spatial consciousness of man. He succeeded in fulfilling the practical demands made on him by his clients (for bookjackets, advertisements etc.) and bringing these into unison with his own specific studies – many in facial forms.

Kurzbiographie Seite 136.
GEORGE GIUSTIS Arbeiten weisen oft eine spezifische Raumvorstellung auf, eine schwebende Allgegenwart des räumlichen Bewusstseins. Dieser Tatbestand entspricht sowohl seinem eigenen Vorstellungsbild wie auch den praktischen Ansprüchen, die seine Auftraggeber an ihn stellten.

Voir la notice biographique en p. 136.
Les travaux de GEORGE GIUSTI incarnent souvent une conception déterminée de l'espace, ainsi cette couverture – une omniprésence géométrique en suspension dans la conscience spatiale de l'être humain. Cette vision a satisfait autant ses clients pour des jaquettes de livres, des travaux publicitaires, etc. que l'artiste lui-même, captivé par des études de géométrie intérieure, notamment celle du visage humain.

ANDRÉ FRANÇOIS, born in Rumania, 1915. He is now a French citizen domiciled in Paris. He studied under A. M. Cassandre. An artist of many genres: graphic designer, children's book illustrator, cartoonist, engraver, stage designer, poster designer, sculptor and author. Widely exhibited. He was awarded the Gold Medal at the Biennale, Warsaw, in 1972 and he won a Gold Medal presented by the New York ADC, among other prizes. Collections of his work can be seen in major museums. He is a member of AGI.

ANDRÉ FRANÇOIS, 1915 in Rumänien geboren, ist heute französischer Staatsbürger und lebt in Paris. Schüler von A. M. Cassandre. Vielfältiger Künstler: Graphik-Designer, Kinderbuch-Illustrator, Karikaturist, Graveur, Bühnenbildner, Plakatentwerfer, Bildhauer und Autor. Seine Werke wurden oftmals ausgestellt. 1972 Goldmedaille anlässlich der Plakatbiennale Warschau sowie Goldmedaille des ADC New York. Verschiedene seiner Werke sind in Museen ausgestellt. Er ist Mitglied der AGI.

ANDRÉ FRANÇOIS, né en Roumanie en 1915. Naturalisé Français, il habite Paris. Elève d'A. M. Cassandre, c'est un artiste aux talents variés: graphiste, illustrateur de livres, dessinateur d'humour, graveur, décorateur de théâtre, affichiste, sculpteur, écrivain. A eu de très nombreuses expositions. Médaille d'or de la Biennale de Varsovie en 1972, il est entre autres médaille d'or de l'ADC de New York. Ses œuvres figurent dans les collections des grands musées. Il est membre de l'AGI.
© 1987 PRO LITTERIS, Zürich

ERBERTO CARBONI, born in Parma, 1899. He studied architecture and specialized in interior design and graphics. He worked as exhibition designer at Sophia, Brussels and Milan, and also designed the decor for La Scala, Milan. His work encompasses publicity campaigns for major clients. Numerous national awards have come his way and his work is represented in many collections in museums in New York.

ERBERTO CARBONI, 1899 in Parma geboren. Er wandte sich nach einem Architekturstudium in Parma der Ausstellungsgestaltung und der angewandten Graphik zu und arbeitete als Ausstellungsdesigner in Sofia, Brüssel und Mailand, wo er das Dekor der Mailänder Scala entwarf. Seine Arbeiten umfassen Werbekampagnen für grosse Unternehmen. Er hat viele nationale Auszeichnungen erhalten, und seine Arbeiten sind in verschiedenen Museen in New York ausgestellt.

ERBERTO CARBONI, né à Parme en 1899. Architecte venu à la décoration intérieure et à l'art publicitaire. A conçu des expositions à Sofia, Bruxelles et Milan, où il a été responsable, entre autres, de la décoration de la Scala. En publicité, a réalisé nombre de campagnes pour d'importants clients. Ses œuvres, récompensées de nombreux prix nationaux, se trouvent dans les collections de divers musées new-yorkais.

YUSAKU KAMEKURA, born in Japan, 1915. He has headed his own design studio Kamekura Design Institute since 1962. He is a founder member and current director of the Japan Design Center and he serves as Chairman of the Japan Graphic Designer Association. He is the recipient of a great many national first prizes and is especially remembered for his posters for the Olympic Games in 1964, the Expo 1970 in Osaka and the Olympic Winter Games in Sapporo in 1972.

YUSAKU KAMEKURA, 1915 in Japan geboren. Leitet seit 1962 sein eigenes Design Studio, Kamekura Design Institute. Mitbegründer und Direktor des Japan Design Center, Vorsitzender der Japan Graphic Designer Association. Gewinner vieler Auszeichnungen. Gestalter vielbeachteter Plakate, wie z. B. für die Olympischen Spiele 1964, Expo 1970 in Osaka und Olympischen Winterspiele 1972 in Sapporo.

YUSAKU KAMEKURA, né au Japon en 1915. Dirige depuis 1962 son propre studio de design, le Kamekura Design Institute. Membre fondateur et directeur actuel du Japan Design Center, il préside la Japan Graphic Designer Association. Lauréat d'un grand nombre de premiers prix nationaux, il s'est surtout signalé par ses affiches pour les Jeux Olympiques de 1964, l'Expo d'Osaka en 1970 et les Jeux Olympiques d'hiver de Sapporo en 1972.

   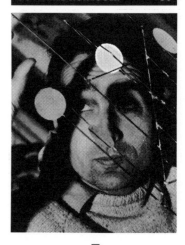

ABRAM GAMES, born in London, 1914. He is self-taught, freelancing at the age of 21, he designed posters for *Shell,* London Transport and the GPO. During the second world war he was appointed official army poster designer and created over 100 posters. After the war he continued designing and publishing posters – and created emblems and postage stamps for Britain and Israel. He is the recipient of some 40 national and international awards. He is the designer of the Queen's Award to Industry and received the OBE for his work as graphic designer in 1957. He was appointed RDI in 1959.

ABRAM GAMES, 1914 in London geboren. Autodidakt. Freischaffend seit seinem 21. Lebensjahr. Gestaltete Plakate für *Shell,* die Londoner Transportbetriebe und für die britische Post. Während des Zweiten Weltkrieges entwarf er über 100 Armeeplakate für das Kriegsministerium. Auch nach dem Krieg gestaltete er Plakate sowie Briefmarken für England und Israel. Er hat rund 40 Preise und Auszeichnungen erhalten. Er entwarf das Emblem für «the Queen's Award to Industry» und erhielt 1957 den OBE für seine Arbeiten als Graphik-Designer. 1959 zum RDI ernannt.

ABRAM GAMES, né à Londres en 1914. Cet autodidacte travaille pour son compte dès l'âge de 21 ans, crée des affiches pour *Shell,* la Régie des transports londoniens et les PTT britanniques. Durant la Seconde Guerre mondiale, il est nommé affichiste officiel du ministère des Armées et réalise à ce titre une bonne centaine d'affiches. Persévérant dans cette voie au lendemain de la guerre, il dessine également des emblèmes et des timbres-poste pour la Grande-Bretagne et Israël. Lauréat d'une quarantaine de prix nationaux et internationaux. A créé le «Designer of the Queen's Award to Industry». Elevé au rang d'OBE en 1957 pour ses créations graphiques. Nommé RDI en 1959.

ARNE UNGERMANN, born 1902 in Odense, Denmark. After a lithographic schooling he was occupied for several years for newspapers in Odense. In 1924 he went to Copenhagen, where he got a position in the advertising department of a large daily newspaper *Politiken.* After educational trips to France, Germany and Austria he was employed in 1930 by the Sunday supplement of the *Politiken, Magasinet.* He developed new finesse in four-color processing and became a contributor to magazines and humorous newspapers. Furthermore, Ungermann created posters, political satires and illustrated books.

ARNE UNGERMANN, 1902 in Odense, Dänemark, geboren. Nach einer Lithographenlehre war er einige Jahre für Zeitungen in Odense tätig. 1924 ging er nach Kopenhagen, wo er in der Reklameabteilung der grossen Tageszeitung *Politiken* eine Anstellung erhielt. Nach Studienreisen nach Frankreich, Deutschland und Österreich wurde er 1930 bei der Sonntagsbeilage von *Politiken,* beim *Magasinet,* angestellt. Er entwickelte neue Finessen im Vierfarbendruck und wurde Mitarbeiter bei Zeitschriften und humoristischen Zeitungen. Ausserdem schuf Ungermann Plakate und politische Satiren und illustrierte Bücher.

ARNE UNGERMANN, né en 1902 à Odense (Danemark). Après un apprentissage de lithographe, il travaille quelques années pour des journaux d'Odense. En 1924, il part pour Copenhague et entre au département publicitaire du grand quotidien *Politiken.* Il fait des séjours d'études en France, en Allemagne et en Autriche, puis entre en 1930 dans l'équipe du *Magasinet,* supplément dominical de *Politiken.* Il se signale par les raffinements qu'il apporte à la quadrichromie et commence à collaborer à des magazines et à des revues satiriques. Ungermann a aussi réalisé des affiches, des satires politiques et a illustré des livres.

For short biography, see page 137.
Is it possible that these three fishes by HANS HARTMANN symbolize the trilingual aspect of *Graphis* magazine? He has here taken an almost biblical fertility symbol as a classical subject. Just as classic is the symbolism of the color blue – fish and water – the element of life.

Kurzbiographie Seite 137.
Ob wohl diese drei Fische von HANS HARTMANN die Dreisprachigkeit des *Graphis* Magazins symbolisieren? Als beinahe biblisches Fruchtbarkeitssymbol hat er hier ein klassisches Thema aufgegriffen. Ebenso klassisch die Symbolik der Farbe blau – Fische und Wasser, das Element des Lebens.

Voir la notice biographique en p. 137.
Ces trois poissons de HANS HARTMANN pourraient fort bien symboliser l'aspect trilingue du magazine *Graphis.* Sujet classique, ce symbole presque biblique de la fertilité est tout naturellement associé au bleu de la vie marine et de sa faune.

GOTTFRIED HONEGGER, born in Zurich, 1917. Painter, sculptor. He divides his time between Paris and Zurich. At first he worked in abstract style, but in 1958 he developed his own technique in which the canvas was geometrically painted in layers and modulated into a relief structure. His sculptures are combinations of elementary forms such as circles or half and quarter spheres.

GOTTFRIED HONEGGER, 1917 in Zürich geboren. Er ist Maler und Bildhauer und lebt in Paris und Zürich. Seine frühen Werke gehören in die Kategorie der abstrakten Malerei. Um 1958 begann er mit konstruktiven Gestaltungen; er entwickelte eine eigene Technik, um das Leinwandbild zum geometrisch gegliederten «Bild-Relief» zu machen. Die plastischen Werke bestehen aus Kombinationen elementarer Körperformen wie Kreisring oder Halb- und Viertelkugel.

GOTTFRIED HONEGGER, né à Zurich en 1917. Peintre et sculpteur. Partage son temps entre Paris et Zurich. A d'abord adopté un style abstrait avant de mettre au point dès 1958 une technique personnelle qui lui fait recouvrir la toile de couches de peinture géométriques qu'il ordonne en une structure présentant un relief. Ses sculptures combinent des formes élémentaires telles que des cercles, des demi- et quarts de sphères.

MARCEL VERTÈS, born in Hungary, 1895. He settled in Paris in 1920 and worked with Jean-Paul Laurens. He took up book and stage design before going to the USA where his chronicle drawings appeared in *Vogue, Harper's Bazaar* etc. He continued to work in Paris and New York doing illustrations, stage design, tapestries, murals, etc. for museums, theaters and private houses. The scenarios and costumes for the film *Moulin Rouge* were designed by him, and it was his hand that was shown as that of Toulouse Lautrec in this film.

MARCEL VERTÈS, 1895 in Ungarn geboren. Geht 1920 nach Paris und arbeitet mit Jean-Paul Laurens. Gestaltung von Buchumschlägen und Bühnenbildern. Er geht in die USA, wo seine Zeichnungen periodisch in *Vogue, Harper's Bazaar* etc. erscheinen. Abwechslungsweise arbeitet er in Paris und in New York. Gestaltung von Illustrationen, Bühnenbildern, Wandteppichen, Wandgemälden etc. für Museen, Theater und Privathäuser. Das Szenario und die Kostüme für den Film *Moulin Rouge* wurden von ihm entworfen, und seine Hand wird in diesem Film als die des Toulouse Lautrec gezeigt.

MARCEL VERTÈS, né en Hongrie en 1895. Etabli à Paris en 1920, il travaille avec Jean-Paul Laurens. Crée des maquettes de livres et des décors de théâtre avant de partir pour les USA où ses dessins paraissent régulièrement dans *Vogue, Harper's Bazaar,* etc. Se partage entre Paris et New York, créant des illustrations, des décors de théâtre, des tapisseries, des murals, etc. pour des musées, des théâtres, des particuliers. On lui doit le scénario et les costumes du film *Moulin Rouge,* où il a prêté sa main à Toulouse-Lautrec.

For short biography, see page 135.
This illustration by PABLO PICASSO related to an article in this issue entitled "War and Peace". In 1952 Picasso was commissioned by the south French town of Vallauris to decorate a 14th century long-disused chapel. Picasso took the subject which had continually influenced him – war and peace. He had two giant panels made (totalling 100 sq mtrs.) and, after trying the composition out in the chapel, he erected the panels in his studio to complete them. Today they are in place in the longitudinal vault-like chapel.

Kurzbiographie Seite 135.
Dieses Bild von PABLO PICASSO bezieht sich auf den Artikel «Krieg und Frieden» in dieser Ausgabe. Picasso wurde 1952 von der südfranzösischen Stadt Vallauris beauftragt, eine seit langem leerstehende Kapelle aus dem 14. Jahrhundert zu bemalen. Picasso wählte ein Sujet, welches ihn bereits seit langem beschäftigte – Krieg und Frieden. Er liess zwei riesige Tafeln (Gesamtfläche 100 m²) herstellen, die er probeweise in der Kapelle aufstellte – um die Gesamtwirkung zu sehen – und dann in seinem Atelier beendete. Die beiden Bilder bedecken die ganze Oberfläche des Gewölbes der Kapelle.

Voir la notice biographique en p. 135.
Cette illustration de PABLO PICASSO se rapporte à un article intitulé «Guerre et Paix» dans le même numéro. En 1952, la municipalité de Vallauris (Alpes-Maritimes) confia à Picasso la décoration d'une chapelle désaffectée du XIVe siècle. Le choix de Picasso se porta sur un sujet qui le préoccupait depuis longtemps – la guerre et la paix. Il réalisa une foule de croquis, qu'il reporta sur deux immenses panneaux d'une surface totale de 100 m² installés dans la chapelle pour juger de l'effet d'ensemble, puis achevés en atelier. Les deux murals sont aujourd'hui en place dans la chapelle, un bâtiment longitudinal en forme de caveau.

For short biography, see page 133.
HANS ERNI had already become well-known abroad at the time of this illustration. Always on the lookout for new media of expression he painted the girl's face with tempera color and then, while still damp, scratched the contours and linaments with a blunt knitting needle.

Kurzbiographie Seite 133.
Das Mädchengesicht dieses Umschlages ist von HANS ERNI mit einer stumpfen Stricknadel auf die noch feuchte Temperafarbe geritzt. Erni sucht in seiner Arbeit dauernd nach neuen Ausdrucksmitteln und ist besonders von der Lithographie fasziniert, die er als schlechthin unerschöpfliches Experimentierfeld für den Graphiker betrachtet.

Voir la notice biographique en p. 133.
HANS ERNI était déjà célèbre à l'époque où il créa cette illustration. Toujours à la recherche de nouveaux moyens d'expression, il peignit ce visage de fille à la détrempe, puis incisa les contours et les traits dans la peinture encore humide en se servant d'une aiguille à tricoter épontée. C'est pourtant la lithographie qui le fascine; il y voit un terrain d'expérimentation illimité pour tout graphiste.

BERTRAM A.TH. WEIHS, born in Salzburg, Austria. He first studied in Vienna but later came to Holland where he enrolled in the Academy of Fine Arts, The Hague. Afterwards he worked for a long time as a typographer in a printing shop in that city and was also teaching at the Academy of Lettering, The Hague. His graphic work has been widely exhibited.

BERTRAM A.TH. WEIHS, in Salzburg, Österreich, geboren. Nachdem er kurze Zeit an der Graphischen Lehranstalt in Wien eingeschrieben war, besuchte er die Akademie für bildende Künste, Den Haag, und arbeitete längere Zeit als Typograph in einer dortigen Druckerei. Er war Lehrer an der Haager Akademie für Schrift und hat seine graphischen Arbeiten verschiedentlich ausgestellt.

BERTRAM A.TH. WEIHS, né à Salzbourg, Autriche. Après avoir été, pour une brève période, inscrit à l'Ecole des Arts graphiques de Vienne, il suivit l'enseignement de l'Académie de La Haye, ville où il travailla assez longtemps auprès d'une imprimerie. Il était professeur d'écriture à la même Académie et a plusieurs fois exposé ses créations graphiques.

HANS FISCHER, born 1909 in Bern, died 1958 in Interlaken. He left behind an extraordinary, rich collection of works. He illustrated 23 books (among them Brentano's *Gockel and Hinkel* and Grimm's Fairytales, which were also published in America and Japan. He finished 26 wall paintings (partly in school buildings) and several hundred papers and drawings. He designed unforgettable stage scenery for the cabaret *Cornichon*. Shortly before his death there still remained over one hundred colored sketches for schoolbooks.

HANS FISCHER, 1909 in Bern geboren, 1958 in Interlaken gestorben. Er hinterliess ein ungemein reiches Werk. Er illustrierte 23 Bücher (darunter Brentanos *Gockel und Hinkel* und Grimms Märchen), die auch in Amerika und Japan publiziert wurden. Er fertigte 26 Wandbilder (z. T. in Schulhäusern) und einige hundert graphische Blätter und Zeichnungen. Er entwarf unvergessliche Bühnenbilder für das Cabaret *Cornichon*. Kurz vor seinem Tod entstanden noch über hundert Farbstift-Zeichnungen für Schulbücher.

HANS FISCHER, né à Berne en 1909, mort à Interlaken en 1958, laissant après lui un œuvre extraordinairement riche. Il a illustré 23 ouvrages, dont le *Gockel et Hinkel* de Brentano et les Contes des frères Grimm, qui parurent aussi en édition américaine et japonaise. Il réalisa 26 murals en partie destinés à des bâtiments scolaires, ainsi que quelques centaines de gravures et de dessins. On lui doit d'inoubliables décors pour le cabaret *Cornichon*. Peu avant son décès prématuré, il avait préparé une bonne centaine de dessins au crayon couleur destinés à des manuel scolaires.

For short biography, see page 135.
This illustration by PABLO PICASSO was executed in 1938. The feature on Picasso's work in this issue concerned the master's use of lithography. Several of Picasso's lithographic works were done on zinc plates instead of the lithographic stone. Many of his compositions were unpremeditated, the products of a swift and sudden impulse, fathered by the pure joy of creation.

Kurzbiographie Seite 135.
Dieses Gemälde von PABLO PICASSO ist 1938 entstanden. Der diesbezügliche Artikel in dieser Ausgabe beschäftigt sich mit dem Lithographen Picasso. Bei vielen seiner lithographischen Werke verwendete er Zinkplatten anstelle des Steins. Viele dieser Kompositionen entstanden spontan, aus einem plötzlichen Impuls, aus reiner Schöpferlust.

Voir la notice biographique en p. 135.
Cette illustration de PABLO PICASSO date de 1938. L'article auquel elle se rapporte étudie les créations lithographiques du maître, réalisées en partie sur des plaques de zinc en lieu et place de la pierre traditionnelle. Un grand nombre de ces compositions sont le fruit de la spontanéité, d'un subit élan créateur où éclate le chant triomphal du démiurge.

BERNARD VILLEMOT, born at Trouville, France, 1911. (Son of cartoonist Jean Villemot.) His wide range of expressive media includes: poster art, murals, lithography, stage design, and painting. He has gained numerous awards, among them: the Gold Medal for advertising art in Tokyo 1957.

BERNARD VILLEMOT, 1911 in Frankreich geboren, als Sohn des Karikaturisten Jean Villemot. Zu seinen ausdrucksstarken Arbeiten gehören Plakate, Wandgemälde, Lithographien, Bühnenbilder, Gemälde. Er hat verschiedene Auszeichnungen erhalten, unter anderen 1957 in Tokio eine Goldmedaille für Werbegraphik.

BERNARD VILLEMOT, né à Trouville (Normandie) en 1911. Fils du caricaturiste Jean Villemot. A révélé son talent expressif dans les médias les plus divers - l'affiche, le mural, la litho, le décor de théâtre, la peinture. Lauréat de nombreux prix, il a décroché à Tokyo, en 1957, la médaille d'or de l'art publicitaire.

For short biography, see Page 141.
ANDRÉ FRANÇOIS' illustration for this cover amusingly symbolizes the responsibilities which weigh heavily upon the graphic artist in his constant attempt to find solutions to very complex problems. (François was forty years old at the time of this illustration.)

Kurzbiographie Seite 141.
ANDRÉ FRANÇOIS' Illustration für diesen Umschlag symbolisiert auf humorvolle Art die Verantwortung, die bei der Lösung komplexer Probleme auf dem Graphiker lastet. (François war vierzig Jahre alt, als er diese Illustration machte.)

Voir la notice biographique en p. 141.
L'illustration d'ANDRÉ FRANÇOIS pour cette couverture symbolise plaisamment les lourdes responsabilités qui incombent au graphiste constamment attelé à la solution de problèmes fort complexes. François avait 40 ans quand il réalisa cette illustration.

For short biography, see page 136.
This work shows one of the many faces by GEORGE GIUSTI. As on the cover of *Graphis* 26, again the tool of the graphic designer is brought into the illustration. The watercolor technique in its softness enhances the rather anxious, dejected expression of the face, the signal-red "nose" in contrast, conveys a livelier, more decisive element.

Kurzbiographie Seite 136.
Diese Arbeit zeigt eines der vielfältigen Gesichter von GEORGE GIUSTI. Wie schon auf dem Umschlag von *Graphis* No. 26, wird auch hier wieder die Darstellung des Handwerkszeugs des Graphikers zur Bildaussage hinzugezogen. Die Aquarelltechnik in ihrer Zartheit fördert den eher ängstlichen, verzagten Ausdruck des Gesichtes, das Signalrot der «Nase» dagegen bringt eine lebhaftere, entschiedenere Komponente.

Voir la notice biographique en p. 136.
On découvre ici l'une des multiples facettes de l'artiste GEORGE GIUSTI. Comme il l'avait fait pour la couverture de *Graphis* 26, il introduit l'instrument du graphiste dans le canevas de l'illustration. La douceur de l'aquarelle fait mieux ressortir la mine anxieuse et défaite, alors que le nez rouge signalise une tonalité plus vivace, plus affirmative.

MICHAEL WOLGENSINGER, born in Zurich, 1915. He studied at the Kunstgewerbeschule in Zurich in the department of photography. He opened his own studio in Zurich and soon became one of Switzerland's most successful photographers.

MICHAEL WOLGENSINGER, 1915 in Zürich geboren. Er studierte in der Klasse für Photographie an der Kunstgewerbeschule in Zürich. Er eröffnete ein eigenes Studio in Zürich und wurde bald einer der erfolgreichsten Photographen der Schweiz.

MICHAEL WOLGENSINGER, né à Zurich en 1915. Fait ses études au département photo de l'Ecole des arts décoratifs de Zurich. Dès l'ouverture de son propre studio à Zurich, il s'est hissé dans le peloton de tête des tout premiers photographes suisses.

YOSHIO HAYAKAWA, born in Osaka, 1917. He studied at the Osaka College of Applied Arts and started his career first as a window dresser and then worked for the city's publicity department. Later he became a freelance designer working in advertising design, packaging, book design, illustration and stage decor. He has won many national awards and examples of his work are held in the MOMA. He was a lecturer at the Kyoto University of Arts.

YOSHIO HAYAKAWA, 1917 in Osaka geboren. Ausbildung an der Kunsthochschule in Osaka. Arbeitete zuerst als Schaufenstergestalter und dann in der Informationsabteilung der Stadtverwaltung. Betätigte sich anschliessend als freier Designer für Werbung, Packungen, Illustrator, Bühnenbildner. Empfänger verschiedener Auszeichnungen. Einige seiner Werke befinden sich im MOMA. Er ist Dozent an der Kunsthochschule Kyoto.

YOSHIO HAYAKAWA, né à Osaka en 1917. Etudes au Collège des arts appliqués de sa ville natale. Il débute comme décorateur d'étalages, puis travaille au département d'information municipal. S'établit par la suite à son compte, réalisant de la publicité, des emballages, des maquettes et illustrations de livres, des décors de théâtre. Lauréat de nombreux prix nationaux. Certaines de ses œuvres figurent dans les collections du MOMA. A enseigné à l'Université des Beaux-Arts de Kyoto.

BEN SHAHN, born in Kovno, Russia, 1898. He went to the USA in 1906 and first studied biology at New York University, later at the National Academy of Design. After extensive travels, he began designing posters – for the War Information Office (1942) and for other government departments. He lectured widely in USA and London. He was awarded many high honors and distinctions for illustration, murals, painting and design. He is represented in major museums, including MOMA.

BEN SHAHN, 1898 in Kovno (Russland) geboren. 1906 wanderten seine Eltern in die USA aus. Er studierte zuerst Biologie an der Universität von New York und besuchte anschliessend die nationale Zeichenakademie. Nach ausgedehnten Reisen begann er Plakate zu entwerfen, z.B. für den Kriegsinformationsdienst (1942) und für andere Ministerien. Er war Dozent an verschiedenen Universitäten in den USA und London und erhielt viele hohe Auszeichnungen für seine Illustrationen, Wandgemälde und Bilder. Seine Werke sind in verschiedenen Museen vertreten, u.a. im MOMA.

BEN SHAHN, né à Kovno (Russie) en 1898. Emigré aux Etats-Unis en 1906, il étudie la biologie à l'Université de New York, puis s'inscrit à la National Academy of Design. Grand voyageur, il revient au pays pour travailler comme affichiste pour le Département d'information des Armées (1942) et d'autres agences ministérielles. Il a enseigné dans diverses universités d'Amérique, ainsi qu'à Londres. De nombreux prix prestigieux sont venus récompenser ses illustrations, ses murals, sa peinture et ses créations d'art publicitaire. Ses œuvres figurent dans les collections des grands musées, notamment dans celles du MOMA.

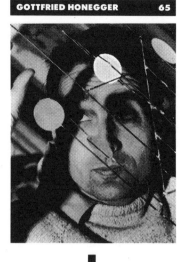

For short biography, see Page 138.
The cover of this issue by ANTONI CLAVÉ was adapted from the decorated box in which his magnificent *Gargantua* (precious book of Clavé's lithographs) was sent to the members of the Comité des Bibliophiles de Provence. Spanish-born Clavé had given up doing illustrations for Spanish authors' works; he readily agreed to illustrate Rabelais as the name opened up for him a tempting pictorial world.

Kurzbiographie Seite 138.
Der Umschlag zu dieser Nummer ist – in einer etwas anderen Farbvariante – die Adaption des Umschlages zu *Gargantua*, einer von ANTONIO CLAVÉ illustrierten Luxusausgabe seiner Lithographien. Clavé hatte schon lange keine Illustrationen mehr zu spanischen Dichtern gemacht, für Rabelais jedoch sagte er spontan zu, weil sich für ihn mit diesem Namen eine verlockende Bilderwelt verband.

Voir la notice biographic en p. 138.
La couverture de ce numéro est une variante chromatique de l'emboîtage décoratif qui servit à distribuer au Comité des Bibliophiles de Provence un livre précieux, le *Gargantua* illustré des lithos d'ANTONIO CLAVÉ. L'artiste espagnol avait renoncé à illustrer des auteurs espagnols; il accepta de s'inspirer de Rabelais dont le nom évoquait pour lui un monde d'images incommensurable.

LEO LONGANESI, born in Italy, 1905. Painter, graphic designer, writer and publisher. In 1927 he founded (with Mino Maccari) a two-weekly magazine entitled *Il Selvaggio* (The Savage) and also *L'Italiano*. In 1937 he published *Omnibus* - a weekly magazine. Since 1950 he has headed his own publishing house.

LEO LONGANESI, 1905 in Italien geboren. Maler, Graphik-Designer, Schriftsteller und Verleger. 1927 gründete er (mit Mino Maccari) eine Zeitschrift mit dem Titel *Il Selvaggio* (Der Wilde) sowie später *L'Italiano*. 1937 folgte das Wochenmagazin *Omnibus*. Seit 1950 leitet er seinen eigenen Verlag.

LEO LONGANESI, né en Italie en 1905. Peintre, graphiste, écrivain et éditeur. Fonde en 1927, avec Mino Maccari, le magazine bimestriel *Il Selvaggio* (Le Sauvage) et aussi *L'Italiano*. En 1937, il lance l'hebdomadaire *Omnibus*. Est à la tête de sa propre maison d'édition depuis 1950.

For short biography, see Page 142.
GOTTFRIED HONEGGER's second *Graphis* cover (after No. 50) is, when one considers that it was done in the mid-fifties, of astonishing modernity and objectivity. Honegger, at that time art director at the Basle chemical firm of Geigy, has emphasized the beauty in cartographic presentation of scientific facts. The brain, undoubtedly today still one of the most mystical of all human organs, serves as model for a well-organized diagram in colour and in form.

Kurzbiographie Seite 142.
GOTTFRIED HONEGGERS zweiter *Graphis*-Umschlag (nach No. 50) ist für die Mitte der Fünfzigerjahre von verblüffender Modernität und Sachlichkeit. Honegger, zu diesem Zeitpunkt Art Direktor des Basler Chemiekonzerns Geigy, verweist hier auf die Schönheit der kühlen kartographischen Darstellung von wissenschaftlichen Sachverhalten. Das Gehirn, bis heute das unangetastet mystischste aller menschlichen Organe, gibt die Vorlage für ein farblich und formal durchgestaltetes Diagramm.

Voir la notice biographic en p. 142.
La deuxième couverture de GOTTFRIED HONEGGER (après celle de *Graphis* 50) est étonnante de modernité et de sobriété si l'on considère qu'elle date du milieu des années 50. Alors directeur artistique de la maison Geigy, Honegger y fait ressortir la beauté de la représentation cartographique placide de données scientifiques. C'est le cerveau, longtemps tenu pour l'organe le plus mystique que nous possédions, qui fournit le modèle de ce diagramme parachevé au double plan chromatique et formel.

CELESTINO PIATTI, born in Switzerland, 1922. Studied at the Kunstgewerbeschule, Zürich. He began in his own studio with advertising campaigns, packaging, posters, exhibition designs. He designed over 5000 book covers for a German paperback publisher. He created the murals for the Swiss Pavilion at the Expo '67 in Montreal. He has gained numerous major awards and distinctions for his art in all fields and his work has been widely exhibited. He is a member of AGI.

CELESTINO PIATTI, 1922 in der Schweiz geboren. Studierte an der Kunstgewerbeschule in Zürich und arbeitete anschliessend als freier Künstler. Seine Arbeiten umfassen Werbekampagnen, Packungen, Plakate, Ausstellungsgestaltung. Für einen deutschen Taschenbuchverlag hat er über 5000 Buchumschläge gestaltet. Für die Expo '67 in Montreal schuf er das Wandgemälde des Schweizer Pavillons. Er hat für sein Schaffen unzählige Auszeichnungen und Würdigungen erhalten. Seine Werke wurden vielfach ausgestellt. Er ist Mitglied der AGI.

CELESTINO PIATTI, né en Suisse en 1922. Ancien élève de l'Ecole des arts décoratifs de Zurich. Quand il s'établit à son compte, c'est pour réaliser des campagnes publicitaires, des emballages, des affiches, des stands d'exposition. Il a créé plus de 5000 couvertures de livres pour un grand éditeur allemand de livres de poche. On lui doit les murals du pavillon suisse à l'Expo 67 de Montréal. Dans tous ses domaines d'activité, il a été récompensé de nombreux grands prix. Ses œuvres ont été exposées maintes fois. Il est membre de l'AGI.

UMETARO AZECHI, born in Japan, 1902. He studied painting at first and later discovered that print-making was for him the ideal mode of expression. He lives in Tokyo.

UMETARO AZECHI, 1902 in Japan geboren. Er studierte Malerei bevor er seine Begabung für den Holzschnitt entdeckte. Er lebt in Tokio.

UMETARO AZECHI, né au Japon en 1902. D'abord peintre, il a découvert dans la gravure son mode d'expression idéal. Il habite Tokyo.

JOAN JORDAN, born in Copenhagen. She studied as a painter and ceramic artist in Denmark, and later specialized in montages of cloth and appliqué work, producing advertisements and children's book illustration using this technique.

JOAN JORDAN, in Kopenhagen geboren. Sie studierte Malerei und Keramik in Dänemark, bevor sie sich auf Montagen mit verschiedenen Materialien und Appliqué-Arbeiten spezialisierte. Diese Arbeiten wurden auch für Werbung und als Kinderbuch-Illustrationen verwendet.

JOAN JORDEN, née à Copenhague. Etudes de peintre et céramiste au Danemark. Elle se spécialise par la suite dans des montages de tissu et d'applications dont elle illustre des annonces et des livres pour enfants.

HERBERT AUCHLI, born in Lucerne, 1921. He studied at the Kunstgewerbeschule, Lucerne, and in Zürich. After extensive travelling, he returned to Switzerland and first worked in advertising agencies in Berne and Zürich and as graphic designer in the machine industry in Geneva before becoming a freelance graphic designer and illustrator with his own studio in Berne (founded 1947). For the past 15 years he has been a member of the professor collegium in the graphic-design department of the Schule für Gestaltung in Berne (School of Design).

HERBERT AUCHLI, 1921 in Luzern geboren. Er studierte an den Kunstgewerbeschulen in Luzern und Zürich. Nach ausgedehnten Reisen kehrte er in die Schweiz zurück und arbeitete für Werbeagenturen in Bern und Zürich und als Graphik-Designer in der Maschinenindustrie in Genf. 1947 gründete er ein eigenes Studio für Graphik-Design und Illustration in Bern. Von 1971 bis 1986 war er Mitglied des Fachlehrerkollegiums in der Graphiker-Fachklasse der Schule für Gestaltung in Bern.

HERBERT AUCHLI, né à Lucerne en 1921. Etudes à l'Ecole des arts décoratifs de Lucerne et à Zurich. Grand voyageur, il se fixe enfin en Suisse pour travailler dans des agences de publicité de Berne et Zurich, puis comme graphiste dans la construction mécanique genevoise. En 1947, il ouvre un studio d'art publicitaire et illustratif à Berne. Ces quinze dernières années, il a fait partie du corps enseignant du département d'art graphique de la Schule für Gestaltung (Ecole de design) de Berne.

RUDOLPH DE HARAK, born in California, 1924. He has been running his own design office in New York since 1950. He does environmental, exhibition and graphic design. He designed the pavilion "Man, his Planet and Space" for Expo '67 in Montreal and was a principal designer of the US pavilion at the Expo '70 in Osaka. He is Professor of Design at Cooper Union and has taught at various other schools. He has held major exhibitions in New York and Paris and has won numerous awards from the AIGA and the New York ADC. His work is held in collections at MOMA and the Warsaw National Museum.

RUDOLPH DE HARAK, 1924 in Kalifornien geboren. Seit 1950 hat er ein eigenes Design-Studio in New York. Zu seinem Arbeitsbereich gehören Signalisierungs- und Ausstellungsgraphik sowie Graphik-Design. Er entwarf den Pavillon «Man, his Planet and Space» für die Weltausstellung '67 in Montreal und war wesentlich an der Gestaltung des US-Pavillons an der Expo '70 in Osaka beteiligt. Er ist Professor für Design an der Cooper Union und hat auch an anderen Schulen unterrichtet. Seine Arbeiten wurden in New York und Paris ausgestellt und u.a. von der AIGA und dem New York Art Directors Club ausgezeichnet. Sie sind in den Sammlungen des MOMA und des Warschauer Nationalmuseums zu finden.

RUDOLPH DE HARAK, né en Californie en 1924. Dirige son propre studio de design à New York depuis 1950. Spécialisé dans le design d'environnements et d'expositions et dans le design graphique. A réalisé pour l'Expo 67 de Montréal le pavillon «L'Homme, sa planète et l'espace». Concepteur en chef du pavillon américain à l'Expo 70 d'Osaka. Professeur de design à Cooper Union, il a enseigné dans diverses autres écoles. De grandes expositions lui ont été consacrées à New York et à Paris. Il est lauréat de nombreux prix de l'AIGA et du New York Art Directors Club. Ses œuvres figurent dans les collections du MOMA et du Musée national de Varsovie.

■

PHILIPPE DELESSERT, born in Switzerland, 1933. He studied jewellery design in Geneva and Paris before turning to the graphic arts. On returning to Switzerland he founded a studio in Lausanne with an advertising artist, Claudine Wick, under the name *Wick and Delessert*.

■

PHILIPPE DELESSERT, 1933 in der Schweiz geboren. Er erlernte in Genf und Paris den Beruf eines Goldschmieds, bevor er seine Neigung für die Werbegraphik entdeckte. Nach seiner Rückkehr in die Schweiz eröffnete er zusammen mit der Graphikerin Claudine Wick in Lausanne ein Atelier unter dem Namen *Wick & Delessert*.

■

PHILIPPE DELESSERT, né en Suisse en 1933. A étudié l'art de la bijouterie à Genève et à Paris avant de s'orienter vers la création graphique. De retour en Suisse, fonde le studio *Wick et Delessert* à Lausanne, en association avec l'artiste publicitaire Claudine Wick.

■

For short biography, see Page 146.
CELESTINO PIATTI was forty-two when he designed this cover. He had found his own style in heavy black contours and color surfaces with the intensity of stained glass. He had already gained many successful advertising campaigns and had just held an important exhibition of his work in Berlin.

■

Kurzbiographie Seite 146.
Das äussere Kennzeichen von CELESTINO PIATTIS Arbeiten, besonders seiner auf Fernwirkung angelegten farbigen Plakate, ist die breite schwarze Kontur, mit der er kleinere farbige Flächen zu akzentuieren und in geometrisch-rhythmische Kompositionen zu bringen versteht. Hinter diesen schwarzen Konturen verbirgt sich der Signetcharakter seiner Werbung. Seine Plakate z. B. sind mit Stich- und Schlagworten zu vergleichen.

■

Voir la notice biographique en p. 146.
CELESTINO PIATTI avait 42 ans quand il réalisa cette couverture. Il avait déjà élaboré sa griffe personnelle – un contourage noir épais de surfaces colorées au petit format, ce qui lui permettait d'accentuer le chromatisme et de l'agencer en des compositions géométriques animées d'un rythme propre. Ces caractéristiques représentatives d'un vitrail éclatant surtout dans les affiches polychromes conçues pour être vues de loin et qui, chez lui, prennent une valeur exemplaire de repères. Notre couverture est née le lendemain d'une exposition importante qui venait de lui être consacrée à Berlin.

■

LE CORBUSIER (1887-1965). French architect, born Charles Edouard Jeanneret in Switzerland. He promoted the international modern style but eventually developed a style of his own. His experiments with modern construction methods resulted in unique designs for houses and entire cities. He used strong cubist forms and often placed his buildings on pillars. After 1940 he developed a complex modular system of harmonious but differing proportions – e.g. the chapel at Ronchamp near Belfort (1954). He also designed the walls of the UN Secretariat in New York.

■

LE CORBUSIER (1887-1965). Französischer Architekt, unter dem Namen Charles Edouard Jeanneret in der Schweiz geboren. Seine Experimente mit modernen Konstruktionsmethoden resultierten in einzigartigen Entwürfen für Häuser und ganze Städte. Er verwendete starke kubistische Formen, und häufig setzte er seine Gebäude auf Pfeiler. Nach 1940 entwickelte er ein komplexes Bausystem aus Elementen mit harmonischen, jedoch unterschiedlichen Proportionen – z. B. die Kapelle in Ronchamp bei Belfort (1954). Er gestaltete u. a. die Wände des UNO-Gebäudes in New York.

■

LE CORBUSIER (1887-1965), de son vrai nom Charles Edouard Jeanneret. Cet architecte français d'origine suisse s'est fait l'avocat du style moderne international tout en développant un style hautement personnel. Expérimentant des méthodes nouvelles de construction, il élabora des plans exceptionnels pour des immeubles comme pour des cités entières. Utilisant des formes résolument cubistes, il a souvent placé ses constructions sur piliers. A partir de 1940, il met au point un système modulaire complexe où des proportions différentes se fondent harmonieusement, ainsi dans la Chapelle de Ronchamp près de Belfort (1954). On lui doit les murs du secrétariat de l'O.N.U. à New York.

■

BERT STERN, born in New York, 1929. He was first employed as an assistant in an art studio. At the age of 20 he bought his first camera and did his military service as cameraman. On return to civilian life he was quickly "discovered" and soon became a highly successful photographer doing editorial annd advertising work.

■

BERT STERN, 1929 in New York geboren. Er arbeitete zuerst als Assistent in einem Graphik-Studio. Mit 20 Jahren kaufte er seine erste Kamera und absolvierte seinen Militärdienst als Kameramann. Bald nach seiner Entlassung aus dem Militär wurde er -entdeckt- und wurde ein sehr erfolgreicher Photograph, der vor allem für Zeitschriften und Werbung arbeitet.

■

BERT STERN, né à New York en 1929. D'abord assistant dans un studio artistique, il s'achète à 20 ans son premier appareil photo et fait son service militaire comme reporter-photographe. Rendu à la vie civile, il se fait rapidement connaître et est aujourd'hui un photographe à succès dans le domaine de l'illustration de presse et de la publicité.

■

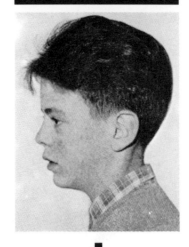

JEAN-MARIE LURÇAT, France 1892–1966. He first studied medicine and then, after meeting the artist Victor Prouvé, became his pupil. He went to Paris to learn typography and engraving. In 1914 he was apprenticed to J. P. Lafitte for whom he began to paint frescoes. He created his first tapestry towards the end of the war and this was followed by decors and ballet costumes. His first exhibitions were held in Paris. He worked in gouaches and oils, and he wove more tapestries at Gobelins in 1936. Largest tapestry, "Le Chant du Monde", 500 sq. m.

JEAN-MARIE LURÇAT, Frankreich 1892–1966. Er studierte Medizin, bis er den Künstler Victor Prouvé kennenlernte und sein Schüler wurde. In Paris lernte er Typographie und Drucktechniken. 1914 wurde er Schüler von J. P. Lafitte, für den er Freskos zu malen begann. Seine ersten Tapisserien machte er gegen Ende des Krieges, und es folgten Dekorationen und Ballett-Kostüme. Seine ersten Ausstellungen hatte er in Paris. Sein bildnerisches Werk besteht vor allem aus Gouachen und Ölbildern. Der grösste Teppich, den er herstellte, ist «Le Chant du Monde», 500 m²gross.

JEAN-MARIE LURÇAT (1892–1966), d'origine française. Etudiant en médecine, il rencontre l'artiste Victor Prouvé, devient son disciple. Etudie à Paris la typo et la gravure. En 1914, il se met au service de J. P. Lafitte, pour qui il commence à peindre des fresques. Sa première tapisserie date de la fin de la guerre. Il crée des décors et des costumes de ballet. Sa première exposition se tient à Paris. Spécialiste de la gouache et de l'huile, il réalise aux Gobelins une série de tapisseries en 1936. Sa tenture la plus importante, «Le Chant du monde», mesure 500 m².

For short biography, see Page 141.
ANDRÉ FRANÇOIS has intentionally adopted a technique of line and color which is at first glance conspicuous through its apparent maliciousness and ineptitude. François is cunningly inept! He blends all the fresh ingenuousness of the child with a clear analytical mind.

Kurzbiographie Seite 141.
ANDRÉ FRANÇOIS hat sich absichtlich eine Technik des Strichs und der Farbe angeeignet, die vorerst durch eine scheinbare und boshafte Ungeschicklichkeit auffällt. François ist durchtrieben ungeschickt! Er verbindet die Frische und Ungeschicktheit eines Kindes mit einem klaren, analysierenden Verstand.

Voir la notice biographique en p. 141.
ANDRÉ FRANÇOIS a intentionnellement adopté une technique du trait et de la couleur qui frappe d'emblée par son apparente malice et maladresse. Maladresse pleine de finasserie! C'est qu'il sait marier à ravir la fraîcheur et l'ingénuité enfantines et un intellect analytique des plus clairvoyants.

CHILD'S PAINTING. This cover illustration shows an aerial view of La Place Saint François, part of Lausanne, Switzerland. A class went with their art teacher to view the area with its great cathedral, its buildings, shops and many tramlines intersecting it. On their return to the classroom the children were left to record their impressions in paint. This is one of them. An 11-year-old said: "I drew the place from the air and then painted it, but I changed the colors a bit to make it more beautiful".

KINDERMALEREI. Der Umschlag zu dieser Nummer zeigt den Platz St. François in Lausanne (Westschweiz) aus der Vogelperspektive. Eine Schulklasse besichtigte in Begleitung ihrer Zeichenlehrerin den verkehrsreichen, von zahlreichen Tramlinien durchkreuzten Platz, auf dem eine alte Kathedrale steht, umgeben von grossen Gebäudekomplexen. Später durften die Kinder ihre Eindrücke mit Farbe ausdrücken. Hier ist eines der Bilder. Der Elfjährige, von dem es stammt, sagt dazu: «Ich habe den Platz von oben gezeichnet und dann gemalt, die Farben habe ich aber etwas geändert, um das Bild schöner zu machen.»

PEINTURE D'ENFANT. La couverture de ce numéro représente une vue d'avion de la place Saint-François à Lausanne. Accompagnée de la maîtresse de dessin, une classe a observé la place: la grande église, les pâtés de maisons, les magasins, les voies de tram. Les enfants ont en suite exprimé leurs impressions sous forme de peintures. Nous avons ici la vision d'un garçon de onze ans. «J'ai dessiné la place en vue d'avion, dit-il, puis je l'ai peinte, mais j'ai changé un peu les couleurs pour que ce soit plus beau.»

For short biography, see Page 136.
This face by GEORGE GIUSTI has the effect of a stained-glass window. It is the face of the sun, but within its heavy "lead" framework it is a ponderous, somewhat ominous sun.

Kurzbiographie Seite 136.
Dieses Gesicht von GEORGE GIUSTI wirkt wie ein mit Blei durchsetztes Kirchenfenster. Es hat eine Sonnenform, aber der Gesamteindruck ist eher düster, fast etwas bedrohlich.

Voir la notice biographique en p. 136.
Ce visage de GEORGE GIUSTI produit un effet de vitrail. Il s'agit bien de la face du soleil, mais sertie de «plomb» de manière à dégager une atmosphère pesante et quelque peu sinistre.

MAURICE SINÉ, born in Paris, 1928. He studied lithography and publicity in Paris from 1942–1946. He joined a French cabaret group and then worked for various advertising agencies and printers. He made his first humorous drawings in 1952. His cartoons and posters were mainly for advertising purposes and among his clients were *Esso, Shell, Metro-Goldwyn-Mayer, Sandoz* and *Schweppes*. His posters were widely acclaimed and he also did book illustrations, TV animated cartoons and publicity films. His series of 3 color films made for *Shell Oil* won the Grand Prix at the Venice International Film Festival 1958.

MAURICE SINÉ, 1928 in Paris geboren, studierte dort von 1942–1946 Lithographie und Werbegraphik. Er tat sich mit einer französischen Kabarett-Gruppe zusammen und arbeitete später für verschiedene Werbeagenturen und Drucker. Seine ersten humoristischen Zeichnungen entstanden 1952. Seine Karikaturen und Plakate wurden hauptsächlich für Werbezwecke verwendet, zu seinen Kunden zählten *Esso, Shell, Metro-Goldwyn-Mayer, Sandoz* und *Schweppes*. Mit seinen Plakaten hatte er grossen Erfolg. Gelegentlich machte er auch Buchillustrationen, Trickfilme und Werbefilme. Seine Serie von 3-Farben-Filmen für *Shell Oil* erhielt den Grand Prix des Internationalen Filmfestivals 1958 in Venedig.

MAURICE SINÉ est né en 1928 à Paris où il a étudié la lithographie et l'art publicitaire de 1942 à 1946. Il fut artiste de cabaret, puis travailla pour diverses agences de publicité et imprimeries. Ses premiers dessins d'humour voient le jour en 1952. Ses caricatures et affiches ont surtout servi à des fins commerciales, ses clients ayant pour nom *Esso, Shell, Metro-Goldwyn-Mayer, Sandoz, Schweppes*, etc. Ses affiches ont connu un très grand succès. Il a aussi démontré ses talents dans l'illustration de livres, le film d'animation TV, le film publicitaire. La série de trois films couleur qu'il réalisa pour *Shell Oil* lui valut le Grand Prix du Festival international du cinéma de Venise en 1958.

RONALD SEARLE, born in Cambridge, England, 1920. Cartoonist, designer of commemorative medals, film credits, film animation, illustrator and graphic designer. His work has been exhibited in many public collections including the Victoria and Albert Museum and various major museums in the USA.

RONALD SEARLE, 1920 in Cambridge, England, geboren. Karikaturen; Zeichnungen für Bücher, Werbezwecke und für Filme; Entwürfe für Medaillen und Graphik-Design. Seine Arbeiten sind in vielen öffentlichen Sammlungen vertreten, u.a. im Victoria and Albert Museum und in einigen grossen Museen der USA.

RONALD SEARLE, né à Cambridge (Royaume-Uni) en 1920. Caricaturiste, médailleur, créateur de génériques de films, de films d'animation, illustrateur, artiste publicitaire. Ses œuvres figurent dans de nombreuses collections publiques, notamment au Victoria and Albert Museum et dans divers grands musées d'Amérique.

© 1987 PRO LITTERIS, Zürich

JACK WOLFGANG BECK, born in the USA, 1923. He is mainly self-taught. In 1950 he established a design-consultancy agency in New York. His scope includes book design, record covers, advertising art and magazine illustration. In 1956 he was represented in AIGA "50 Best Books Show".

JACK WOLFGANG BECK, 1923 in den USA geboren. Er ist Autodidakt. 1950 gründete er eine Design/Beratungs-Firma in New York. Zu seinem Arbeitsbereich gehören Buch-Design, Schallplattenumschläge, Werbegraphik und Zeitschriftenillustrationen. 1956 war er in der AIGA-Ausstellung der 50 besten Bücher («50 Best Books Show») vertreten.

JACK WOLFGANG BECK, né aux Etats-Unis en 1923. Pour le principal de son œuvre, c'est un autodidacte. En 1950, il œvre à New York une agence-conseil en design. Il a réalisé des livres, des pochettes de disques, de la publicité et des illustrations de magazines. L'AIGA l'a inclus en 1956 dans son «Exposition des 50 meilleurs livres de l'année».

KURT WIRTH, born in Switzerland, 1917. After studying graphic design he travelled through Spain and Algeria before setting up his own studio in Berne (1937) mainly for book, newspaper and magazine illustration. In 1951 he continued his studies in Paris and participated in group shows in Canada and the US. His scope encompasses book covers, posters, advertising art, and postage stamps. In 1986 he was made Artist of the Year by the Swiss Sports Journalists. He has taught at the Kunstgewerbeschule in Berne and authored books on drawing. He is a member of AGI.

KURT WIRTH, 1917 in der Schweiz geboren. Er studierte Graphik-Design und reiste durch Spanien und Algerien, bevor er ein eigenes Studio in Bern (1937) hauptsächlich für Buch-, Zeitungs- und Zeitschriften-Illustration eröffnete. 1951 setzte er seine Studien in Paris fort und nahm an Gruppenausstellungen in Kanada und den USA teil. Sein Arbeitsbereich umfasst Buchumschläge, Plakate, Werbegraphik und Briefmarken. 1986 wurde er von den Schweizer Sportjournalisten zum Künstler des Jahres ernannt. Er hat an der Kunstgewerbeschule in Bern unterrichtet und Bücher über das Zeichnen herausgegeben. Er ist Mitglied der AGI.

KURT WIRTH, né en Suisse en 1917. Etudes d'art graphique. Il voyage en Espagne et en Algérie avant de s'établir à son compte à Berne en 1937, réalisant principalement des illustrations de livres, de journaux et de magazines. Poursuit ses études à Paris dès 1951. Participe à des expositions collectives au Canada et aux USA. Son domaine d'activité comprend les couvertures de livres, les affiches, l'art publicitaire, les timbres-poste. Les journalistes sportifs suisses l'élisent en 1986 Artiste de l'Année. Il a enseigné à l'Ecole des arts décoratifs de Berne et consacré divers ouvrages au dessin. Il est membre de l'AGI.

EUGENIO CARMI, born in Genoa, 1920. Graphic designer, industrial designer, painter and sculptor. He studied chemistry before turning to design. During the late 1950's and early 60's he was engaged as Art Director for *Italsider* in Genoa. He is now a freelance designer. He has worked in color TV programs for RAI and been engaged in corporate identity for major firms. He has been awarded numerous prizes. A visual-art teacher, he has lectured widely in the USA and Italy. Collections of his works are held in renowned museums including the Victoria and Albert Museum, MOMA, etc.

EUGENIO CARMI, 1920 in Genua geboren. Graphik-Designer, Industrie-Designer, Maler und Bildhauer. Studierte Chemie bevor er sich dem Design zuwandte. In den späten fünfziger und frühen sechziger Jahren war er Art Direktor für *Italsider* in Genua. Heute arbeitet er als freier Graphiker. Er hat für Farb-TV-Programme für RAI gearbeitet und für grosse Unternehmen Firmenerscheinungsbilder entworfen. Er hat zahlreiche Auszeichnungen erhalten und als Lehrer für visuelle Kunst in Italien und den USA viele Vorlesungen gehalten. Seine Arbeiten befinden sich in den Sammlungen so berühmter Museen wie dem Victoria and Albert Museum, MOMA etc.

EUGENIO CARMI, né à Gênes en 1920. Graphiste, esthéticien industriel, peintre et sculpteur. A fait des études de chimie avant de se consacrer au design. Au tournant des années 1950/60, a fonctionné comme directeur artistique d'*Italsider* à Gênes. Aujourd'hui artiste indépendant. A travaillé pour les programmes TV couleur de la RAI et réalisé des campagnes d'identité globale de marque pour des grandes entreprises. Lauréat de nombreux prix, c'est un professeur d'art visuel et conférencier bien connu en Italie et aux USA. Ses œuvres figurent dans les collections de musées célèbres tels que le Victoria and Albert, le MOMA, etc.

STIG LINDBERG, born in Sweden, 1916. He studied in Stockholm, then joined Gustavsberg Potteries and furthered his study in ceramic design. He was made Art Director of the Potteries before being appointed Head of Ceramics Department at the Art Institute in Stockholm. Besides ceramic design, he also worked in textile design, and did exhibition design, advertising art, posters and book illustration. He has been highly honored for his work and exhibited widely. He is represented in collections at MOMA, Victoria and Albert Museum, and the National Museum, Stockholm.

STIG LINDBERG, 1916 in Schweden geboren. Er studierte in Stockholm und ging zur Porzellanfabrik Gustavsberg, um sein Wissen über Keramik-Design zu vervollkommnen. Er wurde Art Direktor der Porzellanfabrik bevor er die Keramik-Abteilung der Stockholmer Kunstschule übernahm. Ausser Keramik beschäftigte er sich mit Textil-Design, Ausstellungs-Design, Werbegraphik, Plakaten und Buchillustration. Seine Arbeiten wurden mehrfach ausgezeichnet und ausgestellt. Sie sind in den Sammlungen des MOMA, des Victoria and Albert Museum und des National Museum, Stockholm, vertreten.

STIG LINDBERG, né en Suède en 1916. Au terme de ses études à Stockholm, il entre à la manufacture de porcelaine Gustavsberg pour compléter ses connaissances de la céramique d'art. Promu directeur artistique de la manufacture, il quitte l'entreprise pour prendre la direction du département de céramique de l'Institut des Arts appliqués de Stockholm. Outre la création céramique, son domaine d'activité comprend le design textile, le design d'expositions, l'art publicitaire, l'affichisme et l'illustration de livres. Ses travaux ont été maintes fois exposés et primés. On les trouve dans les collections du MOMA, du Victoria et l'Albert Museum et du Musée national de Stockholm.

For short biography, see Page 137.
The third cover which HANS HARTMANN designed for *Graphis* is strongly influenced by the spirit of the fifties. As in the previous cover (No. 49) Hartmann again worked with allusions and symbols. Woman - fruit - fertility- in an exuberant triad of primary colors.

Kurzbiographie Seite 137.
Der dritte Umschlag, den HANS HARTMANN für *Graphis* entwirft, ist stark vom Zeitgeist der fünfziger Jahre geprägt. Wie im vorangegangenen Umschlag (No. 49) arbeitet Hartmann auch hier wieder mit Andeutungen und Symbolen. Frau, Frucht, Fruchtbarkeit im üppigen Dreiklang der Grundfarben.

Voir la notice biographique en p. 137.
La troisième couverture de HANS HARTMANN pour *Graphis* reflète parfaitement l'esprit des années 50. Tout comme dans la couverture (49) précédente, Hartmann a recours à des procédés allusifs et symboliques: la femme – les fruits – la fertilité insérés dans une triade éclatante de couleurs fondamentales.

For short biography, see Page 132.
MAX HUNZIKER, who made a name for himself in the stained-glass medium, also developed a process of original etching for letterpress printing. He drew the reversed design direct on the zinc or copper plate with asphalt varnish, obtaining the full tone by an unbroken layer of asphalt, and grey tones with a burin, wire brush or cottonwool in alcohol. He then etched the plate in nitric acid. Some of these graphic compositions were printed in up to eight colors, in series of 200 to 300 copies.

Kurzbiographie Seite 132.
MAX HUNZIKER ist wohl der erste Künstler, der die Handätzung für Buchdruck entwickelte. Er zeichnet mit Asphaltlack direkt und seitenverkehrt auf die Zink- oder Kupferplatte, wobei er den vollen Ton durch volle Asphaltauflage erreicht und die Grauwerte unter Zuhilfenahme verschiedener Werkzeuge wie Stichel, Drahtpinsel und -bürsten, mit in Spiritus getauchter Watte usw. gewinnt. Darauf ätzt er die Platte selbst in der Salpetersäure an. Die Tiefätzung besorgt dann ein einfühlender Drucker.

Voir la notice biographique en p. 132.
MAX HUNZIKER, qui s'est fait connaître par son art particulier du vitrail, a aussi été le premier à mettre au point une technique de gravure originale en typographie. Il dessine à côtés inversés à même la plaque de zinc ou de cuivre, en utilisant un vernis bitumineux; il obtient les gris en travaillant la couche de bitume au burin, au princeau métallique ou avec de l'ouate imbibée d'alcool. Puis il immerge la plaque dans un bain d'acide nitrique. Un imprimeur expérimenté se charge des retouches. Certaines de ces compositions graphiques ont été tirées en huit couleurs, en 200 à 300 exemplaires.

For short biography, see Page 136.
After a merry face (No. 26), a despondent one (No. 59) and a threatening sun face (No. 78) GEORGE GIUSTI presents here an engineered visage straight out of the machine world. The brain cell is throbbing away driven by what kinetic force? And a ball-bearing eye is staring blankly, expressionless, from a mechanized mind, seeing what steely visions?

Kurzbiographie Seite 136.
Nach einem lustig bis bösartigen (No. 26), einem eher zaghaften (Nr. 59) und einem Sonnengesicht (Nr. 78) konfrontiert uns GEORGE GIUSTI hier mit der «Visage» eines computerhaften Maschinenmenschen. Welche geometrischen Probleme bewegt er in seinem geometrischen Kopf?

Voir la notice biographique en p. 136.
Après nous avoir fait connaître toute une galerie de faces, arborant une expression joyeuse (no 26) ou déprimée (no 59) ou encore solaire et menaçante (no 78), GEORGE GIUSTI nous propose ici un visage mécanique issu d'un univers robotisé. La cellule cérébrale vibre à une force purement cinétique, et l'œil en forme de roulement à billes est dénué d'expression, fixant on ne sait quelle vision d'acier par la grâce d'un cerveau mécanique. Plutôt réfrigérant!

JASON HAILEY, American photographer. He was engaged in advertising photography in the USA, but wider interests led him to gather material for a special project exhibition, *The Selective Eye,* that travelled in the USA; some pieces being added to the permanent collection of the Museum of Modern Art, New York. According to Hailey photography should "achieve a status worthy of fine art".

JASON HAILEY, amerikanischer Photograph. Er befasste sich zur Hauptsache mit Werbephotographie; daneben aber galt sein Interesse der experimentellen Photographie. In einer Wanderausstellung unter dem Titel *The Selective Eye* war eine Auswahl solcher Aufnahmen zu sehen, von denen das Museum of Modern Art, New York, einige in seine ständige Sammlung aufnahm. Haileys Anliegen war es immer, dass die Photographie als eine freie Kunstgattung anerkannt werde.

JASON HAILEY, photograph américain. Il a surtout travaillé comme photographe publicitaire aux Etats-Unis, mais s'est aussi intéressé à la photo expérimentale, d'où son exposition itinérante aux USA, *The Selective Eye* (L'Œil sélectif); certaines des pièces exposées figurent aujourd'hui dans les collections permanentes du Museum of Modern Art de New York. Hailey a toujours cherché à hisser la photographie au rang d'un grand art.

For short biography, see Page 133.
The "Pomegranate" on this cover was executed by IMRE REINER in wax-tempera technique – in which he experimented for some time early in his career, using tempera colors in conjunction with oil and wax. As well as painting, he also did copper and wood engraving and lithography, and designed the typefaces *Corvinus* and *Reiner Script.*

Kurzbiographie Seite 133.
Der «Granatapfel» dieses Umschlages wurde von IMRE REINER in einer Wachs-Tempera Technik ausgeführt, mit der er in der letzten Zeit experimentiert hatte. Er hat sich auch als Entwerfer von Drucktypen einen Namen gemacht, so mit der *Corvinus* und der *Reiner Script.* Neben der Malerei pflegte er auch den Kupferstich, den Holzschnitt und die Lithographie.

Voir la notice biographique en p. 133.
Pour réaliser la «grenade» de cette couverture, IMRE REINER s'est servi d'une technique de détrempe associée à de l'huile et à de la cire, technique à laquelle il avait consacré d'intéressantes expériences en début de carrière. Ce peintre est aussi graveur sur cuivre et sur bois, ainsi que lithographe. Il s'est également fait connaître par ses créations de caractères intitulées *Corvinus* et *Reiner Script.*

This cover illustration (collection E. Erickson, New York) relates to a feature inside the magazine entitled: Coptic Textiles from Burial Grounds in Egypt. It dealt with the fragments of clothing and furnishing textiles which were discovered in burial grounds in Upper Egypt in 1884 and which are held in leading museums throughout the world. This example is a Coptic weaving from a portrait of an African head, bunch of grapes and ritual colored ribbon.

Diese Umschlagillustration (Sammlung E. Erickson, New York) bezieht sich auf einen Artikel in dieser Ausgabe mit dem Titel: Koptische Textilien aus ägyptischen Gräbern. Es ging darin um Fragmente von Kleidungsstücken und Heimtextilien, die 1884 in Grabstätten in Oberägypten gefunden wurden und heute in führenden Museen der ganzen Welt zu sehen sind. Dieses Beispiel koptischer Wirkerei zeigt einen afrikanischen Kopf mit Weintraube und farbigem Ritualband.

Cette illustration de couverture, qui figure à New York dans la collection E. Erickson, se rapporte à un article du magazine qui étudie les tissus coptes trouvés dans les nécropoles d'Egypte. Il s'agit de fragments de vêtements et de tissus d'ameublement découverts sur les lieux funéraires de Haute-Egypte en 1884 et conservés aujourd'hui dans les grands musées du monde. On voit ici un portrait nilotique accompagné de grappes de raisin et du traditionnel bandeau polychrome.

■

MARINO MARINI, Italy, 1901–1980. He studied painting and sculpture at the Academy in Florence. From 1929–1940 he taught art in Monza and he was then made Professor of Sculpture at the Academia di Belle Arti di Brera (Milan). Apart from his paintings and sculpture work (especially noted for the equestrian figures) he has also illustrated numerous books.

■

MARINO MARINI, Italien, 1901–1980. Er studierte Malerei und Bildhauerei an der Akademie in Florenz. 1929-1940 unterrichtete er Kunst in Monza, danach wurde er Professor für Bildhauerei an der Academia di Belle Arti di Brera (Mailand). Neben der Malerei und Bildhauerei (Menschen- und Tierfiguren, vor allem Reiter) widmete er sich auch der Buchillustration.

■

MARINO MARINI, Italie, 1901–1980. Etudie la peinture et la sculpture à l'Académie de Florence. Enseigne de 1929 à 1940 les arts à Monza, puis est nommé professeur de sculpture à l'Academia di Belle Arti di Brera, à Milan. Sculpteur et peintre (surtôt noté pour ses statues et images equestres) il a aussi illustré de nombreux ouvrages.

■

ALAN FLETCHER, born in Nairobi, Kenya, of British parentage, in 1931. He studied at the Royal College of Art, London. At the start of his career he was engaged at the Container Corporation, USA. In 1958 he worked as designer for renowned US magazines and, after freelancing in London, he became founder and partner of Fletcher/Forbes/Gill Design Studio (and with Colin Forbes he executed many famous designs for *Pirelli*. He is currently partner in the international studio Pentagram. He has served on various design-contest juries and gained numerous awards, including D&AD Gold Medals and D&AD President's Award.

■

ALAN FLETCHER, 1931 als Sohn britischer Eltern in Nairobi, Kenya, geboren. Er studierte am Royal College of Art, London. Seine Karriere begann bei der Container Corporation, USA. 1958 arbeitete er als Designer für führende Zeitschriften in den USA. Später machte er sich in London selbständig und wurde dann Gründer und Partner von Fletcher/Forbes/Gill Design Studio. Zusammen mit Colin Forbes schuf er viele berühmte Designs für *Pirelli*. Heute ist er Partner des internationalen Studios Pentagram. Er war Mitglied von vielen Design-Juries und erhielt selbst zahlreiche Auszeichnungen, u.a. D&AD Goldmedaillen und den «President's Award».

■

ALAN FLETCHER, né à Nairobi (Kenya) des parents britanniques en 1931. Etudes au Royal College of Art de Londres. Débute à la Container Corporation aux Etats-Unis. En 1958, il travaille comme designer pour de grands magazines américains. Etabli à son compte à Londres, il est cofondateur et associé du Fletcher/Forbes/Gill Design Studio. Avec Colin Forbes, il réalise des campagnes spectaculaires pour *Pirelli*. Il est aujourd'hui l'un des associés du studio international Pentagram. Membre de nombreux jurys de design, il a lui-même remporté toute une série de prix, dont des médailles d'or D&AD et le «President's Award» de D&AD.

■

BEN NICHOLSON (1894-1982). English painter. He was a leading member of the abstract art movement in England influenced by the cubism of Georges Braque and the neoplasticism of Piet Mondrian. His work consisted mainly of abstract still lifes in the 1920's. In 1930 he began working on reliefs and in the 1940's he worked on landscapes with elements of still lifes. His later work took a geometric form.

■

BEN NICHOLSON (1894-1982). Englischer Maler. Er war einer der wichtigsten Vertreter einer abstrakten Kunst in England, die u.a. von der kubistischen Malerei Georges Braques beeinflusst wurde. In den zwanziger Jahren malte er vor allem abstrakte Stilleben. 1930 begann er an Reliefs zu arbeiten, und in den 40er Jahren schuf er vor allem Landschaften mit Elementen von Stilleben. Spätere Arbeiten weisen vor allem geometrische Formen auf.

■

BEN NICHOLSON (1894-1982). Peintre anglais, l'un des principaux représentants du mouvement d'art abstrait anglais influencé par le cubisme de Georges Braque et le néoplasticisme de Mondrian. Dans les années 1920, il se voua surtout à la nature morte abstraite. Les années 30 le virent créer des reliefs. Dans les années 40, il réalisa notamment des paysages à partir d'éléments tirés de natures mortes. Par la suite, il s'investit dans une peinture axée sur des formes géométriques.

■

FRANCO GENTILINI, born in Faenza, Italy, 1909. He started work in a ceramic factory where his creative talent was soon noticed by the painter Mario Ortolani. He furthered his art studies in Rome and Paris. He became a much sought after painter and illustrator – primarily for books of Italian classics. His work was exhibited widely in Italy and also in Paris.

■

FRANCO GENTILINI, 1909 in Faenza, Italien, geboren. Er arbeitete in einer Keramikfabrik, wo sein Talent bald von dem Maler Mario Ortolani entdeckt wurde. In Rom und Paris besuchte er darauf Kunstschulen. Als Maler und Illustrator, vor allem für italienische Klassiker, hatte er viel Erfolg. Zahlreiche Ausstellungen in Italien und Paris zeigten seine Werke.

■

FRANCO GENTILINI, né en 1909 dans la ville italienne de Faenza. Il commence à travailler dans une fabrique de céramique, où le peintre Mario Ortolani remarque ses talents créatifs. Grâce à son aide, Gentilini part étudier à Rome et à Paris. Peintre et illustrateur couru, il a surtout été sollicité pour illustrer les ouvrages des classiques italiens. Ses œuvres sont été exposées un peu partout en Italie, ainsi qu'à Paris.

■

JAN LENICA, born in Poland, 1928. He began to publish his satirical drawings in *Szpilki* and various other magazines in 1945, and he designed his first poster in 1950. Since then he has been gaining many prizes for his poster design, including two first prizes in Warsaw (1955 and 1966), first and second prizes at the film poster exhibition in Karlsbad (1962) and the Toulouse-Lautrec prize in Paris (1961). In 1972 he was commissioned to design a poster for the Munich Olympics. From 1957 he has made films and stage decor – and won many prizes for both. He is represented in collections in MOMA and in Warsaw. He lives in Paris.

JAN LENICA, 1928 in Polen geboren. 1945 begann er, satirische Zeichnungen in *Szpilki* und verschiedenen anderen Zeitschriften zu veröffentlichen. 1950 entstand das erste Plakat. Seitdem erhielt er zahlreiche Preise für seine Plakate, u.a. zwei erste Preise in Warschau (1955 und 1966), den ersten und zweiten Preis bei der Filmplakat-Ausstellung in Karlsbad (1962) und den Toulouse-Lautrec-Preis in Paris (1961). 1972 erhielt er den Auftrag für ein Plakat für die Olympiade in München. Seit 1957 beschäftigt er sich auch mit Filmen und Bühnenbildern – und wurde mehrfach ausgezeichnet. Er ist im MOMA und in Warschauer Museen vertreten. Er lebt in Paris.

JAN LENICA, né en Pologne en 1928. Commence à publier en 1945 ses dessins satiriques dans *Szpilki* et divers autres périodiques. Sa première affiche date de 1950. Depuis, de nombreux prix sont venus récompenser ses affiches, notamment deux premiers prix à Varsovie (1955, 1966), un premier et un deuxième prix à l'exposition des affiches de cinéma à Karlovy Vary (1962) et le prix Toulouse-Lautrec de Paris (1961). En 1972, il fut chargé de créer une affiche pour les Jeux Olympiques de Munich. Sa carrière de cinéaste et de décorateur de théâtre, qui a débuté en 1957, lui a valu de nombreux prix. Ses œuvres sont au MOMA, à Varsovie. Il habite Paris.

WILLY EIDENBENZ, born in Zürich, 1909. (Brother of graphic designer Hermann Eidenbenz.) He studied at the Kunstgewerbeschule, Zürich, under Ernst Keller and O. Meyer-Amden. He developed a technique based on arithmetical and algebraic progressions which he labelled "neo-naturalism". His compositions, ranging from very small sizes to 25 sq. meter murals, found admirers in Switzerland and also from far afield.

WILLY EIDENBENZ, 1909 in Zürich geboren. (Bruder des Graphik-Designers Hermann Eidenbenz.) Er studierte unter Ernst Keller und O. Meyer-Amden an der Kunstgewerbeschule, Zürich. Er entwickelte eine Technik, der arithmetische und algebraische Progressionen zugrunde liegen und die er «Neo-Naturalismus» nannte. Seine Kompositionen, vom kleinsten Format bis zum Wandbild von 25 m², fanden nicht nur in der Schweiz viele Bewunderer.

WILLY EIDENBENZ, né à Zurich en 1909. Frère du graphiste Hermann Eidenbenz. Etudie à l'Ecole des arts décoratifs de Zurich sous Ernst Keller et O. Meyer-Amden. Elabore une technique basée sur des progressions arithmétiques et algébriques qu'il baptise «néonaturalisme». Ses compositions, du format miniature jusqu'au mural de 25 m², ont trouvé des admirateurs en Suisse et à l'étranger.

HOOT VON ZITZEWITZ, born in Germany, 1927. He moved to the USA and became an American citizen. From 1952–56 he worked as a designer for the US Airforce. He later devoted his time to photojournalism, abstract painting and graphic design. He won major accounts including: *Lukens Steel, Shell Oil, Union Carbide, Remington Rand*, etc. He has held a number of exhibitions of his work.

HOOT VON ZITZEWITZ, 1927 in Deutschland geboren. Er wanderte in die USA aus und wurde amerikanischer Bürger. 1952–56 arbeitete er als Designer für die US Air Force. Später widmete er sich dem Photojournalismus, der abstrakten Malerei und dem Graphik-Design. Zu seinen Kunden gehören *Lukens Steel, Shell Oil, Union Carbide, Remington Rand*, etc. Seine Arbeiten wurden verschiedentlich ausgestellt.

HOOT VON ZITZEWITZ, né en Allemagne en 1927. Emigré en Amérique, il a pris la nationalité américaine. A travaillé de 1952 à 1956 comme designer pour l'Armée de l'air américaine, puis s'est orienté vers le reportage photo, la peinture abstraite et l'art publicitaire. Compte parmi ses clients importants *Lukens Steel, Shell Oil, Union Carbide, Remington Rand*, etc. A eu de nombreuses expositions.

HEIRI (HEINRICH) STEINER, born in Switzerland, 1906. He studied at the Kunstgewerbeschule under Ernst Keller and in Berlin under Prof. O.H.W. Hadank. He formed his own graphic-design studio in Zurich in 1930. He designed part of the Swiss Pavilion at the Paris International Exhibition (1937). In 1947 he went to Paris and became Art Director for UNESCO publications. In the early fifties he did design work for the US Information Service. He returned to Zurich in 1959. One-man exhibitions of his work were held in London (1967), Stuttgart (1968), Zurich (1977), Ludwigsburg (1978).

HEIRI (HEINRICH) STEINER, 1906 in der Schweiz geboren. Er studierte an der Kunstgewerbeschule Zürich bei Ernst Keller und in Berlin bei Prof. O.H.W. Hadank. 1940 gründete er sein eigenes Graphik-Design-Studio in Zürich. Er entwarf einen Teil des Schweizer Pavillons für die Weltausstellung Paris 1937. 1947 ging er nach Paris und wurde dort Art Direktor für die UNESCO-Publikationen. In den frühen fünfziger Jahren arbeitete er als Designer für den US Informationsdienst. 1959 kehrte er nach Zürich zurück. Seine Arbeiten wurden in Einzelausstellungen in London (1967), Stuttgart (1968), Zürich (1977) und in Ludwigsburg (1978) gezeigt.

HEIRI (HEINRICH) STEINER, né 1906 en Suisse. Etudes auprès d'Ernst Keller, Ecole des arts appliqués, Zurich, et d'O.H.W. Hadank à Berlin. Il a fondé à Zurich en 1930 un atelier d'où sont sortis des travaux graphiques et aussi des conceptions pour l'aménagement d'expositions, entre autres pour le pavillon suisse à l'Exposition mondiale de Paris en 1937. En 1947 il fut nommé directeur artistique des publications de l'UNESCO à Paris. Depuis 1950 il y a travaillé comme designer pour le Service d'information américain. Depuis 1959 il vit de nouveau à Zurich. Expositions individuelles à Londres (1967), Stuttgart (1968), Zurich (1977) et à Ludwigsburg (1978).

REID MILES, born in the USA. He studied at the Chouinard Art School in Los Angeles and later taught there. In the early fifties he moved to New York and his work appeared in a large number of major US publications.

REID MILES, Bürger der Vereinigten Staaten. Er studierte an der Chouinard Art School in Los Angeles, wo er später unterrichtete. In den frühen fünfziger Jahren zog er nach New York. Seine Arbeiten erschienen in zahlreichen wichtigen Publikationen in den USA.

REID MILES, né aux Etats-Unis. Il a étudié à la Chouinard Art School de Los Angeles, où il est retourné comme professeur. Depuis le début des années 50, il est installé à New York et publie ses travaux dans un grand nombre de publications américaines de premier plan.

ANTONIO FRASCONI, born in Uruguay, 1919. He studied in Montevideo and in the USA. Since 1973 he has been Professor of the Art Faculty of the State University of New York. He specializes in woodcuts, engravings and lithography for illustration in major magazines and record covers. A film with 100 of his woodcuts won the Grand Prix at the Venice Film Festival (1960). Many international awards have been conferred on him and he was included for five years in AIGA "50 Books of the Year".

ANTONIO FRASCONI, 1919 in Uruguay geboren. Er studierte in Montevideo und in den USA. Seit 1973 ist er Professor der Fakultät für bildende Kunst an der State University, New York. Er hat sich auf Holzschnitt, Radierungen und Lithographie spezialisiert, die als Illustrationen für führende Zeitschriften und als Plattenhüllen verwendet wurden. Ein Film mit 100 seiner Holzschnitte gewann den Grand Prix des Filmfestivals in Venedig (1960). Er erhielt für seine Arbeiten viele internationale Preise, und war fünfmal in der AIGA-Publikation «Die 50 Bücher des Jahres» vertreten.

ANTONIO FRASCONI, né en Uruguay en 1919. Etudes à Montevideo et aux Etats-Unis. Depuis 1973, professeur à la Faculté des Arts de l'Université de l'Etat de New York. Spécialiste de la gravure sur bois, de la taille-douce et de la lithographie, ses illustrations ont paru dans des grands magazines et sur des pochettes de disques et couvertures d'albums. Un film réunissant cent de ses bois a remporté le Grand Prix du Festival du cinéma de Venise en 1960. Ses travaux ont été récompensés de nombreux prix internationaux. Pendant cinq années de suite, il a figuré dans la liste des «50 Livres de l'année» de l'AIGA.

© 1987 PRO LITTERIS, Zürich

FELIX MÜLLER, born in Solingen, Germany, 1923. He studied in Antwerp and Wuppertal before becoming assistant to Jupp Ernst, Director of the Werkkunstschule in Wuppertal (1949-50). In 1949 he also founded the *Müller-Blase Studio*. He was appointed Head of the graphic-art department of the State School of Art in Bremen in 1954 and was made Director of this school in 1959.

FELIX MÜLLER, 1923 in Solingen, Deutschland, geboren. Er studierte in Antwerpen und Wuppertal, bevor er Assistent von Jupp Ernst, dem Direktor der Werkkunstschule in Wuppertal (1949-50) wurde. 1949 gründete er das *Müller-Blase Studio*. 1954 wurde er zum Leiter der graphischen Abteilung der Staatlichen Kunsthochschule in Bremen und 1959 zum Direktor ernannt.

FELIX MÜLLER, né à Solingen (RFA) en 1923. Etudiant à Anvers et Wuppertal avant de devenir l'assistant de Jupp Ernst, directeur de la Werkkunstschule Wuppertal, de 1949 à 1950. C'est en 1949 qu'il fonde le *Müller-Blase Studio*. En 1954, il accède à la direction du département d'art graphique de l'Ecole d'art du Land de Brême, école qu'il dirige depuis 1959.

SEYMOUR CHWAST, born in New York, 1931. He studied at Cooper Union, New York, and cofounded *Push Pin Studios* (1954). For this studio he originated the internal publication *Push Pin Graphic*. His wide scope ranges from advertising art, film and TV art, poster and book design, packaging, lettering, woodcuts, etc. He was one-time Vice President of AIGA and is a visiting Professor at Cooper Union. He has participated in numerous group shows and has staged a one-man exhibition in Paris. Many awards have been conferred on him and his work is held in the collections of MOMA and the Library of Congress, Washington DC.

SEYMOUR CHWAST, 1931 in New York geboren. Er studierte an der Cooper Union, New York, und ist Mitbegründer der *Push Pin Studios* (1954), für die er später die Kundenzeitschrift *Push Pin Graphic* ins Leben rief. Sein immenser Arbeitsbereich umfasst Werbe-, Film- und TV-Graphik, Plakate, Buchgestaltung, Verpackungen, Typographie, Holzschnitte etc. Er war Vize-Präsident der AIGA. Als Gast-Professor hält er Vorlesungen an der Cooper Union. Er war in vielen Gruppenausstellungen vertreten und hatte eine Einzelausstellung in Paris. Er hat zahlreiche Auszeichnungen für seine Arbeiten erhalten, und ist in den Sammlungen des MOMA und der Library of Congress, Washington DC vertreten.

SEYMOUR CHWAST, né à New York en 1931. Ancien élève de Cooper Union, il est cofondateur des *Push Pin Studios* en 1954, pour lesquels il lance la revue d'entreprise *Push Pin Graphic*. Son champ d'activité embrasse l'art publicitaire, la création graphique au cinéma et à la TV, la conception de livres et d'affiches, les emballages, la création de caractères, la gravure sur bois, etc. Il a été vice-président de l'AIGA. Professeur associé, il enseigne à Cooper Union. Ses travaux ont fait l'objet de nombreuses expositions collecitves et d'une exposition personnelle à Paris. Lauréat de nombreux prix, il est représenté dans les collections du MOMA et de la Library of Congress de Washington.

PINO TOVAGLIA, born in Milan, 1923. He studied under G. Usellini and E. Siuti and later taught poster and graphic art at the Scuola Superiore d'Arte del Castello in Milan (1946-53). He also taught at the Umanitaria, Scuola del Libro in Milan (1959). He was the recipient of numerous awards for advertising campaigns for major clients. An exhibition of his work was held in Milan in 1961.

PINO TOVAGLIA, 1923 in Mailand geboren. Er studierte bei G. Usellini und E. Siuti und unterrichtete später selber Plakatkunst und Graphik an der Scuola Superiore d'Arte del Castello in Mailand (1946-53) und an der Umanitaria, Scuola del Libro (1959). Er erhielt zahlreiche Preise für Werbekampagnen für wichtige Kunden. 1961 wurden seine Arbeiten in Mailand ausgestellt.

PINO TOVAGLIA, né à Milan en 1923. Ancien élève de G. Usellini et E. Siuti, il enseigne de 1946 à 1953 l'affichisme et l'art graphique à l'Ecole supérieure d'art du Castello à Milan. Il a aussi enseigné en 1959 à l'Umanitaria, Scuola del Libro de Milan. Lauréat de nombreux prix pour les campagnes publicitaires qu'il a réalisées pour des clients importants, une exposition a fait connaître ses œuvres à Milan en 1961.

SAM FRANCIS, born 1923 in California. American painter. He studied medicine before joining the US airforce in 1943. On the occasion of a stay in a military hospital, he began to paint and after his convalescence he returned to the University of California to study painting. Among his teachers were Mark Rothko and Clifford Still. In 1950 the artist moved to Paris. 1956-58 he completed wall paintings for the Art Auditorium in Basle. He created a further wall painting for the Sofu School for Flower Arrangements. His pictures were shown among others in the travelling exhibition "Presenting New American Painting".

SAM FRANCIS, 1923 in Kalifornien geboren. Amerikanischer Maler. Er studierte Medizin, bevor er 1943 der US Airforce beitrat. Anlässlich eines Aufenthaltes in einem Militärspital begann er zu malen, und er kehrte nach seiner Genesung an die University of California zurück, um Malerei zu studieren. Zu seinen Lehrern gehörten Mark Rothko und Clifford Still. 1950 zog der Künstler nach Paris. 1956-58 führte er Wandbilder für die Kunsthalle in Basel aus. Ein weiteres Wandbild schuf er für die Sofu-Schule für Blumenarrangements. Seine Bilder wurden u.a. in der Wanderausstellung «Neue amerikanische Malerei» gezeigt.

SAM FRANCIS, né en Californie en 1923. Ce peintre américain a étudié la médecine avant d'entrer dans l'Armée de l'air américaine en 1943. Durant un séjour à l'hôpital militaire, il se mit à peindre et retourna étudier la peinture à l'Université de Californie sitôt rendu à la vie civile. Parmi ses professeurs, Mark Rothko et Clifford Still l'ont particulièrement marqué. En 1950, il part pour Paris. De 1956 à 1958, il peint des murals pour le Musée d'art moderne (Kunsthaus) de Bâle. Un autre de ses murals vint embellir l'Ecole Sofu d'arrangements floraux. Ses tableaux ont figuré dans l'exposition itinérante consacrée à «la nouvelle peinture américaine».

ROBERT DELPIRE, born in Paris, 1926. He first studied medicine, and founded an art magazine for his fellow medical students. Shortly afterwards he published his first book. He later devoted his time to the publishing of illustrated books of outstanding quality. In 1955 he was also technical director of the art magazine *L'Œil*. He organized many photographic exhibitions. His publishing activities later included advertising and film.

ROBERT DELPIRE, 1926 in Paris geboren. Er studierte zuerst Medizin und wurde Herausgeber einer Kunstzeitschrift für seine Mitstudenten. Kurz darauf veröffentlichte er sein erstes Buch. Später widmete er seine Zeit ausschliesslich der Veröffentlichung illustrierter Bücher von herausragender Qualität. 1955 wurde er technischer Direktor des Kunstmagazins *L'Œil*. Er organisierte viele Photoausstellungen und beschäftigte sich später auch noch mit Werbung und Film.

ROBERT DELPIRE, né à Paris en 1926. Alors qu'il est encore étudiant en médecine, il lance un magazine d'art pour ses camarades d'études. Peu après, il publie son premier livre et entame une carrière qui le conduira à publier ou illustrer des livres de grande classe. En 1955, on le trouve directeur technique du magazine d'art *L'Œil*. Il a organisé de nombreuses expositions photo. Ses activités dans l'édition l'ont plus tard amené à la publicité et, de là, au cinéma.

For short biography, see Page 141.
To this illustration, ANDRÉ FRANÇOIS said: "When I was asked to design the next cover, I was just working on a series of pictures on sheet iron to try to catch the atmosphere of a fair. As I was fixing the separate silhouette of the head on a white ground, the stapler in my hand turned into the gun of a shooting-range. Out of curiosity and love of experiment I kept on shooting staples in the head and around it. I then realized I had produced a piece of anatomy."

Kurzbiographie Seite 141.
Zu seinem Entwurf für diesen *Graphis*-Umschlag erzählt ANDRÉ FRANÇOIS: »Als mich Walter Herdeg bat, den nächsten Umschlag zu entwerfen, arbeitete ich gerade an einer Bilderfolge auf Blech, wobei ich die Stimmung eines Jahrmarktes wiedergeben wollte. Beim Fixieren der separaten Kopfsilhouette auf weissem Grund wurde die Heftpistole in meiner Hand zum Gewehr einer Schiessbude. Aus reiner Experimentierlust und Neugierde fuhr ich fort, Klammern in und um den Kopf zu schiessen. Unversehens entstand eine Struktur, ein anatomisches Gebilde.«

Voir la notice biographique en p. 141.
ANDRÉ FRANÇOIS commente ainsi son illustration de couverture: «Quand Walter Herdeg m'a demandé de réaliser la couverture suivante, j'étais en train de créer une série d'images sur tôle qui étaient censées restituer l'atmosphère d'une fête foraine. Fixant la silhouette de la tête sur fond blanc, l'agrafeuse que j'avais à la main a pris la forme d'un fusil de stand de tir forain. La curiosité et le goût de l'expérimentation m'ont alors poussé à mitrailler d'agrafes la tête et son pourtour. Et c'est ainsi qu'est née cette structure anatomique.»

RICCARDO MANZI, born in Rome, 1913. He studied in Naples and first worked in Rome and then Milan for various newspapers. He began doing series of cartoons and later turned to painting and advertising art. He participated in the Biennale of Venice (1956) and in an exhibition in New York (1959). In 1954 he won a prize for costume design and was aware the Premio Graziano in 1956. His work is held in collections in Italy, Switzerland and Caracas.

RICCARDO MANZI, 1913 in Rom geboren. Er studierte in Neapel und arbeitete zuerst in Rom, später in Mailand, für verschiedene Zeitungen. Er begann mit Karikaturen und wandte sich später der Malerei und Werbegraphik zu. 1956 war er an der Biennale in Venedig vertreten, und 1959 hatte er eine Ausstellung in New York. Er erhielt einen Preis für Kostümentwürfe (1954) und den Premio-Graziano-Preis (1956). Seine Arbeiten befinden sich in Sammlungen in Italien, der Schweiz und Caracas.

RICCARDO MANZI, né à Rome en 1913. Après ses études à Naples, il part travailler à Rome, puis à Milan pour divers quotidiens. Il débute dans la caricature pour s'orienter plus tard vers la peinture et l'art publicitaire. Ses travaux ont été exposés à la Biennale de Venise 1956 et à New York en 1959. En 1954, il remporte un prix pour ses costumes. en 1956 le Premio Graziano. Ses œuvres figurent dans des collections italiennes, suisses et vénézuéliennes (Caracas).

FRANCO GRIGNANI, born in Italy, 1908. He studied architecture before devoting himself to graphic design, painting and photography. He was Art Director of *Bellezza d'Italia* for many years. He has participated in many international exhibitions and he has received numerous awards. He is represented in many famous collections and is a member of AGI.

FRANCO GRIGNANI, 1908 in Italien geboren. Er studierte Architektur bevor er sich dem Graphik-Design, der Malerei und der Photographie zuwandte. Er war viele Jahre Art Direktor von *Bellezza d'Italia*, in zahlreichen internationalen Ausstellungen vertreten, und er hat zahlreiche Auszeichnungen erhalten. Seine Arbeiten sind in vielen berühmten Sammlungen vertreten. Er ist Mitglied der AGI.

FRANCO GRIGNANI, né en Italie en 1908. Il fut architecte avant de se vouer à l'art graphique, à la peinture et à la photo. Il a été directeur artistique de *Bellezza d'Italia* durant de longues années. Il a participé à de nombreuses expositions internationales, et a remporté de nombreux prix. Ses œuvres figurent dans nombre de collections prestigieuses. Il est membre de l'AGI.

RAYMOND SAVIGNAC, born in Paris, 1907. He worked with A.M.Cassandre in 1935. He was well-known to the public through his newspaper ads for countless commodities, for his UNICEF posters and for film posters. He also designed magazine covers and did stage decor. The Grand Prix of 1955 and of 1957 were conferred on him at the Chicago Open Air Exhibitions. His posters gained him the nickname "l'homme de choc".

RAYMOND SAVIGNAC, 1907 in Paris geboren. 1935 arbeitete er mit A.M. Cassandre zusammen. Durch seine Inserate für zahlreiche Konsumgüter, UNICEF-Plakate und Film-Plakate machte er sich schnell einen Namen. Ausserdem entwarf er Zeitschriftenumschläge und Bühnenbilder. Bei den Chicago Open Air Exhibitions erhielt er 1955 und 1957 den Grand Prix. Seine Plakate brachten ihm den Übernamen «l'homme de choc» ein.

RAYMOND SAVIGNAC, né à Paris en 1907. Fut le collaborateur d'A.M. Cassandre en 1935. S'est fait rapidement connaître du public par ses annonces pour d'innombrables biens de consommation, par ses affiches UNICEF et ses affiches de cinéma. A aussi réalisé des couvertures de magazines, des décors de théâtre. A remporté le Grand Prix des Chicago Open Air Exhibitions en 1955 et 1957. Ses affiches lui ont valu le surnom de «l'homme de choc».

WALTER GRIEDER, born in Basle, 1914. He grew up in France. He studied in Basle and founded his own studio there in 1956. He continued his studies in Paris and London. Specializing primarily in children's book illustration, he became one of the most sought-after and acclaimed juvenile book illustrators in Europe.

WALTER GRIEDER, 1914 in Basel geboren. Er wuchs in Frankreich auf, studierte in Basel und gründete dort 1956 sein eigenes Studio. Weitere Studien brachten ihn nach Paris und London. Als Spezialist für Kinderbücher wurde er zu einem der gesuchtesten und anerkanntesten Jugendbuchillustratoren Europas.

WALTER GRIEDER. Né à Bâle en 1914, il a grandi en France. Etudes à Bâle, où il ouvre son propre studio en 1956. Complément d'études à Paris et à Londres. Spécialisé avant tout dans l'illustration de livres d'enfants, il est devenu l'un des illustrateurs de littérature enfantine les plus recherchés et les plus fêtés d'Europe.

RITVA PUOTILA, born in Finland, 1935. This cover illustration shows a rug made in Helsinki to a design by this artist. She studied architecture in Helsinki and, in 1960, was awarded a Gold Medal at the Milan Triennale for one of her rug designs. She has gone on to win many more high awards in Finland and abroad.

RITVA PUOTILA, 1935 in Finnland geboren. Dieser Umschlag zeigt einen Ausschnitt aus einem Teppich, der nach einem Entwurf dieser Künstlerin in Helsinki hergestellt wurde. Sie studierte Architektur in Helsinki. 1960 erhielt sie an der Triennale in Mailand die Goldmedaille für einen ihrer Teppichentwürfe. Es folgten viele weitere wichtige Auszeichnungen in Finnland und im Ausland.

RITVA PUOTILA, née en Finlande en 1935. Cette illustration de couverture représente le détail d'un tapis réalisé à Helsinki d'après une maquette de l'artiste. Ritva Puotila a étudié l'architecture à Helsinki. En 1960, la Triennale de Milan lui décerna sa médaille d'or pour l'un de ses dessins de tapis. Ce fut le début de toute une série de prix importants remportés tant en Finlande qu'à l'étranger.

Short biography, see page 135.
Cover illustration by PABLO PICASSO. This illustration, reduced from its original size of 25½ x 21 inches, shows a 5-color linocut: "Buste de Femme au Chapeau" (1962). This issue contained a feature on the new series of 60 linocuts, mostly in color, which Picasso completed between 1961 and 1965. Picasso was, at this time eighty-three.

Kurzbiographie Seite 135.
Umschlagillustration von PABLO PICASSO. Es handelt sich um eine verkleinerte Wiedergabe eines fünffarbigen Linolschnitts: «Buste de Femme au Chapeau» entstanden 1962, Format 64 x 53 cm. Diese Ausgabe enthielt einen Artikel über die zwischen 1961 und 1963 von Picasso geschaffene neue Folge von 60 meist farbigen Linolschnitten. Picasso war damals 83 Jahre alt.

Voir la notice biographique en page 135.
Illustration de couverture par PABLO PICASSO. Il s'agit d'une gravure sur linoléum, reproduite en format reduit: «Buste de Femme au Chapeau» (64 x 53cm). Dans cette édition de GRAPHIS il y avait un article sur la nouvelle série de 60 gravures sur linoléum crée par Picasso de 1961 à 1963. A ce temps là il avait 83 ans.

HEINZ EDELMANN, born in Czechoslovakia of German parents, 1934. He studied at the Kunstakademie, Düsseldorf. After working in an advertising agency he became a freelance designer – at first in Düsseldorf and then in The Hague. His work includes designs for animated films (he designed the Beatles film *Yellow Submarine* in 1967), posters (for the WDR Radio Channel) and for films and theaters. He is also engaged in advertising and book design. He has taught at many art institutes in Germany and in Holland. He is a member of AGI.

HEINZ EDELMANN, 1934 in der Tschechoslowakei als Sohn deutscher Eltern geboren. Er studierte an der Staatlichen Kunstakademie, Düsseldorf. Nachdem er in einer Werbeagentur gearbeitet hatte, machte er sich als Gebrauchsgraphiker selbständig – zuerst in Düsseldorf und später in Den Haag. Er hat u.a. Zeichentrickfilme gemacht (z.B. 1967 den Beatles-Film *Yellow Submarine)* und Plakate für Film, Theater und den Rundfunk (WDR) entworfen. Ausserdem befasst er sich mit Werbung und Buchillustrationen. Er hat an vielen Kunstschulen in Deutschland und Holland unterrichtet und ist Mitglied der AGI.

HEINZ EDELMANN, né de parents allemands en Tchécoslovaquie en 1934. Ancien élève de l'Académie des beauxarts de Düsseldorf, il s'établit à son compte à Düsseldorf, puis à La Haye après un passage obligé par une agence de publicité. Son œuvre de designer comprend des films d'animation – on lui doit le film des Beatles *Le Sous-Marin vert* réalisé en 1967 –, des affiches pour la Radio WDR (station régionale de RFA), des affiches de cinéma et de théâtre. Il s'est aussi occupé de publicité et de maquettes de livres. Professeur dans de nombreux instituts d'art en Allemagne et aux Pays-Bas, il est membre de l'AGI.

For short biography, see Page 141.
The cover of *Graphis* 106 shows one of ANDRÉ FRANÇOIS' experiments with staples which had occurred partly by chance. In this illustration he attempts another – with equal success – with plaster and various other materials. Has *Graphis* 114 been awarded the winner's medal for reaching the summit?

Kurzbiographie Seite 141.
Der Umschlag von *Graphis* No. 106 zeigte eine Nagelarbeit von ANDRÉ FRANÇOIS, hier versucht er sich ebenso erfolgreich mit Gips und diversen anderen Materialien. Ist *Graphis* No. 114 eine Siegermedaille, die dem Erfolgreichsten zugesprochen wird?

Voir la notice biographique en p. 141.
La couverture de *Graphis* 106 montrait l'un des travaux expérimentaux qu' ANDRÉ FRANÇOIS réalise à coups de tirs d'agrafes partiellement aléatoires. Ici, il obtient un résultat équivalent à l'aide de plâtre et de divers autres matériaux. *Graphis* 114 a-t-il remporté la médaille du vainqueur pour avoir escaladé le sommet?

For short biography, see Page 146.
CELESTINO PIATTI's distinguishing mark is that he does not advertise with the anecdote and the association but directly with a pictorial slogan, a straight forward symbol which is compact – a graphic message that has something of simple folk art and of the woodcut. His typography is similarly non-formalist, factual and clear.

Kurzbiographie Seite 146.
CELESTINO PIATTIS Eigenart liegt nach wie vor darin, dass er nicht auf anekdotisch-assoziative Art wirbt, sondern mit dem einfachen, schlagwortartigen «Signet», das von meistens sehr treffenden Slogans begleitet wird. Und seine «Signete» sind lapidare graphische Formen, die etwas Holzschnittartiges, volkstümlich Einfaches haben.

Voir la notice biographique en p. 146.
La griffe de CELESTINO PIATTI se reconnaît aisément, hier comme aujourd'hui: il ne traite pas le problème publicitaire de manière anecdotique et/ou associative, mais directement par le biais d'un slogan imagé, d'un symbole condensé. Ce message graphique évoque l'immédiateté et la simplicité de l'art populaire et de la gravure sur bois. Sa typo semblablement non formaliste respire l'objectivité et la clarté.

EDUARD PRÜSSEN, born in Cologne, 1930. He studied at the Kölner Werkschulen and in 1953 was artistic adviser to Cologne's Folklore Museum for which he did scientific drawings and designed the exhibition posters. From 1956 on he worked as graphic and exhibition designer for America House in Cologne. He has freelanced since 1959. His scope encompasses editorial and book illustration, graphic and advertising design. He specializes in woodcuts and linocuts and he is the publisher of a small-format, handmade house organ entitled: *Donkey Post.*

EDUARD PRÜSSEN, 1930 in Köln geboren. Er studierte an den Kölner Werkschulen. 1953 wurde er künstlerischer Berater des Volkskundemuseums Köln, für das er wissenschaftliche Zeichnungen machte und Ausstellungsplakate entwarf. Ab 1956 war er als Graphiker und Ausstellungsgestalter für das Kölner Amerikahaus tätig. Seit 1959 arbeitet er freiberuflich als Maler und Graphiker, wobei er sich sowohl mit redaktioneller als auch mit Werbegraphik und Buchillustrationen befasst. Er hat sich auf Holz- und Linolschnitte spezialisiert. Ausserdem gibt er eine kleine, mit der Handpresse gedruckte Kundenzeitschrift mit dem Titel *Donkey Post* heraus.

EDUARD PRÜSSEN, né à Cologne en 1930. Ancien élève des Werkschulen de Cologne. En 1953, on le trouve conseiller artistique du Musé d'art populaire de Cologne pour lequel il réalise des dessins scientifiques et des affiches d'expositions. Dès 1956, il travaille comme graphiste et concepteur d'expositions pour la Maison d'Amérique de Cologne. Artiste indépendant depuis 1959, il cumule les fonctions de peintre, de graphiste, d'illustrateur au service de magazines et de livres et crée de l'art publicitaire. Il s'est spécialisé dans le bois et le lino et publie pour sa clientèle, sous le titre de *Donkey Post* (Courrier du Baudet), une revue d'entreprise au petit format qu'il tire sur une presse à bras.

FLAVIO COSTANTINI, born in Rome, 1926. He first served as an officer in the Merchant Navy. In 1956 he began experimentation in serigraphy for textile printing and in the same year founded, with friends, a graphic studio which soon won accounts from major Italian clients, including *Shell, Italsider,* and *Olivetti.* Many of his very detailed drawings are of machinery. He also does book and magazine illustrations, stage sets and posters. He has held numerous one-man exhibitions in Italy and his screen-prints have been shown in London (1971).

FLAVIO COSTANTINI, 1926 in Rom geboren. Er diente in der italienischen Kriegs- und Handelsmarine. 1956 begann er mit Textildruck zu experimentieren, und im gleichen Jahr gründete er mit Freunden ein Graphik-Studio, das bald so wichtige Kunden wie *Shell, Italsider* und *Olivetti* hatte. Viele seiner realistischen Zeichnungen zeigen Maschinen. Er macht auch Buch- und Zeitschriftenillustrationen, Bühnenbilder und Plakate. In Italien hatte er zahlreiche Einzelausstellungen, und seine Siebdrucke wurden 1971 in London ausgestellt.

FLAVIO COSTANTINI, né à Rome en 1926, a d'abord été officier dans la marine de guerre et la marine marchande italiennes. En 1956, il se met à expérimenter l'impression sérigraphique. La même année, il fonde avec des amis un studio d'art publicitaire qui s'assure rapidement une audience nationale: *Shell, Italsider, Olivetti,* etc. Une grande partie de ses dessins circonstanciés concernent des machines. Il crée également des illustrations destinées à des ouvrages et à des magazines, décore des théâtres, réalise des affiches. Il a eu de nombreuses expositions personnelles en Italie. Ses sérigraphies ont été présentées au public londonien en 1971.

HERBERT LEUPIN, born in Switzerland, 1916. He formed his own studio in 1937 in Basle for advertising art and design consultancy. His scope encompasses lithography, illustration, and poster creation and he has won many awards for his work. He is now a freelance painter living in Basle.

HERBERT LEUPIN, 1916 in der Schweiz geboren. 1937 gründete er in Basel ein eigenes Studio für Werbegraphik und Design. Sein Arbeitsfeld umfasst Lithographie, Illustration und Plakat-Design. Er wurde mehrfach für seine Arbeiten ausgezeichnet. Heute lebt er als freier Maler in Basel.

HERBERT LEUPIN, né en Suisse en 1916. En 1937, il fonde à Bâle un studio d'art publicitaire et de conseils en matière de design, où il réalise des lithos, des illustrations, des affiches qui lui ont valu de nombreux prix. Il se voue aujourd'hui à la peinture à Bâle en artiste indépendant.

In 1962 three young graphic designers formed a partnership studio in London called: *Fletcher/Forbes/Gill.* ALAN FLETCHER was born in Nairobi in 1931, and studied at the Royal College of Art, London. COLIN FORBES was born in London in 1928, studied at the Central School and headed the graphic-design department there. BOB GILL was born in New York in 1931 and studied at the Philadelphia School of Art. He worked in New York as designer before going to London as design consultant.

1962 gründeten drei junge Graphik-Designer ein gemeinsames Studio in London, das sie *Flechter/Forbes/Gill* nannten. ALAN FLETCHER, 1931 in Nairobi geboren, studierte am Royal College of Art in London. COLIN FORBES, 1928 in London geboren, studierte an der Central School und leitete dort die Graphik-Design-Abteilung. BOB GILL, 1931 in New York geboren, studierte an der Philadelphia School of Art. Er hatte bereits in New York als Designer gearbeitet, bevor er nach London ging.

En 1962, trois jeunes graphistes ouvraient à Londres un studio conjoint sous la raison sociale de *Fletcher/Forbes/Gill.* ALAN FLETCHER, né à Nairobi en 1931, a fait ses études au Royal College of Art de Londres. COLIN FORBES, né à Londres en 1928, est un ancien élève de Central School, dont il a dirigé le département de design graphique. BOB GILL, né à New York en 1931, a fait des études à la Philadelphia School of Art. Designer à New York, il était venu à Londres en qualité de conseiller en design.

TOMI UNGERER, born in Strasbourg (French nationality), 1931. He had no formal art training. In his youth he travelled extensively. In 1956 he went to New York and there he began his career as cartoonist, painter and illustrator – he is also the author of many books, for children and for adults. He has gained more than fifty awards, including the Gold Medal from the Society of Illustrators and the ADC. In 1971 he did a series of advertisements for the West German government. Exhibitions of his work have been held throughout the world. Today, he is living in Ireland.

TOMI UNGERER, 1931 in Strassburg geboren, französische Staatsangehörigkeit. Er hatte keine Kunstausbildung, sondern sammelte in jungen Jahren seine Erfahrungen auf zahlreichen Reisen. 1956 ging er nach New York, wo seine Karriere als Karikaturist, Maler und Zeichner begann. Daneben machte er zahlreiche Bücher, für Kinder und für Erwachsene. Er hat mehr als fünfzig Preise erhalten, einschliesslich der Goldmedaille der Society of Illustrators and des Art Directors Club. 1971 gestaltete er eine Anzeigenserie für die westdeutsche Regierung. Ausstellungen seiner Arbeiten waren in aller Welt zu sehen. Heute lebt Tomi Ungerer in Irland.

TOMI UNGERER, né à Strasbourg en 1931, de nationalité française. N'a pas suivi d'études artistiques spécifiques, mais a parcouru le monde dans sa jeunesse, à la recherche d'impressions et d'expériences visuelles. S'installe à New York en 1956, débute comme caricaturiste, peintre et illustrateur. A conçu de nombreux livres pour enfants et adultes. Lauréat d'une cinquantaine de prix, y compris la médaille d'or de la Society of Illustrators et celle de l'ADC. En 1971, il réalise une série d'annonces pour le gouvernement de la République Fédérale. Des expositions font connaître ses œuvres dans le monde entier. Il habite aujourd'hui l'Irlande.

EBERHARD G. RENSCH, born in Halle, GDR, 1929. He worked in advertising studios and was for a time Director of Exhibitions for the US Consulate in Frankfurt before going freelance in 1955. He is engaged primarily in advertising and graphic design.

EBERHARD G. RENSCH, 1929 geboren in Halle, DDR. Er arbeitete in Werbeagenturen und war einige Zeit Ausstellungsdirektor beim US-Konsulat in Frankfurt, bevor er 1955 freiberuflich tätig wurde. Er befasst sich hauptsächlich mit Werbegraphik und Graphik-Design.

EBERHARD G. RENSCH, né à Halle (RDA) en 1929. A travaillé dans diverses agences de publicité et en qualité de directeur des expositions du consulat américain de Francfort avant de s'établir à son compte en 1955. Il travaille principalement dans le secteur publicitaire et dans le design graphique.

VICTOR VASARELY, born in Hungary, 1908, (French nationality). He studied at the Academy of Art in Budapest. In 1930 he moved to Paris and began his career with graphic design before turning to painting in 1944. In 1955 he entered his most important genre – kinetics, and in the same year he won the Prix de la Critique in Brussels, the Gold Medal at Milan Triennale and the International Prize in Venezuela. Throughout the 1960's he gained major prizes, awards in Europe, USA and Japan for his environmental work and the plastic arts. His optical illusions earned him the nickname "Father of Op Art".

VICTOR VASARELY, 1908 in Ungarn geboren, französische Staatsangehörigkeit. Er studierte an der Mühely-Akademie in Budapest. 1930 übersiedelte er nach Paris, wo er einige Zeit als Werbegraphiker arbeitete. 1944 wandte er sich der Malerei zu, nach gut 10 Jahren begann die Phase der berühmt gewordenen kinetischen Bilder. 1955 erhielt er den Kritikerpreis in Brüssel, die Goldmedaille der Mailänder Triennale und den Internationalen Preis in Venezuela. In den sechziger Jahren erhielt er für seine Plastiken und Objekte zahlreiche wichtige Preise und Auszeichnungen aus Europa, den USA und Japan. Seine optischen Illusionen brachten ihm den Namen «Vater der Op Art» ein.

VICTOR VASARELY, né en Hongrie en 1908, de nationalité française. Etudes à l'Académie Mühely de Budapest. Artiste publicitaire à Paris dès 1930, il s'oriente vers la peinture en 1944, aborde en 1955 le genre qui le rendra célèbre: l'art cinétique virtuel. La même année, il est Prix de la critique à Bruxelles, médaille d'or à la Triennale de Milan, Prix international au Venezuela. Les années 60 lui apportent une riche moisson de grands prix internationaux en Europe, aux Etats-Unis et au Japon pour ses créations plastiques et environnementales mariant lumière et mouvement virtuel. Ses illusions d'optique lui ont valu le titre honorifique de «père de l'op art».

SAUL STEINBERG, born in Rumania, 1914. He studied psychology and sociology in Bucharest. From 1932–41 he lived in Milan where he studied architecture. He joined the staff of the *New Yorker* in 1941 and lived in New York, becoming a US citizen. His graphic parody cartoons have been published in book form. His drawings were used to illustrate ads and also to decorate walls, e.g. Plaza Hotel, Cincinnati, and the US Pavilion in Brussels. Exhibited in New York, London, Paris etc. His work is held in MOMA, Whitney Museum and the Victoria and Albert Museum.

SAUL STEINBERG, 1914 in Rumänien geboren. Er studierte Psychologie und Soziologie in Bukarest. Von 1932 bis 1941 lebte er in Mailand, wo er Architektur studierte. 1941 ging er nach New York zu der Zeitschrift *New Yorker*. Er wurde amerikanischer Staatsbürger. Seine parodistischen Zeichnungen sind in Buchform erschienen. Sie wurden auch für Werbezwecke verwendet. Seine Bilder dekorieren u.a. die Wände des Plaza-Hotels, Cincinnati, sie wurden für den US-Pavillon in Brüssel verwendet und in zahlreichen Ausstellungen in New York, London, Paris etc. gezeigt. Seine Arbeiten sind in den Sammlungen des MOMA, des Whitney Museums und des Victoria and Albert Museums vertreten.

SAUL STEINBERG, né en Roumanie en 1914. Après ses études de psychologie et de sociologie à Bucarest, on le trouve de 1932 à 1941 à Milan, où il étudie l'architecture. En 1941, il part pour New York, rejoint l'équipe du magazine *New Yorker*, prend la nationalité américaine. Ses caricatures, parues aussi en volume, ont enrichi l'art publicitaire et la décoration murale, ainsi celle du Plaza Hotel de Cincinnati et du pavillon américain de l'Expo de Bruxelles. A eu des expositions à New York, Londres, Paris et dans de nombreuses autres villes. Ses œuvres figurent dans les collections du MOMA, du Whitney Museum et du Victoria and Albert Museum.

TOSHIHIRO KATAYAMA, born in Osaka, 1928. He is a self-taught artist. After working as a freelance graphic designer he co-founded the Nippon Design Center. In 1966 he moved to the USA and is currently senior lecturer and designer at Carpenter Center for Visual Arts, Harvard University. He has designed over 20 exhibitions and is engaged in environmental graphics, exhibition design, advertising art, packaging, etc. He designed the murals for the Boston City Subway. His work is in the MOMA collections.

TOSHIHIRO KATAYAMA, 1928 in Osaka geboren. Er ist Autodidakt. Er arbeitete als freier Graphiker, bevor er 1960 einer der Art Direktoren des Nippon Design Centers wurde. 1963 ging er als Graphiker zu Geigy in die Schweiz. 1966 übersiedelte er in die USA. Am Carpenter Center for Visual Arts der Harvard-Universität ist er jetzt als Designer tätig und hält Vorlesungen. Er hat über 20 Ausstellungen gestaltet und beschäftigt sich mit Umweltgraphik, Ausstellungs-Design, Werbegraphik, Verpackungen etc. Er hat die Wände für die U-Bahn in Boston gestaltet. Seine Arbeiten befinden sich in den Sammlungen des MOMA.

TOSHIHIRO KATAYAMA, né à Osaka en 1928. Graphiste autodidacte, il a travaillé à son compte avant d'être l'un des cofondateurs du Nippon Design Center en 1960. Part en Suisse en 1963 comme graphiste chez Geigy. S'installe aux USA en 1966. Aujourd'hui maître de conférences et designer au Carpenter Center for Visual Arts de l'Université Harvard. A réalisé une bonne vingtaine d'expositions, œuvre dans le domaine de la création graphique environnementale, de la conception d'expositions, de l'art publicitaire, de l'emballagisme, etc. On lui doit les murals du métro de Boston. Ses œuvres figurent dans les collections du MOMA.

EUGENE HOFFMAN, born in Pennsylvania, 1933. He studied at the Arizona State Teachers College at first and is mainly self-taught as graphic designer and artist. He had many vocations before finally settling down as a freelance humorous illustrator and designer. His work has been widely exhibited.

EUGENE HOFFMAN, 1933 in Pennsylvania geboren. Er studierte am Arizona State Teacher College und ist als Graphik-Designer und Künstler im wesentlichen Autodidakt. Er hatte viele Angebote, bevor er sich schliesslich als freischaffender Karikaturist und Designer niederliess. Seine Arbeiten sind an vielen Orten ausgestellt worden.

EUGENE HOFFMAN, né en Pennsylvanie en 1933. D'abord tourné vers l'enseignement, il a étudié à l'Arizona State Teachers College. En art, il est essentiellement autodidacte. A beaucoup bourlingué avant de s'établir à son compte comme dessinateur d'humour et designer. Ses travaux ont fait l'objet de nombreuses expositions.

For short biography, see Page 157.
WALTER GRIEDER writes as follows on the technique used for the cover design: "I apply a ground color to cardboard and paint my picture idea on this ground. I then brush over the surface with white and score out the drawing with the end of the brush while the layer is moist. Finally I add the color values."

Kurzbiographie Seite 157.
WALTER GRIEDER berichtete über seine Technik: «Ich trage auf Karton eine Grundfarbe auf und male die Bildidee auf diesen Grund. Dann überstreiche ich die Fläche mit weisser Farbe und ritze die Zeichnung mit dem Pinselende auf die noch feuchte Schicht. Zum Schluss füge ich die Farbwerte hinzu.»

Voir la notice biographique en p. 157.
Voici ce que WALTER GRIEDER nous dit de la technique utilisé pour cette couverture: «J'étends sur un carton une couleur fondamentale. Sur le fond ainsi constitué, je peins ce que j'ai en tête. Je recouvre le tout de peinture blanche et j'incise le dessin du bout de mon pinceau avant que ça sèche. Pour finir, j'ajoute les couleurs.»

ANGEL GRAÑENA, born in Spain, 1929. He studied art and sculpture before specializing in advertising design in 1943. In 1955 he founded his own studio in Barcelona. He was also Art Director of the *Cid* agency in Barcelona and taught advertising art at the Escuela Massana. This cover design won the first prize in a cover competition organized by the Spanish advertising journal *I.P.*

ANGEL GRAÑENA, 1929 in Spanien geboren. Er studierte Kunst und Bildhauerei, bevor er 1943 als Werbegraphiker zu arbeiten begann. 1955 eröffnete er sein eigenes Atelier in Barcelona. Er war Art Director der Agentur *Cid* und unterrichtete Werbegraphik an der Escuela Massana. Mit dem Entwurf dieses Umschlags gewann er den ersten Preis in einem Wettbewerb der spanischen Zeitschrift für Werbung *I.P.*

ANGEL GRAÑENA, né en Espagne en 1929. A étudié l'art et la sculpture avant de se spécialiser en art publicitaire en 1943. En 1955, il ouvre son propre studio à Barcelone. Il a été directeur artistique de l'agence *Cid* de Barcelone et a enseigné l'art publicitaire à l'Escuela Massana. Cette illustration lui a valu le premier prix d'un concours de couvertures organisé par la revue de publicité espagnole *I.P.*

ETIENNE DELESSERT, born in Lausanne, Switzerland, 1941. He started in Switzerland as graphic designer and then, after two years in Paris, he moved to New York. He is a regular contributor to many of the most prestigious US publications. His children's books have been published in the USA and in various European countries. His illustrations for *Thomas et l'infini* gained him the award: "Best European Book for Children, 1977". He also does murals, advertising art, animated cartoons and film art. His work has been extensively exhibited. He divides his time between New York and Switzerland.

ETIENNE DELESSERT, 1941 in Lausanne, Schweiz, geboren. Seine Karriere begann als Graphik-Designer in der Schweiz, nach zwei Jahren in Paris zog er schliesslich nach New York. Seine Arbeiten erscheinen regelmässig in führenden amerikanischen Publikationen. Seine Kinderbücher wurden in den USA und verschiedenen europäischen Ländern verlegt. Seine Illustrationen für *Thomas et l'infini* wurden mit dem Preis für das beste europäische Kinderbuch 1977 ausgezeichnet. Zu seinem Arbeitsbereich gehören auch Wandbilder, Werbegraphik und Trickfilme. Er ist in New York und der Schweiz tätig.

ETIENNE DELESSERT, né à Lausanne en 1941. D'abord graphiste en Suisse, il passe deux années à Paris, puis part pour New York. Ses travaux paraissent régulièrement dans la plupart des périodiques américains de prestige. Ses livres d'enfants ont été publiés aux Etats-Unis et dans divers pays européens. Ses illustrations pour *Thomas et l'infini* lui ont valu le Prix du meilleur livre d'enfant européen en 1977. Il réalise aussi des murals, travaille pour la publicité, le cinéma d'animation, les bancs-titres au cinéma. A eu de nombreuses expositions. Partage son temps entre New York et la Suisse.

For short biography, see Page 150.
RONALD SEARLE has taken up a subject for this cover which is only too well-known to many designers – the creative pangs and misery at the sight of a blank, white sheet. A chaos of possible solutions runs through his confused mind: from the simplest graphic formulations to the baroque and whimsical. Somewhere the artist sits as an immovable figure between consciousness and unconsciousness. Here, however, Searle conquers fate, or rather remembers Freud: "when man sets his conflicts in the open, they are settled in no time."

Kurzbiographie Seite 150.
RONALD SEARLE hat sich für diesen Umschlag mit einem Thema beschäftigt, das vielen Graphikern wohl nur allzu bekannt ist: die schöpferischen Qualen und Nöte beim Anblick des grossen, weissen Blattes. Ein wahres Durcheinander von möglichen Lösungen spukt durch den verwirrten Kopf: von den schlichtesten graphischen Formulierungen bis zu barocken und grillenhaften Hirngespinsten. Noch sitzt der Künstler als unbewegliche Figur irgendwo zwischen Sein und Nichtsein. Hier jedoch schlägt Searle dem Schicksal ein Schnippchen, oder vielmehr erinnert er sich an die Lehre Freuds – indem der Mensch seinen Konflikt an den Tag bringt, löst er ihn im Handumdrehen.

Voir la notice biographique en p. 150.
RONALD SEARLE s'attaque dans cette couverture à un sujet bien connu des graphistes: les affres de la création face à la page blanche. Un tohu-bohu de solutions possibles se déverse dans l'esprit de l'artiste en proie au doute et à la confusion, de la formule graphique linéaire jusqu'aux élucubrations les plus baroquisantes. Le créateur se situe encore, immobile, aux confins de l'être et du non-être. Ici, pourtant, Searle déjoue la malédiction de l'impuissance, en se souvenant peut-être de Freud: en mettant à jour le conflit qui le paralyse, l'individu le résout en un tournemain.

JEAN MICHEL FOLON, born in Belgium, 1934. He gave up architectural studies to devote himself to drawing. Apart from designing covers and doing illustrations for major magazines and for advertising, he also works in TV and film art and has designed cartoons and titles for French TV channels. More recently he has turned to watercolor painting and engraving. His work has been exhibited in Italy, France, Belgium and the USA. He is co-author (with Giorgio Soavi) of *Le Message (Olivetti*, 1967). Awarded the Grand Prix in 1973 at the Biennale in Sao Paulo.

JEAN MICHEL FOLON, 1934 in Belgien geboren. Er gab sein Architektur-Studium auf, um sich dem Zeichnen zu widmen. Neben der Gestaltung von Umschlägen und Illustrationen für bedeutende Magazine und für Werbezwecke, arbeitet er auch für Film und Fernsehen, u.a. entwarf er Titel und Trickfilme für das französische Fernsehen. In letzter Zeit befasst er sich vor allem mit Aquarellen und Radierungen. Seine Arbeiten wurden in Italien, Frankreich, Belgien und den USA ausgestellt. Er ist Co-Autor (mit Giorgio Soavi) von *Le Message* («Die Botschaft», *Olivetti*, 1967. 1973 erhielt er den Grand Prix der Biennale in Sao Paulo.

JEAN MICHEL FOLON, né en Belgique en 1934. Interrompt ses études d'architecture pour se vouer au dessin. Réalise des couvertures et des illustrations pour des grands magazines, travaille aussi pour le cinéma et le cinéma d'animation, a créé des titres et des séquences animées pour la télévision française. Ces derniers temps, s'est tourné vers l'aquarelle et la gravure. Ses travaux ont été exposés en Italie, en France, en Belgique, aux USA. Co-auteur, avec Giorgio Savi, de l'ouvrage *Le Message (Olivetti*, 1967). Lauréat du Grand Prix de la Biennale de Sao Paulo 1973.

ELEONORE SCHMID, born in Lucerne, Switzerland, 1939. She was educated at the Applied Arts School Lucerne and afterwards worked as a graphic artist in a publishing company. She made illustrations for a children's newspaper, books and games. Her illustrations for *Treasure Island* by R.L. Stevenson received special recognition. During a long stay in Paris her first picture book *The Tree*, in collaboration with Etienne Delessert, evolved, for which she received the gold medal at the Biennale in Bratislava. Today she is in Zürich again working as a freelance graphic artist and illustrator. Apart from many children's books, she illustrated a picture bible for children.

CHRISTIAN HERDEG, born in Zürich, 1942. He studied photography and filming in Zürich, and furthered his studies in Canada and in the USA where his first "light objects" were exhibited. In 1971 he returned to Europe and gave up professional photography to work as freelance artist in the medium of argon and neon-light tubes. His works have been bought by large industrial firms and cultural institutes: seven light tubes on water for the Swiss Bank Corp., Zürich, a light-prism group at Zürich airport, design of the main information hall at the Technical High School, Zürich etc. He has had numerous one-man shows at home and abroad.

MILTON GLASER, born in New York, 1929. He studied at Cooper Union, and was awarded a Fulbright Scholarship to the Academia delle Belle Arti in Bologna. He is a founder member of *Push Pin Studios* (1954). He served on the Board of *New York Magazine* in 1968 and in 1975 was appointed Vice President and Design Director of *The Village Voice*. His own studio, Milton Glaser Inc., was founded in 1974. In 1979 he was made Honorary Fellow of the Royal Soc. of Arts. His scope encompasses all areas of design and his awards are manifold. He is represented in MOMA, the Israel Museum, Victoria and Albert Museum and Musée de l'affiche, Paris.

For short biography, see Page 155.
The motif of this cover is borrowed from the book *Quattro Facciate* by ANTONIO FRASCONI, printed by hand in a limited edition in 1967. This book, of unusually large format (21¼ x 14½ inches), contains woodcut renderings of four of Florence's proudest buildings: the Batistery of the Cathedral, the Basilicas of Santa Maria Novella and San Miniato al Monte and the Badia Fiesolana. The illustration on this cover is an impression of the façade of San Miniato.

ELEONORE SCHMID, 1939 in Luzern, Schweiz, geboren. Ihre Ausbildung erhielt sie an der Kunstgewerbeschule Luzern und arbeitete anschliessend als Graphikerin in einem Verlag. Sie machte Illustrationen für eine Kinderzeitschrift, Bücher und Spiele. Besondere Anerkennung fanden ihre Illustrationen für die *Schatzinsel* von R.L. Stevenson. Während eines längeren Aufenthalts in Paris entstand in Zusammenarbeit mit Etienne Delessert ihr erstes Bilderbuch *The Tree*, für das sie eine goldene Plakette der Biennale Bratislava erhielt. Heute ist sie wieder in Zürich als freischaffende Graphikerin und Illustratorin tätig. Neben mehreren Bilderbüchern illustrierte sie eine Bilderbibel für Kinder.

CHRISTIAN HERDEG, 1942 in Zürich geboren. Er studierte Photographie und Film in Zürich und vervollständigte seine Studien in Kanada und in den USA, wo seine ersten «Lichtobjekte» ausgestellt wurden. 1971 kehrte er nach Europa zurück und gab die professionelle Photographie auf, um als freischaffender Künstler mit Argon und Neon-Röhren zu arbeiten. Seine Arbeiten wurden von grossen Firmen und Kulturinstituten gekauft, z.B: Sieben Lichtkörper auf Wasser vom Schweizerischen Bankverein. Herdeg hatte zahlreiche Einzelausstellungen in verschiedenen Ländern.

MILTON GLASER, 1929 in New York geboren. Er studierte an der Cooper Union, New York, und erhielt das Fulbright-Stipendium für ein Studium an der Academia delle Belle Arti, Bologna. Er ist Mitbegründer der *Push Pin Studios* (1954). 1968 wurde er u.a. Design-Direktor des *New York Magazine*, 1975 Vize-Präsident und Design-Direktor der *Village Voice*. Sein eigenes Studio, Milton Glaser Inc., besteht seit 1974. Sein Arbeitsbereich umfasst alle Sparten des Designs. Er hat unzählige Auszeichnungen erhalten und seine Arbeiten befinden sich im MOMA, Israel Museum, Victoria and Albert Museum und Musée de l'affiche, Paris.

Kurzbiographie Seite 155.
Das Motiv dieses Umschlages ist dem Buch *Quattro Facciate* von ANTONIO FRASCONI entnommen, welches 1967 in einer beschränkten Auflage von Hand gedruckt wurde. Von ungewöhnlich grossem Format (54 x 37 cm), enthält das Buch Holzschnitt-Wiedergaben von vier der erhabensten Gebäuden in Florenz: Baptisterium der Kathedrale, Basiliken Santa Maria Novella und San Miniato al Monte, Badia Fiesolana. Der Umschlag zeigt eine Impression der Fassade von San Miniato al Monte.

ELEONORE SCHMID, née en 1939 à Lucerne, en Suisse. A suivi les cours de l'Ecole des arts décoratifs de sa ville natale, puis a travaillé comme graphiste chez un éditeur, réalisant des illustrations pour un journal d'enfants, des livres et des jouets. Ses illustrations pour *l'Île au trésor* de R.L. Stevenson ont suscité l'admiration. D'un séjour prolongé à Paris naquit son premier album illustré *The Tree* (l'Arbre) en collaboration avec Etienne Delessert. Il lui valut la médaille d'or de la biennale de Bratislava. De retour à Zurich, elle travaille comme graphiste et illustratrice indépendante. Elle a illustré nombre de livres d'enfants et aussi une Bible imagée pour les petits.

CHRISTIAN HERDEG, né à Zurich en 1942. A étudié la photo et le cinéma à Zurich, au Canada et aux Etats-Unis où ses premiers «objets lumineux» ont fait sensation dans les expositions. Revenu en Europe en 1971, il renonce à la photographie professionnelle pour travailler à son compte dans le domaine des créations artistiques à base de tubes d'argon et de néon. Ses œuvres ont été acquises par de grands investisseurs industriels et culturels: sept tubes lumineux flottant sur l'eau par la Société de Banque Suisse de Zurich, un groupe de prismes lumineux par l'aéroport de Zurich, etc. Il faut y ajouter la décoration du hall d'information de l'Ecole polytechnique de Zurich, entre autres. Nombreuses expositions individuelles.

MILTON GLASER, né à New York en 1929. Ancien élève de Cooper Union, il obtient une bourse Fulbright pour l'Academia delle Belle Arti de Bologne. Co-fondateur des *Push Pin Studios* en 1954, il sera entre autres directeur du design au *New York Magazine* dès 1968, vice-président et dircteur du design du *Village Voice* dès 1975. Son studio Milton Glaser, Inc. voit le jour en 1974. Honorary Fellow de la Royal Society of Arts en 1979, il a exercé ses talents de designer dans toutes les spécialités, obtenu un nombre important de prix et récompenses et vu ses œuvres accueillies dans les collections du MOMA, de l'Israel Museum, du Victoria and Albert Museum, du Musée parisien de l'affiche.

Voir la notice biographique en p. 155.
Le thème de cette couverture est emprunté à l'ouvrage d'ANTONIO FRASCONI intitulé *Quattro Facciate* (Quatre Façades) imprimé sur une presse à bras en 1967. Ce livre au tirage limité a un grand format peu usuel - 54 x 37 cm. Il renferme des gravures en bois consacrées à quatre merveilles architecturales de Florence: le baptistère de la Cathédrale, les basiliques de S. Maria Novella et S. Miniato al Monte, la Badia Fiesolana. On voit ici la façade de S. Miniato al Monte.

PETER MAX, born in Germany, 1940. After first travelling to Shanghai and Israel he settled in the USA and in 1962 he founded an art studio there together with Tom Daly. The partnership achieved rapid success with modernistic designs appealing to the younger generation. (He earned himself the label "the Walt Disney of the future generation".) The studio turns out a vast volume of work – posters and designs for advertising purposes: foodstuffs, crockery, clocks, furnishings.

PETER MAX, 1940 in Deutschland geboren. Über Shanghai und Israel kam er in die USA und eröffnete dort 1962 ein Atelier mit Tom Daly. Diese Zusammenarbeit brachte sofortigen Erfolg. Max zog sich für zwei Jahre zurück und kreierte Tausende von Zeichnungen, die ihm den Titel «Walt Disney der kommenden Generation» eintrugen. Seine aufreizenden Farben und leicht verrückten Ideen tragen dazu bei, Uhren und Geschirr, Lebensmittel und Möbel zu verkaufen, und seine Plakate, die besonders die Jugendlichen ansprechen, sind für ihn zu einem grossen Erfolg geworden.

PETER MAX, né en Allemagne en 1940. Après des séjours à Chang-hai et en Israël, il s'installe aux Etats-Unis et y fonde en 1962 un studio conjointement avec Tom Daly. Les associés s'imposent rapidement par des designs modernistes qui leur valent l'approbation de la jeune génération. (Max a même été appelé «le Walt Disney de la génération à venir».) Le studio a une production importante d'affiches et de travaux publicitaires dans les secteurs de l'alimentation, des articles ménagers, de l'horlogerie, des ameublements, etc.

GRAPHICTEAM of Cologne. This is a team of five members who joined forces after working together in the design studios of *Bayer* Chemical Company in Leverkusen. They left in 1966 and, apart from the *Bayer* account, they soon won many more major clients and now work in all fields of advertising and graphic art. The team is headed by Coordt von Mannstein, and the other four members are: Hans Buschfeld, Siegfried Himmer, Winfried Holtz and Heinz Lippert.

GRAPHICTEAM in Köln. Es handelt sich hier um die fünf Mitglieder eines Teams, die sich zusammenschlossen, nachdem sie sich im graphischen Atelier der chemischen Fabrik *Bayer*, Leverkusen, kennengelernt hatten. 1966 eröffneten sie ein eigenes Atelier in Köln und gewannen neben *Bayer* andere wichtige Kunden. Das Team arbeitet auf allen Gebieten der Werbung und Graphik und wird von Coordt von Mannstein geleitet. Die anderen vier Mitglieder sind: Hans Buschfeld, Siegfried Himmer, Winfried Holtz und Heinz Lippert.

GRAPHICTEAM, Cologne. Il s'agit de cinq associés qui se sont connus dans les studios de design du groupe chimique *Bayer* à Leverkusen (RFA). Constitué en 1966, Graphicteam s'est assuré une clientèle importante à part *Bayer*, pour laquelle il œuvre dans tous les secteurs du design et de la publicité. L'équipe dirigée par Coordt von Mannstein comprend Hans Buschfeld, Siegfried Himmer, Winfried Holtz et Heinz Lippert.

For short biography, see Page 160.
Beneath the deceptively naive style of this artist runs a vein of mordant satire. TOMI UNGERER has depicted the duel-to-the-death of modern advertising – but luckily – thanks to their functional tectonics – their passionate anger is not likely to cost much blood.

Kurzbiographie Seite 160.
Hinter dem trügerisch naiven Stil TOMI UNGERERS verbirgt sich eine beissende satirische Ader. Auf seinem Umschlag hat der unbarmherzige Kampf in der modernen Werbung auch ihre primitivsten Vertreter angesteckt. Aber glücklicherweise wird dank ihrer funktionellen Tektonik in diesem Duell wohl kaum viel Blut fliessen.

Voir la notice biographique en p. 160.
Le style faussement naïf de TOMI UNGERER recouvre une veine satirique virulente. Il a ici décrit la lutte implacable que se livre les tenants de la publicité moderne. La tectonique fonctionnelle aidant, l'ardeur assassine des adversaires ne risque guère de dégénérer en un bain de sang.

SOFU TESHIGAHARA, born in Sakai, Japan, 1900. For this special double issue devoted to the art of Japan, each feature opened with a title in Japanese characters. This design is the artist's rendering of the word *Nippon* (The Land of the Rising Sun). Teshigahara, a famous sculptor, whose works have been exhibited in Europe, the USA and Japan, also founded the *Sogetsu* school of Ikebana and is considered to be one of Japan's leading exponents on the art of flower arranging.

SOFU TESHIGAHARA, 1900 in Sakai, Japan, geboren. Die von ihm für den Umschlag gemalten japanischen Schriftzeichen bedeuten *Nippon*, Land der aufgehenden Sonne. Teshigahara ist ein bekannter Bildhauer, dessen Werke schon in vielen Ausstellungen gezeigt wurden. 1925 gründete er in Japan die *Sogetsu*-Schule für Ikebana. Er gilt als einer der führenden Kenner Japans in der Kunst des Blumenarrangements.

SOFU TESHIGAHARA, né à Sakai (Japon) en 1900. Dans ce numéro double spécial consacré à l'art du Japon, chaque article était introduit par un titre calligraphié en caractères japonais. Cette composition représente la version artistique que Sofu Teshigahara donne du mot *Nippon* (Pays du soleil levant). Sculpteur célèbre dont les œuvres ont été exposées en Europe, aux Etats-Unis et au Japon, Teshigahara a aussi fondé l'école d'ikebana *Sogetsu*; il est considéré comme l'un des principaux représentants japonais de cet art floral aux savantes combinaisons.

GENE LAURENTS, born in Louisiana, 1931. He studied art in Lafayette and Ohio State University. After working in advertising design in New York for a few years he won a Fulbright Scholarship to Hamburg and Munich where he worked on poster art. He later took up photography as his medium and in 1960 he began working for leading women's magazines in Paris, London and Munich. He now lives in New York. His works have been exhibited in the Modern Art Museum in Munich and at the Photokina in Cologne.

GENE LAURENTS, 1931 in Louisiana, USA, geboren. Er studierte Kunst an der Lafayette und an der Ohio State University. Anschliessend arbeitete er als Werbegraphiker in New York. Ein Fulbright-Stipendium brachte ihn 1959 nach Hamburg und München, wo er Plakate entwarf. Später widmete er sich verstärkt der Photographie, und ab 1960 begann er für führende Frauenmagazine in Paris, London und München zu arbeiten. Er lebt heute in New York. Seine Arbeiten wurden in der Staatsgalerie für moderne Kunst in München und an der Photokina in Köln ausgestellt.

GENE LAURENTS, né en Louisiana en 1931. A étudié l'art à Lafayette et à l'Université d'Etat de l'Ohio. Après quelques années d'art publicitaire à New York, il obtient une bourse Fulbright pour Hambourg et Munich, où il crée surtout des affiches. Il se tourne ensuite vers la photo et travaille dès 1960 pour les grands magazines féminins de Paris, Londres et Munich. Il habite aujourd'hui New York. Ses œuvres ont été exposées au Musée d'art moderne de Munich et à la Photokina de Cologne.

OLAF LEU, born in Germany, 1936. After technical studies at Ulm he worked as a graphic designer in Frankfurt. From 1957–59 he was Assistant Art Director of an advertising agency. He then turned freelance and in 1971 he founded the *Olaf Leu Design Bureau*, Frankfurt. His one-man shows have been held in Europe, USA and Chile and he has taken part in several exhibitions in Europe, USA and Japan. He has been awarded some 200 awards, including the Silver Medal at Brno Biennale (1970) and the Gold Medal at the ADC Philadelphia (1970) – he also won two awards from AIGA in 1972 for the best packaging design.

OLAF LEU, 1936 in Deutschland geboren. Nach einer technischen Ausbildung in Ulm wurde er Graphik-Designer in Frankfurt. Von 1957 bis 1959 war er Assistant Art Director einer Werbeagentur. Dann machte er sich selbständig und gründete 1971 das *Olaf Leu Design-Studio*, Frankfurt. Er hatte Einzelausstellungen in Europa, den USA und in Chile und nahm an Gruppenausstellungen in Europa, den USA und Japan teil. Insgesamt erhielt er 200 Auszeichnungen, darunter die Silbermedaille der Biennale in Brno (1970) und die Goldmedaille des ADC Philadelphia (1970) – und zwei Preise der AIGA für das beste Packungs-Design (1972).

OLAF LEU, né en Allemagne en 1936. Après des études techniques à Ulm, il travaille comme graphiste à Francfort. De 1957 à 1959, il est directeur artistique adjoint d'une agence de publicité. Il prend ensuite sa liberté, travaille en indépendant. En 1971, il fonde le *Olaf Leu Design Bureau* à Francfort. Il a eu des expositions individuelles en Europe, aux USA et au Chili et a participé à plusieurs expositions en Europe, aux USA et au Japon. Il a reçu quelque 200 prix, dont la médaille d'argent de la Biennale de Brno 1970, la médaille d'or de l'ADC de Philadelphie en 1970 et deux prix de l'AIGA en 1972 pour le meilleur design d'emballage.

KEITH GODARD (cover photography by John T. Hill) was born in London, 1938. He studied at the London College of Printing and Graphic Arts. He later went to Yale and took his MFA degree. He now lives in the USA, heads his own design group and also teaches at the Philadelphia College of Art.

KEITH GODARD (Umschlag-Photographie von John T. Hill) wurde 1938 in London geboren. Er studierte am London College of Printing and Graphic Arts. Später setzte er seine Studien an der Yale University fort (Abschluss: Master of Fine Arts). Er lebt heute in den USA, leitet eine eigene Design-Gruppe und unterrichtet ausserdem am Philadelphia College of Art.

KEITH GODARD (photo de la couverture de John T. Hill) né à Londres en 1938, il a étudié au London College of Printing and Graphic Arts. Plus tard, il a passé son MFA à Yale. Aujourd'hui installé aux Etats-Unis, il dirige son propre groupe de design tout en enseignant au Philadelphia College of Art.

CHRISTINE CHAGNOUX, born in Paris, 1937. She studied at the Ecole des Beauxarts, Paris. She specializes in plant and animal life illustration and has contributed regularly to many French magazines. Since 1970 she has turned toward etching and engraving. She illustrated a series of children's books in which the hero is a hippopotamus (Petit Potam). For her animated cartoon of this figure she won First Prize at Lido di Venezia (1969). Many one-man shows of her work have been staged in the USA and France. She has participated in several group exhibitions and has gained numerous awards.

CHRISTINE CHAGNOUX, 1937 in Paris geboren. Sie studierte an der Ecole des Beaux-Arts in Paris. Sie hat sich auf Illustrationen aus dem Pflanzen- und Tierreich spezialisiert, und ihre Arbeiten werden regelmässig in französischen Zeitschriften gezeigt. Seit 1970 befasst sie sich auch mit Druckgraphik. Eine Kinderbuchreihe, deren Held ein Flusspferd ist (Petit Potam), wurde durch ihre Illustrationen zu einem grossen Erfolg. Für einen Zeichentrickfilm mit dieser Figur erhielt sie den Ersten Preis am Lido di Venezia (1969). In den USA und Frankreich wurden ihre Arbeiten in vielen Einzelausstellungen gezeigt. Hinzu kommen verschiedene Gruppenausstellungen und zahlreiche Preise.

CHRISTINE CHAGNOUX, née à Paris en 1937. A fait l'Ecole des Beaux-Arts à Paris. S'est spécialisée dans l'illustration végétale et animale pour le compte de nombreux magazines français. Depuis 1970, elle s'oriente vers la gravure en général, l'eau-fort en particulier. Elle a illustré une série de livres pour enfants dont le héros est un petit hippopotame, Petit Potam. Son dessin animé sur le même sujet lui a valu le premier prix au Festival cinématographique de Venise en 1969. De nombreuses expositions individuelles de ses œuvres lui ont été consacrées aux Etats-Unis et en France. Elle a participé à plusieurs expositions collectives et remporté toute une série de prix.

JOSSE GOFFIN, born in Brussels, 1938. He studied advertising design in his native city and continued his studies in Paris. He became freelance in 1962. His wide scope encompasses illustration, serigraphy, advertising art, murals, engraving, posters, animated cartoons etc. His clients include publishers, paper producers, chemical firms, chain stores and trade fairs. His poster for the Dutch Railways won an award conferred by the Amsterdam ADC. He has held numerous one-man exhibitions.

JOSSE GOFFIN, 1938 in Brüssel geboren. Er studierte Werbegraphik in seiner Heimatstadt und setzte diese Studien in Paris fort. 1962 machte er sich selbständig. Zu seinem umfassenden Arbeitsbereich gehören Illustration, Serigraphie, Werbegraphik, Druckgraphik, Plakate, Zeichentrick-Serien usw. Zu seinem Kundenkreis gehören Verleger, Papierhersteller, chemische Unternehmen, Ladenketten und Messen. Sein Plakat für die holländischen Eisenbahnen erhielt einen Preis des Amsterdamer ADC. Zahlreiche Einzelausstellungen waren seinen Arbeiten gewidmet.

JOSSE GOFFIN, né à Bruxelles en 1938. Il a étudié l'art publicitaire dans sa ville natale, puis à Paris. Artiste indépendant depuis 1962, il crée à tour de bras des illustrations, des sérigraphies publicitaires, des murals, des gravures, des affiches, des dessins animés, etc. Il a pour clients, entre autres, des éditeurs, des papetiers, des sociétés de produits chimiques, des grands magasins, des foires-expositions. Son affiche pour les Chemins de Fer Néerlandais lui a valu un prix de l'Art Directors Club d'Amsterdam. De nombreuses expositions individuelles lui ont été consacrées.

For short biography, see Page 154.
From the many greetings we received from artists for *Graphis'* 25th birthday, we selected the one by JAN LENICA for the cover. When Lenica designed his 25 he was on holiday in Finland where, in his own words, "there are only lakes and forests, but no artists' shops. I therefore created a page as well as I could, from nothing." With a little black, some white paper scraps and a rose basket from granny's poetry album, he managed to bring to life two numerals that speak for themselves.

Kurzbiographie Seite 154.
Von den vielen Glückwünschen, die wir von verschiedenen Künstlern zum 25. *Graphis*-Jubiläum erhielten, wählten wir denjenigen von JAN LENICA für diesen Umschlag aus. Als Lenica seine 25 entwarf, weilte er in Finnland in den Ferien, wo es - nach seinen eigenen Worten - «nur Seen und Wälder gibt, aber keine Farbgeschäfte. So habe ich ein Blatt gebastelt, wie ich es konnte, aus nichts». Mit ein wenig Schwarz, einigen weissen Papierschnitzeln und einem Rosenkörbchen aus Grossmutters Poesiealbum ist es ihm gelungen, zwei Zahlen ins Leben zu rufen, die für sich selber sprechen.

Voir la notice biographique en p. 154.
Parmi les nombreux vœux d'artistes reçus à l'occasion du 25e anniversaire de *Graphis*, nous avons retenu pour cette couverture celui de JAN LENICA. Il en a eu l'idée lors d'un séjour de vacances en Finlande où, nous dit-il, «il n'y a que des lacs et des forêts, mais pas de magasins de peinture. C'est pourquoi j'ai bricolé mon dessin à partir de rien.» Un peu de noir, des bouts de papier blanc, une de ces corbeilles de roses chères à nos grand-mères qui en émaillaient leurs albums de poésies ont suffi à notre artiste pour concocter deux nombres qui en disent long.

RICHARD GUYATT, born in Spain, 1914. He started his career as painter and freelance graphic designer (his earliest commissions were posters for *Shell*). After the war he worked as exhibition designer and was co-designer of pavilions for the Festival of Britain (1951). He also designed ceramics for *Wedgewood* and was advisor to the Bank of England on banknote design. In 1948 he was appointed Professor at the Royal College of Art, and started up the School of Graphic Design there. He was awarded the CBE for his services to graphic design in 1969.

RICHARD GUYATT, 1914 in Spanien geboren. Er begann seine Laufbahn als Maler und freischaffender Graphik-Designer (seine ersten Aufträge waren Plakate für *Shell*). Nach dem Krieg arbeitete er als Ausstellungs-Designer, u.a. war er an dem Entwurf von Pavillons für das Festival of Britain (1951) beteiligt. Er hat auch Keramik für *Wedgewood* entworfen und hat die Bank von England beim Entwurf von Banknoten beraten. 1948 wurde er Professor am Royal College of Art und rief dort die Abteilung für Graphik-Design ins Leben. 1969 erhielt er den CBE für seine Verdienste im Graphik-Design.

RICHARD GUYATT, né en Espagne en 1914. A débuté comme peintre et graphiste indépendant - ses premières affiches lui ont été commandées par *Shell*. Après la guerre, il a travaillé comme concepteur d'expositions. A ce titre, il a apporté sa contribution à divers pavillons du Festival of Britain 1951. Il a aussi créé des céramiques pour *Wedgewood* et a conseillé la Banque d'Angleterre pour l'esthétique de ses billets de banque. En 1948. il est nommé professeur au Royal College of Art, où il installe une Ecole d'art graphique. Pour les services qu'il a rendus à la cause de l'art graphique, il a été élevé en 1969 à la dignité de C.B.E.

For short biography, see Page 141.
ANDRÉ FRANÇOIS has always been a fertile inventor of new species. In this illustration he has come up with a simplified subhuman genus possessing only one of the senses at a time. Of course it goes without saying that these "one-sense" creatures must live in groups in order to communicate at all.

Kurzbiographie Seite 141.
ANDRÉ FRANÇOIS ist, neben vielen anderen Tätigkeiten, auch schöpferischer Erfinder von neuen Lebewesen. Hier stellt er uns eine vereinfachte, menschenähnliche Gattung vor, die immer nur einen der fünf Sinne besitzt. Natürlich müssen diese Geschöpfe, um in den Genuss aller Lebensfreuden zu gelangen, in Gruppen leben.

Voir la notice biographique en p. 141.
ANDRÉ FRANÇOIS est un inventeur prolifique d'espèces nouvelles. Les soushumains qu'il nous présente ici ne possèdent chacun qu'un seul des cinq sens de l'homo sapiens. Il est donc inévitable que ces créatures monosensorielles sont condamnées à vivre en groupe pour accéder à la plénitude de la communication et donc de l'existence.

■

FRITZ GOTTSCHALK, born in Zürich, 1937. He studied at the Kunstgewerbeschule in Zurich und Basle. After freelancing for a time in Paris, he moved to London and from there to Canada (1963) where he was engaged on the Expo '67. He took on Canadian citizenship in 1968 and founded (with Stuart Ash) *Gottschalk + Ash Int'l* in 1968. The firm has gained numerous awards in advertising art, industrial design and architectural graphics. In 1978 he returned to Switzerland and opened *Gottschalk + Ash Int'l, Zurich*.

■

FRITZ GOTTSCHALK, 1937 in Zürich geboren. Er besuchte die Kunstgewerbeschule in Zürich und Basel. Er arbeitete einige Zeit lang in Paris und London bevor er nach Kanada zu Paul Arthur & Associates ging. Hier war er u.a. wesentlich an der Vorbereitung der Expo 1967 in Montréal beteiligt. 1968 wurde er Kanadier und gründete zusammen mit Stuart Ash die Firma *Gottschalk + Ash Int'l*. Sie erhielten zahlreiche Auszeichnungen für Werbegraphik, Industrie-Design und Architektur-Graphik. 1978 kehrte er in die Schweiz zurück und leitet seitdem die Zürcher Niederlassung von *Gottschalk + Ash Int'l*.

■

FRITZ GOTTSCHALK, né à Zurich en 1937. Ancien élève des Ecoles des arts décoratifs de Zurich et de Bâle. Artiste indépendant à Paris, il part pour Londres, puis pour le Canada en 1963. Il est appelé a participer à la conception de l'Expo 67. Naturalisé Canadien en 1968, il fonde en 1968 avec Stuart Ash la société *Gottschalk+Ash Int'l* qui remporte de nombreux prix pour ses créations publicitaires, ses études d'esthétique industrielle et ses réalisation graphiques architecturales. De retour en Suisse en 1978, il y fonde *Gottschalk + Ash Int'l, Zurich*.

■

F.G. BOES (cover photography by H. Hansen), born in Germany. Creative consultant and designer whose name is given to a number of wellknown brand products. In 1970 he founded GO with two partners: "a company for the systematic development and introduction of products and services". He has won numerous awards, including a Gold Medal of the IAA in Mexico for advertisement design. He is a member of the TDC New York, ICTA, and the German designers' association.

■

F.G. BOES (Umschlag-Photographie von H. Hansen), deutscher Designer und Creative Consultant. Bekannte Markenartikel-Konzeptionen stammen aus seinem Atelier. 1970 gründete er mit zwei Partnern die GO, Gesellschaft zur systematischen Entwicklung und Durchsetzung von Produkten und Dienstleistungen. Er erhielt verschiedene Auszeichnungen, darunter eine Goldmedaille für das international beste Anzeigenkonzept IAA, Mexiko. Er ist Mitglied des TDC, New York, der ICTA und der Deutschen Designer Vereinigung.

■

F.G. BOES (photo H. Hansen), né en Allemagne. Conseiller créatif et designer dont le nom a été donné à toute une série de produits de marque connus. En 1970, il fonde avec deux associés GO, «société pour le développement systématique et l'introduction de produits et services». Il a remporté de nombreux prix, dont une médaille d'or de l'IAA au Mexique pour ses annonces. Boes est membre du TDC de New York, de l'ICTA et de l'association allemande des designers.

■

TAKEJI IWAMIYA, born in Yonago City, Japan, 1920. He is one of Japan's best-known photographers. This is a photograph of "The Tower of the Sun" on top of the Symbol Area, the focal point of Expo '70. Architect Kenzo Tange and artist Taro Okamoto designed the tower and Iwamiya took the shot. He wandered over the Expo site for 5 months taking photos that would express its theme and atmosphere. He is Professor at Osaka University of Arts.

■

TAKEJI IWAMIYA, 1920 in Yonago City, Japan, geboren, ist einer der bekanntesten Photographen Japans. Er unterrichtet an der Kunstakademie in Osaka. Der Umschlag dieser Graphis-Ausgabe zeigt eine Photographie des Turms der Sonne, Brennpunkt der Expo '70. Dieser wurde vom Architekten Kenzo Tange und dem Künstler Taro Okamoto gestaltet und von Iwamiya photographiert. Iwamiya besuchte monatelang das Expo-Gelände, um Thematik und Atmosphäre mit seiner Kamera einzufangen.

■

TAKEJI IWAMIYA, né à Yonago (Japon) en 1920. C'est l'un des photographes japonais les plus en vue. Il s'agit ici d'une photo de la «Tour du Soleil» au sommet de l'Aire symbolique, le point central de l'Expo 70. La Tour est due à l'architecte Kenzo Tange et à l'artiste Taro Okamoto. Cette photo figure dans la riche moisson qu'Iwamiya a engrangée en parcourant pendant cinq mois le site de l'Expo à l'affût d'images propices à capter le thème et l'ambiance de cette grande manifestation. Takeji Iwamiya est professeur à l'Université des arts d'Osaka.

■

ROLAND TOPOR, born in Paris, 1938. After leaving the Ecole des Beaux-Arts, he began to draw and to write, having found that his ideas divided themselves into the literary and the visual. He has since continued to publish albums of drawings interspersed with novels and short stories. He also illustrated books and contributed drawings to periodicals. He has also occupied himself with animated films. One of his films was awarded the Prix Spécial at the Film Festival, Cannes. One-man exhibitions of his work have taken place all over the world.

■

ROLAND TOPOR, 1938 in Paris geboren. Nach Studien an der Ecole des Beaux Arts begann er sich zeichnerisch und schriftstellerisch zu betätigen, weil er festgestellt hatte, dass sich seine Gedanken in eine visuelle und in eine literarische Richtung bewegen. Seitdem hat er verschiedene Alben mit Zeichnungen, aber auch Novellen und Kurzgeschichten veröffentlicht. Er illustrierte auch Bücher und zeichnete für Zeitschriften. Er befasst sich ausserdem mit Trickfilmen. Für einen seiner Filme erhielt er den Prix Spécial am Filmfestival in Cannes. Einzelausstellungen seiner Werke fanden in aller Welt statt.

■

ROLAND TOPOR, né à Paris en 1938. Après l'Ecole des beaux-arts, il s'adonne au dessin et à l'écriture, constatant que ses idées prennent un tour à la fois littéraire et visuel. Depuis, il produit des albums de dessins entremêlés de nouvelles et de récits. Il a aussi illustré des livres et alimenté divers périodiques en dessins. Créateur de films d'animation, il a été récompensé d'un Prix Spécial du Festival du cinéma de Cannes. Des expositions personnelles lui ont été consacrées dans le monde entier.

■

RICHARD LINDNER, 1901–1978. He studied in Munich and worked as Art Director there, but fled from Nazi Germany to Paris in 1933. He moved to New York in 1941 and worked as illustrator for leading US publications. He taught at Pratt Institute (from 1952). His first one-man exhibition was held in 1954. A successful graphic designer, he was over fifty when he decided to give up his profession and turn to fine art.

RICHARD LINDNER, 1901–1978. Er studierte an der Münchner Akademie und wurde 1929 Art Director eines grossen Verlages. 1933 floh er aus Nazi-Deutschland nach Paris und ging 1941 nach New York, wo er als Illustrator für Buchverlage und Zeitschriften tätig war. 1952 übernahm er ein Lehramt am Pratt Institute. Seine erste Einzelausstellung fand 1954 statt. Mehr als fünfzigjährig entschliesst sich der erfolgreiche Graphiker, sein Metier an den Nagel zu hängen und Maler zu werden.

RICHARD LINDNER, 1901–1978. A étudié à Munich, où il a ensuite travaillé comme directeur artistique. Quitte l'Allemagne pour Paris à l'avènement du national-socialisme en 1933. Emigré à New York en 1941, il y travaille comme illustrateur pour des grandes publications américaines. Dès 1952, il enseigne au Pratt Institute. Une première exposition personnelle lui est consacrée en 1954. Au faîte de sa carrière de graphiste, la cinquantaine franchie, il tourne le dos au succès commercial et se voue désormais aux beaux-arts.

For short biography, see Page 160.
VICTOR VASARELY has designed another of his works in optical art, demonstrating how two-dimensional yet skilfully staggered circles can conjure up a spiralled body floating in space in which the subtle modulation of browns and golds sucks our eyes down in its dynamic center.

Kurzbiographie Seite 160.
Auf diesem Umschlag von VICTOR VASARELY sieht man, wie zweidimensionale und kunstvoll angeordnete Kreise die räumliche Wölbung eines spiraligen Körpers heraufbeschwören können und wie durch subtile Abstufung von Braun- und Goldtönen unsere benommenen Sinne magisch hineingezogen werden in das Zentrum des gelben Strudels.

Voir la notice biographique en p. 160.
VICTOR VASARELY a réalisé ici un autre chef-d'œuvre de l'op art en montrant que des cercles bidimensionnels judicieusement échelonnés peuvent créer l'illusion d'un corps spiralé flottant dans l'espace, vers le centre duquel l'œil est aspiré par la magie subtile des bruns et des ors en une dynamique hypnotisante.

© 1987 PRO LITTERIS, Zürich

VIN GIULIANI, born in New York, 1930. He began his career as industrial designer and later studied at Pratt Institute before freelancing. He is a leading exponent of the art of assemblage, working chiefly with wood, nails and assorted objects for advertising and editorial purposes. His clients include large corporations as well as many leading magazines. His work has been widely exhibited in the USA.

VIN GIULIANI, 1930 in New York geboren. Er begann seine Laufbahn als Industrie-Designer, studierte später am Pratt Institute und arbeitete anschliessend freiberuflich. Er gilt als einer der bedeutendsten Exponenten der Kunst der Assemblage. Er arbeitet vorwiegend mit Holz, Nägeln und einem ganzen Arsenal von gesammelten Raritäten. Zu seinen Auftraggebern gehören verschiedene grosse Unternehmen und auch führende Zeitschriften. Seine Werke wurden in vielen Ausstellungen in den USA gezeigt.

VIN GIULIANI, né à New York en 1930. Il débute comme esthéticien industriel, puis s'en va étudier au Pratt Institute avant de se mettre à son compte. C'est l'un des ténors de l'art de l'assemblage à partir de bois, de clous et d'objets assortis, pour des besoins publicitaires ou illustratifs. Il compte parmi ses clients des grandes sociétés aussi bien qu'un nombre important de magazines de premier plan. Ses travaux ont été exposés sur tout le territoire des Etats-Unis.

For short biography, see Page 157.
WALTER GRIEDER is one of Switzerland's most prominent children's book illustrators. The cover shows how reality is transformed into fantasy. In this «reversal of roles» it is not the children who are looking upwards to flying ducks and flowing clouds, but the children themselves flying under cloud umbrellas while a family of ducks watches them enviously from the ground. Quite likely the ducks (as earthbound children) are saying to themselves: "If only we could fly!"

Kurzbiographie Seite 157.
WALTER GRIEDER ist einer der prominentesten Kinderbilderbuch-Illustratoren der Schweiz. Der Umschlag zeigt, wie durch die Phantasie die Realität vertauscht wird. Nicht Kinder schauen hoch zu fliegenden Enten und schwebenden Wolken, sondern die Kinder fliegen selbst unter Wolken-Schirmen und eine Entenfamilie beobachtet sie. Vielleicht denken die Enten: «Ach, könnten wir doch fliegen.»

Voir la notice biographique en p. 157.
WALTER GRIEDER est l'un des meilleurs illustrateurs de livres d'enfants que connaisse la Suisse. Sa couverture montre comment le réel se transforme sous l'influence de l'imagination. Ce ne sont pas les enfants qui admirent depuis le plancher des vaches des canards qui volent et des nuages qui passent; ce rôle contemplatif est dévolu aux canards qui regardent passer les enfants accrochés aux parapluies des nuages en pensant peut-être: «Ah, si seulement on savait voler!»

© 1987 PRO LITTERIS, Zürich

For short biography, see Page 162.
The subject of JEAN MICHEL FOLON's cover is taken from a poster which he designed in silkscreen on aluminium foil for the O.P.G. Conseil in Paris. The theme was the use of audiovisual media in modern communications, and as usual, Folon contrived to reduce it to its simplest terms. Snippets of information with a silver nucleus – the audio and the visual – flow on two wavelengths in the complementary colors red and green, from the human head. They are then mixed, shuffled and reassembled, and rise into a dark blue firmament as creations of the spirit.

Kurzbiographie Seite 162.
Das Motiv des Umschlages von JEAN MICHEL FOLON stammt von einem Plakat, welches er für den O.P.G. Conseil in Paris entworfen hatte. Das Thema war die Anwendung audiovisueller Kommunikationsmedien, und wie gewöhnlich gelang Folon dessen Gestaltung mit den einfachsten Mitteln. Die Schwingungen von Sprache und Musik, in den Komplementärfarben Rot und Grün dargestellt, fliessen im menschlichen Kopf zusammen. Das vorherrschende Blau, eine Farbe, die von Geist aber auch von Einsamkeit spricht, erfährt durch das Rot-Grün der audiovisuellen Spulen eine freundliche Bereicherung.

Voir la notice biographique en p. 162.
Le motif de la couverture de JEAN MICHEL FOLON s'inspire d'une affiche conçue pour O.P.G. Conseil à Paris. Il y était question de l'application des techniques médiatiques audiovisuelles. Comme à son habitude, Folon a su l'exprimer de manière très simple. Les vibrations du langage et de la musique interprétées dans les deux couleurs complémentaires rouge et vert se conjuguent à l'intérieur du crâne. Le bleu qui domine en tant que couleur de l'esprit, mais aussi de la solitude, s'enrichit au contact des bobines audiovisuelles rouges et vertes, qui introduisent de la variété et un sens certain de la solidarité.

FRANEC STAROWIEYSKI, born in Cracow, Poland, 1930. He studied in Warsaw and Cracow. In the last 25 years he has published some 200 posters, designed stage decors and he is devoted to Baroque calligraphy. His wide scope encompasses: posters, illustration, lettering, film-making, murals, lithography, book design, stage decor and painting. In 1980 he was visiting Professor at the Berlin Hochschule der Künste. One-man exhibitions in Europe and USA. Many awards have been conferred on him for his poster creations. He is a member of AGI.

FRANEK STAROWIEYSKI, 1930 in Krakau, Polen, geboren, studierte Malerei in Warschau und in seiner Geburtsstadt. In den letzten 25 Jahren hat er rund 200 Plakate geschaffen und sich auch Bühnenbildern und der Barockkalligraphie gewidmet. Sein umfangreicher Arbeitsbereich umfasst: Plakate, Illustrationen, Beschriftungen, Filme, Wandbilder, Lithographien, Buchentwürfe, Bühnenbilder und Gemälde. 1980 war er Gastdozent an der Berliner Hochschule der Künste. Einzelausstellungen seiner Werke fanden in Europa und den USA statt. Für seine Plakate hat er viele Auszeichnungen erhalten. Er ist Mitglied der AGI.

FRANEK STAROWIEYSKI, né à Cracovie (Pologne) en 1930. A fait ses études à Varsovie et à Cracovie. Durant le dernier quart de siècle, il a publié quelque 200 affiches, conçu des décors de théâtre et perfectionné sa calligraphie baroque. On lui doit aussi des illustrations, des caractères, des films, des murals, des lithos, des maquettes de livres, des peintures. En 1980, il a été professeur associé à l'Université berlinoise des arts. Des expositions individuelles lui ont été consacrées en Europe et aux Etats-Unis. Ses affiches lui ont valu de nombreux prix. Il est membre de l'AGI.

MERVYN KURLANSKY, born in South Africa, 1936. He studied at the Central School of Art and Design in London and has been working in London since 1960. After freelancing, he joined with Crosby and Forbes *(Crosby, Fletcher, Forbes Partnership)* - regrouped as *Pentagram Design Partnership* in 1972. He has been highly awarded for his work and is the recipient of a Bronze Medal at the Brno Biennale, Silver Medal from the D&AD, Gold Medals from the Packaging Design Council and Ministry of Trade & Technology, Japan. He is a member of AGI.

MERVYN KURLANSKY, 1936 in Südafrika geboren. Er studierte an der Central School of Art and Design in London und arbeitet seit 1960 in dieser Stadt. Nachdem er einige Zeit freischaffend tätig war, schloss er sich der Gruppe Crosby, Fletcher, Forbes an, 1972 umgruppiert in *Pentagram Design Partnership*. Unter seinen zahlreichen Auszeichnungen befinden sich eine Bronzemedaille der Brno Biennale, eine Silbermedaille der D&AD, Goldmedaillen des Packaging Design Council und des Ministry of Trade & Technology, Japan. Er ist Mitglied der AGI.

MERVYN KULANSKY, né en Afrique du Sud en 1936. A étudié à la Central School of Art and Design de Londres, travaille dans cette ville depuis 1960. Il a d'abord été indépendant, puis a rejoint Crosby and Forbes (associés dans Crosby, Fletcher, Forbes) au sein du *Pentagram Design Partnership* en 1972. Ses travaux lui ont valu des prix importants, tels qu'une médaille de bronze à la Biennale de Brno, une médaille d'argent de D&AD, des médailles d'or du Packaging Design Council et du ministère japonais du Commerce et de la Technologie. Il est membre de l'AGI.

WINSOR McCAY (cover designer Claude LeGallo). This issue was devoted to the comic strip and, as Winsor McCay was one of the pioneers and greatest talents in this medium, a sample of his creative comic illustrations was used for the cover.

WINSOR McCAY (Umschlag Design von Claude LeGallo). Diese *Graphis*-Ausgabe war dem Comic Strip gewidmet. Da Winsor McCay ein Pionier und einer der grössten Talente auf diesem Gebiet war, war es naheliegend, eine seiner Illustrationen für diesen Umschlag zu verwenden.

WINSOR McCAY (designer: Claude LeGallo). Ce numéro étant consacré à la bande dessinée, et Winsor McCay faisant figure de pionnier et de talent exceptionnel dans ce média, un choix de ses images de B.D., où explose sa créativité, a été utilisé pour cette couverture.

OTL AICHER, born in Germany, 1922. He studied at the Akademie der Bildenden Künste in Munich before founding his own graphic studio in Ulm in 1948. He was a co-founder of the Hochschule für Gestaltung (Ulm) and was its Vice Chancellor in the early 60's. He coordinated the visual image of the 1972 Olympics in Munich. One-man shows of his posters have been held in USA, Brazil and Germany and he has participated in international exhibitions. His awards include the Prix d'Honneur at the 1954 Milan Triennale, and First Prize for typography in Innsbruck, 1958. He is represented in MOMA.

■

OTL AICHER, 1922 in Deutschland geboren. Er studierte an der Akademie der Bildenden Künste in München und gründete 1948 in Ulm sein eigenes Graphikstudio. Er ist Mitbegründer der Hochschule für Gestaltung Ulm und war deren Rektor von 1962-64. Er war für die visuelle Gestaltung der Olympischen Spiele in München 1972 verantwortlich. Seine Plakate wurden in den USA, Brasilien und Deutschland ausgestellt. Nebst vielen anderen Auszeichnungen erhielt er den Prix d'Honneur der Triennale Mailand 1954 und den ersten Preis für Typographie in Innsbruck 1958. Seine Werke sind in den Sammlungen des MOMA vertreten.

■

OTL AICHER, né en Allemagne en 1922. A fait des études à l'Académie des Beaux-Arts de Munich. En 1948, il ouvre un studio à Ulm. Cofondateur de l'Université de design (Hochschule für Gestaltung) d'Ulm, il en fut le vice-chancelier au début des années 60. C'est à lui qu'est revenue la coordination de l'image visuelle des Jeux Olympiques de Munich en 1972. Des expositions personnelles lui ont été consacrées aux USA, au Brésil, en Allemagne. Il a participé à diverses expositions internationales. Il est entre autres lauréat du Prix d'honneur de la Triennale de Milan 1954 et du Premier Prix de typographie à Innsbruck en 1958. Ses œuvres figurent dans les collections du MOMA.

■

ALAIN LE FOLL, born in Brittany, France, 1934. He studied in Paris and first worked for an advertising agency, for the *Lafayette* department store and for women's magazines. His scope also encompasses other fields of design: pottery, stage settings, wallpapers, cloth and animated films. More recently he has devoted his time to drawing and lithography. His fine art has been regularly exhibited.

■

ALAIN LE FOLL, 1934 in der Bretagne, Frankreich, geboren. Er studierte in Paris und arbeitete anschliessend in der Werbeabteilung des Kaufhauses *Lafayette* sowie für Frauenzeitschriften. Seine Arbeiten umfassen verschiedene Bereiche des Designs: Töpferei, Bühnenbilder, Tapeten, Stoffe, Trickfilme. In letzter Zeit hat er jedoch hauptsächlich Zeichnungen und Lithographien gemacht. Seine Arbeiten sind in verschiedenen Ausstellungen gezeigt worden.

■

ALAIN LE FOLL, né en Bretagne en 1934. A fait ses études à Paris. D'abord au service d'une agence de publicité, des grands magasins *Lafayette* et de magazines féminins, il a élargi progressivement son champ d'action à la céramique, au décor de théâtre, au papier peint, au design textile et au cinéma d'animation. S'est orienté ces derniers temps vers le dessin et la litho. Ses créations non commerciales ont fait l'objet d'expositions à intervalles réguliers.

■

OLGA SIEMASZKO, born in Cracow, Poland. She studied in Warsaw and from 1945 till 1956 she was Art Director of the publishing house *Czytelnik* and also of the children's weekly *Swierszczyk*. She was also engaged on stage decor and posters before concentrating on children's literature. She has won numerous prizes for her work, including first prizes at the Polish Book Exhibition and a Gold Medal at the IBA in Leipzig. She has held several one-man exhibitions.

■

OLGA SIEMASZKO wurde in Krakau, Polen, geboren und beendete 1939 ihre Studien in Warschau. Von 1945 bis 1956 war sie Art Director im *Czytelnik*-Verlag und bei der Kinderwochenzeitung *Swierszczyk*. Während sie früher auch Bühnenbilder und Plakate gestaltete, widmet sie sich heute der Kinderliteratur. Ihre Arbeiten wurden mehrmals ausgezeichnet, so mit zwei ersten Preisen an polnischen Buchausstellungen und mit der Goldmedaille der IBA in Leipzig. Sie hatte verschiedene Einzelausstellungen.

■

OLGA SIEMASZKO, né à Cracovie (Pologne). A fait ses études à Varsovie. De 1945 à 1956, elle est directrice artistique de la maison d'édition *Czytelnik* en même temps que de l'hebdomadaire de la jeunesse *Swierszczyk*. On lui doit aussi des décors de théâtre et des affiches, délaissés dès qu'elle dut se concentrer sur la création d'illustrations pour livres d'enfants. Ses travaux ont été récompensés de nombreux prix, dont des Premiers Prix à l'Exposition polonaise du Livre et une médaille d'or de l'IBA à Leipzig. Plusieurs expositions personnelles lui ont été consacrées.

■

WALTER BREKER, born in Germany, 1904. He was an apprentice lithographer before he took up design studies. In 1930 he was appointed assistant to Professor W. Deffke, Magdeburg. Later he was made Head of the department of applied graphics and book design at the Werkkunstschule in Krefeld and remained there for 20 years. In 1954 he was appointed Professor of the State Art Academy in Düsseldorf. He is the recipient of many prizes, including 9 (from 1950-1966) in contests for the Best German Posters.

■

WALTER BREKER, 1904 in Deutschland geboren, studierte nach einer Lithographenlehre an der Kunstgewerbeschule Bielefeld. Ab 1930 war er Lehrassistent bei Prof. Deffke an der Kunstgewerbeschule Magdeburg und anschliessend während 20 Jahren Leiter der Abteilung für Angewandte Graphik und Buchkunst an der Werkkunstschule Krefeld. 1954 wurde er als Professor an die Staatliche Kunstakademie Düsseldorf berufen. Er hat für seine Arbeiten viele Preise erhalten, darunter neun in Wettbewerben für das beste deutsche Plakat.

■

WALTER BREKER, né en Allemagne en 1904. Apprenti lithographe avant que d'entreprendre des études de design. En 1930, il devient l'assistant du professeur W. Deffke, directeur de l'Ecole des arts décoratifs de Magdeburg. Appelé plus tard à la tête du département du Livre et des Arts appliqués de la Werkkunstschule de Krefeld, il en assume la direction pendant 20 ans. En 1954, il est nommé professeur à l'Académie d'Etat de Düsseldorf. Parmi les nombreux prix qu'il a reçus figurent, entre 1950 et 1966, neuf prix décernés par le jury du concours annuel de la meilleure affiche allemande.

■

JEAN LAGARRIGUE, born in France. He went to the USA in 1963 and studied at the School of Visual Arts, New York. He returned to France in 1965 and was Art Director of the women's magazine *Marie-Claire*. In 1968 he went back to America and became Art Director of *Esquire* magazine. Now back in France, he is freelance. His work has been exhibited in Paris.

JEAN LAGARRIGUE wurde in Frankreich geboren. Er studierte zwei Jahre an der School of Visual Arts in New York. Nach seiner Rückkehr nach Frankreich wurde er 1965 Art Director bei der Frauenzeitschrift *Marie-Claire*. 1968 ging er zurück nach Amerika und wurde Art Director bei der Zeitschrift *Esquire*. Heute lebt Lagarrigue wieder in Frankreich und arbeitet freischaffend. Seine Arbeiten wurden wiederholt in Paris ausgestellt.

JEAN LAGARRIGUE, né en France. En 1963, il part aux USA étudier à la School of Visual Arts. De retour en France en 1965, il sera directeur artistique du magazine féminin *Marie-Claire*. En 1968, il repart pour l'Amérique, où il devient directeur artistique du magazine *Esquire*. Aujourd'hui il vit en France comme artiste indépendant. Ses travaux ont fait l'objet d'expositions à Paris.

For short biography, see Page 133.
The relationship of man to science was always a major concern for HANS ERNI. His illustration dates back to 1941 and is entitled "Page from the diary of an urbanist". Painted on rough boards and depicting Erni's own face, there is a human being no longer whole – a mere framework of nerves, arteries and sinews. The work is born out of the chaos and adversity of a time of war.

Kurzbiographie Seite 133.
Der Schweizer Künstler HANS ERNI hat sich schon immer mit den Beziehungen des Menschen zur Wissenschaft befasst, und sein auf dem Umschlag verwendetes Bild scheint uns die verschiedenen Bereiche, in denen Kunst wissenschaftlichen Zwecken dient, in treffender Weise zusammenzufassen. Botanik, Anatomie, Biologie und Technik sind dargestellt, aber das Bild hat noch eine tiefere Bedeutung. Erni gab ihm den ungewöhnlichen Titel «Tagebuchblatt eines Urbanisten».

Voir la notice biographique en p. 133.
Les rapports entre l'homme et la science ont toujours constitué l'une des grandes préoccupations de HANS ERNI. Cette illustration de l'artiste suisse, intitulée «Page du journal d'un urbaniste», est de 1941. L'homme peint sur la palissade, et qui a les traits d'Erni, n'est plus complet; il est réduit à un simple assemblage de nerfs, de vaisseaux sanguins et de tendons. Cette œuvre née du chaos et de l'adversité de la guerre est prophétique. Elle n'a pas pris un pli et parle à nos consciences sensibilisées aux impératifs écologiques.

For short biography, see Page 158.
HEINZ EDELMANN's creations have a tendency to confuse the onlooker. On closer inspection the teeth and feet of the dog shown in the illustration look more human than canine: he has bitten off a piece of the rainbow. Is this animal a symbol for the creative man who chases after colorful images, attempting to catch them and bring them down to earth?

Kurzbiographie Seite 158.
HEINZ EDELMANNS Schöpfungen neigen dazu, den Betrachter zu verwirren. Gebiss und Füsse des abgebildeten Hundes stellen sich bei näherer Betrachtung als eher menschlich denn tierisch heraus. Ungewöhnlich sind auch die Jagdgewohnheiten unseres Vierbeiners: Er hat sich ein Stück aus dem Regenbogen herausgerissen. Ist dieses Tier ein Symbol für den Kreativ-Schaffenden, der seinen bunten Vorstellungen nachpirscht, sie einfangen und auf die Erde bringen will?

Voir la notice biographique en p. 158.
Les créations de HEINZ EDELMANN tendent à déconcerter l'observateur. La dentition et les pieds du molosse sont bien plus humains que canins si l'on y regarde de près. Ses habitudes de chasse sont également insolites. Sa proie: un morceau de l'arc-en-ciel. Cet animal est-il censé incarner le créatif toujours à l'affût de ses visions en couleurs et tout heureux de pouvoir s'en emparer et les ramener sur terre?

ROGER HANE, born in Pennsylvania, 1939. He graduated from Philadelphia Museum School of Art in 1961 and went to New York in 1965. He has since established himself as one of America's outstanding illustrators. He has worked for almost all the leading magazines in the USA as well as doing illustrations for publishers and for promotional purposes. He has participated regularly in exhibitions and shows.

ROGER HANE, 1939 in Pennsylvania geboren. 1961 graduierte er an der Philadelphia Museum School of Art, und 1965 ging er nach New York. Inzwischen ist er einer der herausragendsten Illustratoren Amerikas geworden. Er hat für fast alle führenden Magazine der USA gearbeitet sowie für verschiedene Verleger und Unternehmer. Seine Arbeiten werden regelmässig an den wichtigsten amerikanischen Graphikausstellungen gezeigt.

ROGER HANE, né en Pennsylvanie en 1939, Diplôme de la Philadelphia Museum School of Art en 1961, il s'installe à New York en 1965. Depuis, il s'est fait reconnaître comme l'un des grands illustrateurs américains. Il a travaillé pour la presque totalité des grands magazines américains, sans compter les illustrations qu'il a fournies aux éditeurs et aux commanditaires d'actions promotionnelles. Hane a participé régulièrement aux expositions spécialisées.

■

For short biography, see Page 141.
The creature portrayed on this cover is rare nowadays. But not so long ago the green horned head, long claws and armoured tail were familiar to every child, and no story-book-adventure of knights and fair damsels would have been complete without it. The secondary features shown on this one – the colored pencils and the convincing fiery flame-message – are enough to make us pleased though that such a reputed artist and designer as ANDRÉ FRANÇOIS saw and recorded it before it was once and for all slayed.

■

Kurzbiographie Seite 141.
Obwohl die auf diesem Umschlag dargestellte Kreatur heute nur noch selten vorkommt, besteht kaum ein Zweifel über ihre Artszugehörigkeit. Der grüne, gehörnte Kopf, die gekrallten Zehen und der gepanzerte Schwanz sind jedem Kind bestens bekannt. Zugegeben, einige sekundäre Züge des Ungeheuers dürften den konventionellen Zoologen verwirren, so die kasperle-köpfigen Panzerhökker oder die bunten Stifte. Was seine Echtheit betrifft, genügt es eigentlich zu wissen, dass ein so bekannter Künstler und Designer wie ANDRÉ FRANÇOIS das Tier gesichtet und aufgezeichnet hat, bis es ein für allemal in Vergessenheit gerät.

■

Voir la notice biographique en p. 141.
La créature représentée ici est devenue plutôt rare de nos jours. La tête verte cornue, les pieds griffus et la queue cuirassée sont familières à tous les bambins, et aucun livre relatant les aventures des preux chevaliers et des gentes damoiselles ne serait complet sans leur intervention. Certains traits secondaires détonnent évidemment dans le tableau zoologique: les crayons couleur, les bosses à guignols, le message que composent les flammes sortant de la gueule. Quel bonheur qu'un artiste et designer de la stature d'ANDRÉ FRANÇOIS ait pu voir et décrire l'animal avant qu'on l'ait terrassé une fois pour toutes!

■

For short biography, see Page 150.
Although we know that most artists dislike their graphic work interpreted for them, we can only assume that RONALD SEARLE didn't invent this bittersweet scene without some mordant ulterior motive. Is this the archetypal graphic designer's greatest frustration? A colorful butterfly wants to rest on a rose, but it is already occupied by a grey, grim-faced newspaper reader. Are we to imply then that often designers are not able to realize their own visual conceptions because businesslike materialists engage them for their own purposes?

■

Kurzbiographie Seite 150.
Wir wissen zwar, dass die meisten Künstler eine Deutung ihrer graphischen Vorstellungen ablehnen, aber es ist kaum anzunehmen, dass RONALD SEARLE diese bittersüsse Szene ohne irgendwelche beissenden Hintergedanken gemacht hat. Ist hier der Archetypus der grössten Frustration des Graphikers dargestellt? Ein bunter Schmetterling will eine Rose aufsuchen, aber sie ist besetzt von einem grauen, grimmigen Zeitungsleser. Heisst das, dass Graphiker sehr oft die eigenen visuellen Vorstellungen nicht realisieren können, weil geschäftstüchtige Materialisten sie für ihre Zwecke beanspruchen?

■

Voir la notice biographique en p. 150.
Même si nous savons que la plupart des artistes refusent toute interprétation de leurs conceptions graphiques, il n'en reste pas moins évident que RONALD SEARLE avait sa petite idée derrière la tête en créant cette scène douce-amère. A-t-il voulu interpréter l'archétype de la frustration majeure des graphistes? Un papillon multicolore aborde une rose déjà occupée par un lecteur tout gris, tout morose. Cela signifierait-il que le graphiste doit trop souvent renoncer à mettre en œuvre ses convictions visuelles personnelles parce que des matérialistes habiles en affaires s'en emparent pour les dénaturer?

■

HANS-GEORG RAUCH, born in Berlin, 1939. He studied at the Hochschule für Bildende Kunst at Hamburg. He went to the USA and began contributing regularly to the leading publications there. He is also engaged on advertising illustration for major international corporations. He has received a number of awards for illustration. He works in mixed technique: watercolor, colored pencil, pen-and-ink and collage.

■

HANS-GEORG RAUCH, 1939 in Berlin geboren. Er studierte an der Hochschule für Bildende Künste in Hamburg und ist freier Mitarbeiter verschiedener europäischer und auch amerikanischer Zeitschriften. Er beschäftigt sich ausserdem mit Werbeillustrationen für führende internationale Unternehmen und hat verschiedene Preise bekommen. Er arbeitet in verschiedenen Techniken: Wasserfarbe, Farbstift, Feder und Tinte und Collage.

■

HANS-GEORG RAUCH, né à Berlin en 1939. Ancien élève de l'Université des Beaux-Arts de Hambourg. En 1986 il quitte l'Allemagne pour les Etats-Unis, où il travaille régulièrement pour les grandes publications américaines et réalise des illustrations publicitaires pour d'importantes sociétés internationales. Il est lauréat de nombreux prix d'illustration. Sa technique mixte unit l'aquarelle, le crayon couleur et le collage.

■

TADANORI YOKOO, born in Japan, 1936. He trained as a graphic designer. From 1959-60 he was designer at the National Advertisement Laboratory, Osaka. In the early sixties he worked with the Nippon Design Center and was then director of various design studios and since 1971 has his own studio in Tokyo. His scope embraces advertising design, print-making, architectural design illustrating and poster design, and it is this last for which he has won international acclaim. He participates in many shows and his awards are numerous. He is represented in the MOMA collection and in other major museums.

■

TADANORI YOKOO, 1936 in Japan geboren. Nach einer Graphik-Design Ausbildung war er als Designer am National Advertisement Laboratory in Osaka tätig. Anfang der 60er Jahre war er Mitglied des Nippon Design Center in Tokio, dann Direktor verschiedener Studios, und 1971 gründete er ein eigenes Studio in Tokio. Neben Werbe-Design, Druckgraphik und Architektur-Design beschäftigt er sich auch mit Plakatkunst und erntete besonders hierfür internationalen Ruhm. Er nahm an zahlreichen Ausstellungen teil und erhielt viele Preise. Arbeiten von Yokoo befinden sich im MOMA und den wichtigsten Museen in Europa, Kanada, Japan und den USA.

■

TADANORI YOKOO, né au Japon en 1936. A subi une formation de designer. De 1959 à 1960, designer au National Advertisement Laboratory d'Osaka. Au début des années 60, il collabore avec le Nippon Design Center, puis assume la direction de divers studios de design. En 1971, il ouvre son propre studio à Tokyo. Son champ d'activité embrasse l'art publicitaire, la gravure, le design architectural, l'illustration et l'affiche. Ce sont notamment ses affiches qui l'ont fait connaître au plan international. Il participe à de nombreuses expositions et a remporté toute une série de prix. Ses œuvres figurent dans les collections du MOMA et dans divers autres grands musées.

■

CHRISTIAN PIPER, born in Breslau, Germany (now Poland), 1941. He studied at the Werkkunstschule in Aachen from 1964-1966 and later in Essen. After graduation he became a freelance illustrator for several German magazines (including *TWEN*). In Germany his work embraced theater posters, TV animation, book and magazine illustration. In 1972 he went to New York where he joined *Push Pin Studios*. His illustrations have appeared in many of the leading US magazines.

CHRISTIAN PIPER, 1941 in Breslau, heute Polen, geboren. 1964-1966 studierte er an der Werkkunstschule in Aachen, danach an der Folkwangschule in Essen. Nach seinem Abschluss war er freiberuflicher Illustrator bei mehreren deutschen Zeitschriften, u.a. bei *TWEN*. Piper machte Theaterplakate, Fernseh-Zeichentrick, Buch- und Zeitschriftenillustrationen. 1972 kam er nach New York, wo er sich den *Push Pin Studios* anschloss. Seine Illustrationen erschienen in führenden US-Zeitschriften.

CHRISTIAN PIPER, né à Breslau (Allemagne; aujourd'hui Wroclaw, Pologne) en 1941. Etudes à la Werkkunstschule d'Aix-la-Chapelle de 1964 à 1966, poursuivies à Essen. Le jeune diplômé s'établit à son compte comme illustrateur de divers magazines allemands, dont *TWEN*. Durant sa carrière allemande, il crée des affiches de théâtre, des séquences d'animation pour la télévision, des illustrations de livres et magazines. En 1972, il part pour New York, où il entre aux *Push Pin Studios*. Ses illustrations ont été publiées dans un grand nombre de magazines américains de premier plan.

JEAN MAZENOD, photographer. The illustration on this cover followed up on a feature in the previous issue which was devoted to the photographs Jean Mazenod took on the treasures of Greek art for a volume in the series published by Lucien Mazenod: *Art and the Great Civilization*. The work was awarded a UNESCO diploma at an exhibition of handsome books in East Berlin. On this cover he proved that his talents were not limited to such ancient beauty.

JEAN MAZENOD, Photograph. Der Entwurf dieses Umschlags folgte auf einen Artikel im vorhergehenden *Graphis*, der den Photographien gewidmet war, die Mazenod von den Schätzen griechischer Kunst machte. Sie sind Gegenstand des dritten Bandes seines grossen Sammelwerkes: *Die Kunst und die grossen Kulturen*. In einer Ausstellung der schönsten Bücher der Welt in Ost-Berlin wurde das Werk mit einem UNESCO-Diplom ausgezeichnet. Mit dem Umschlagentwurf von *Graphis* Nr. 173 bewies Mazenod, dass er sich nicht nur auf altertümliche Schönheit versteht.

JEAN MAZENOD, photographe. Cette illustration de couverture fait suite à un article dans le précédent numéro consacré aux photos des trésors d'art grecs que Jean Mazenod a réalisées pour un volume de la collection que dirige Lucien Mazenod, *Art and the Great Civilization*. L'ouvrage a été récompensé d'un diplôme de l'UNESCO à une exposition de beaux livres organisée à Berlin-Est. Mazenod nous démontre sur cette couverture que ses talents ne se limitent pas à l'évocation des splendeurs du passé.

LES MASON, born in California, 1924. He studied in Los Angeles and founded *West Coast Designers* before moving to Australia in 1961. Opened *Les Mason Graphic Design* in South Melbourne in 1962. He acts as design consultant and marketing-research counsellor to Australian agencies as well as doing corporate identity programs, architectural graphics, packaging, advertising art, and illustration. He designed the murals and graphics for the Melbourne Underground Railway. He is the winner of numerous Gold and Silver awards in Australia and his work is held in collections of the National Gallery Western Australia.

LES MASON, 1924 in Kalifornien geboren. Er studierte in Los Angeles und gründete *West Coast Designers* bevor er 1961 nach Australien ging, wo er 1962 *Les Mason Graphic Design* gründete. Er arbeitet als Design- und Marktforschungsberater für australische Agenturen, beschäftigt sich aber auch mit Firmenerscheinungsbildern, Architektur-Graphik und mit Packungs-, Werbe- und redaktioneller Graphik. Er entwarf Wandbilder und Graphiken für die Untergrundbahn Melbourne. Er gewann zahlreiche Preise in Australien, und seine Arbeiten befinden sich in anerkannten Sammlungen.

LES MASON, né en Californie en 1924. A fait ses études à Los Angeles et fondé *West Coast Designers* avant d'émigrer en Australie en 1961. En 1962, il fonde à South Melbourne le studio *Les Mason Graphic Design*. Il fonctionne comme conseiller en matière de design et d'études de marchés pour les agences australiennes tout en réalisant des programmes d'identité globale de marque, des créations graphiques appliquées à l'architecture, des emballages, des travaux publicitaires, des illustrations. On lui doit les murals et la décoration graphique du métro de Melbourne. Lauréat de nombreuses médailles d'or et d'argent en Australie, ses œuvres figurent dans les collections de la National Gallery of Western Australia.

For short biography, see Page 155.
SEYMOUR CHWAST has drawn, painted and sculpted many heads in his time. This one is a collage – a passing face at the window – the slick, sunglassed, cigarette-smoking, dentifriced, sophisticated face of the present-day consumer, just looking in.

Kurzbiographie Seite 155.
SEYMOUR CHWAST hat im Laufe der Zeit zahlreiche Köpfe gezeichnet, gemalt oder modelliert. Diesmal ist es eine Collage: kein aufgeblasener, statischer Kopf, aber ein blasiertes, sich spiegelndes Gesicht – das glatte, mit Brille kamouflierte, stereotyp-lächelnde, zigaretten-behangene, unechte Konsumentengesicht des 20. Jahrhunderts.

Voir la notice biographique en p. 155.
SEYMOUR CHWAST a dessiné, peint et sculpté d'innombrables têtes au fil des années. Celle-ci est un collage: le visage d'un passant qui fait du lèche-vitrines et qui incarne parfaitement le consommateur blasé du XXᵉ siècle, jusques y compris l'assurance insolente, les lunettes de soleil étincelantes, la cigarette fichée au coin des lèvres, la sophistication d'un sourire dentifricé à souhait.

EUGÈNE MIHAESCO, born in Rumania, 1937. He studied art in Bucharest. In 1967 he left Rumania and, after first settling for a while in Switzerland, he went to New York, becoming a contributor to some of the major US publications. He taught at Pratt Institute and had one-man shows in New York in 1981 and 1984. Among his many awards is the 1985 Gold Medal from the Art Directors Club New York.

EUGÈNE MIHAESCO, 1937 in Rumänien geboren. Er studierte Kunst in Bukarest, verliess 1967 Rumänien und ging nach New York, nachdem er sich für eine Weile in der Schweiz niedergelassen hatte. Seit 1971 ist er ständiger Mitarbeiter der *New-York Times* und gestaltet auch regelmässig Umschläge für *The New Yorker*. Er lehrte am Pratt Institute und hatte 1981 und 1984 Einzelausstellungen in New York. Einer seiner vielen Preise ist die Goldmedaille des Art Directors Club New York, die er 1985 erhielt.

EUGÈNE MIHAESCO, né en Roumanie en 1937. Etudes d'art à Bucarest. Quitte la Roumanie en 1967 pour la Suisse, puis pour New York, où il alimente en illustrations plusieurs grandes publications américaines. Il a enseigné au Pratt Institute. Des expositions personnelles lui ont été consacrées à New York en 1981 et 1984. Lauréat de nombreux prix, il a obtenu en 1985 la médaille d'or de l'Art Directors Club de New York.

For short biography, see Page 162.
ETIENNE DELESSERT brought together a black and a white child, symbolizing all children on earth, and sharing a common joy and a common heritage – the reading of a book. As they turn the pages with rapt attention, out pops the King of the Golden River – a butterfly with pearls on its wings ready to bear them to a world of excitement, adventure, beauty and fantasy – plus a pinch or two of horror.

Kurzbiographie Seite 162.
Diese Kinder von ETIENNE DELESSERT, das eine weiss und das andere dunkelhäutig, sind symbolisch für alle Kinder dieser Welt, gleich welcher Rasse, für einmal eine gemeinsame Freude, ein gemeinsames Erbe teilend. Er stellt in eindrucksvoller Weise dar, mit welcher Magie das Kind beim Öffnen eines Bilderbuches in den Bann einer Welt voll Faszination gezogen wird: der König des goldenen Flusses kommt zum Vorschein und ein zart bemalter Schmetterling, stellvertretend für Spannung, Abenteuer, Schönheit, Phantasie und leichtes Gruseln.

Voir la notice biographique en p. 162.
ETIENNE DELESSERT a réuni ici deux enfants, un noir et un blanc représentant tous les enfants du monde et partageant une même joie, un même héritage: le plaisir de la lecture. Au fur et à mesure qu'ils tournent émerveillés les pages du livre, il en émerge le Roi du Fleuve d'or, un papillon aux ailes serties de perles, qui les invitent à les rejoindre au pays de tous les frissons d'excitation, de toutes les aventures, de la beauté et de l'imagination – sans oublier un zeste ou deux d'horreurs secrètes.

RICHARD HESS, born in the USA, 1934. He studied at Michigan State University then joined *Palmer Paint Company* where he painted originals of "Paint by Number" sets. He was Art Director with *J. Walter Thompson* in Detroit (1955–57) After working as Art Director for various companies he founded *Richard Hess Inc.* His scope embraces graphic and film art consultancy (for *CBS, IBM, Xerox,* etc.) as well as illustration, corporate identity programs, cartoons, packaging, exhibition design, etc. He has gained many awards from the New York ADC and has held one-man exhibitions in the USA and Japan.

RICHARD HESS, 1934 in den USA geboren. Er studierte an der Michigan State University, wurde dann Angestellter der *Palmer Paint Company* und zuständig für die «Malen-mit-Zahlen» Entwürfe. Er war Art-Direktor bei *J. Walter Thompson* in Detroit (1955–1957) und für verschiedene Agenturen bevor er die *Richard Hess Inc.* gründete. Neben Arbeiten für Fernsehanstalten, Plattenfirmen und Verlage (u. a. für *CBS, IBM, Xerox,* etc.), beschäftigte er sich auch mit Illustrationen, Firmenerscheinungsbildern, Cartoons, Packungen, Ausstellungsdesign, etc. Er gewann viele Preise und hatte Einzelausstellungen in den USA und in Japan.

RICHARD HESS, né aux Etats-Unis en 1934. Après ses études à l'Université d'Etat du Michigan, il entre à la *Palmer Paint Company* où il peint les originaux des séries «Paint by Number». Directeur artistique de *J. Walter Thompson* à Detroit (1955–57), puis de diverses autres sociétés, il s'établit à son compte en fondant la *Richard Hess Inc.* Ses spécialités: conseils en matière de design et de réalisations cinématographiques pour *CBS, IBM, Xerox,* etc., illustrations, programmes d'identité globale de marque, dessins d'humour, emballages, conception d'expositions, etc. Il a remporté un grand nombre de prix de l'Art Directors Club de New York. Des expositions personnelles lui ont été consacrées aux Etats-Unis et au Japon.

For short biography, see Page 167.
Some more of ROLAND TOPOR's satirical visions appear on this cover. Outsiders see only one person, Topor sees two and he has placed them one behind the other. It is himself and his alter ego – half-hidden – giving each word he writes an alien twist.

Kurzbiographie Seite 167.
Diese Zeichnung zeigt erneut eine von ROLAND TOPORS satirischen Visionen (wie bereits der Umschlag zu Graphis 151). Der flüchtige Betrachter sieht nur eine Person, Topor hingegen sieht zwei: das Ego und das Alter-Ego, halb versteckt. Gleich und doch verschieden, so dass jedes Wort, das er schreibt, um eine Nuance anders ausfällt, als es gemeint ist.

Voir la notice biographique en p. 167.
Après Graphis 151, ROLAND TOPOR récidive ici en nous proposant une nouvelle vision satirique. Là où les gens de l'extérieur ne voient qu'une seule personne, Topor en voit deux: le moi et son double, placés l'un derrière l'autre. C'est l'Autre, à moitié caché, qui imprime une subtile torsion à toute pensée que pond le moi, la dénaturant et compliquant la communication avec autrui.

■

■

■

■

For short biography, see Page 157.
FRANCO GRIGNANI moves with ease between fine art and graphic design without changing style. Here he has flung a brightly-colored streamer out into black space. Everyone knows that the red and white stripes continue on the back of the streamer where it is turned in. Only they don't. Grignani tricks you into seeing three dimensions – four if you feel the streamer is in motion – and there are only two. Spaceman Grignani is fond of probing the nature of the visual world.

■

Kurzbiographie Seite 157.
FRANCO GRIGNANI bewegt sich zwischen freier Kunst und Graphik, ohne vom eigenen Stil abzuweichen. Auf diesem Umschlag lässt er einen bunten Wimpel mit rot-weissen Streifen im schwarzen Feld aufsteigen. Man würde schwören, dass sich diese Streifen auch auf der Rückseite des Wimpels fortsetzen. Aber sie tun es nicht. Grignani hat uns überlistet, indem er uns drei Dimensionen suggeriert – oder sogar vier, wenn man sich den Wimpel in Bewegung vorstellt – aber es sind nur zwei.

■

Voir la notice biographique en p. 157.
FRANCO GRIGNANI évolue à son aise entre l'art pur et l'art publicitaire sans rien changer à son style. Sur cette couverture, il projette une bande multicolore de tissu rayée de rouge et de blanc dans l'espace figuré en noir. Le rouge et le blanc devraient se retrouver au verso de la bande. Pourtant, il n'en est rien. Grignani nous a bernés en suggérant trois, voire quatre dimensions si vous imaginez le mouvement de la bande, là où il n'y en a que deux. Le cosmonaute Grignani aime interroger de la sorte la nature même du monde visuel.

■

ROY CARRUTHERS, born in South Africa, 1938. He studied at Port Elizabeth Technical College before working as Art Director with advertising agencies in South Africa. In 1961 he moved to London where he was Art Director for *Town* magazine. He moved on to the USA in 1968 and in 1971 became a freelance illustrator, contributing to many major US magazines. In 1974 he gave up illustrating to concentrate on painting. Many one-man shows of his work have been staged in the US and he is the recipient of many awards conferred by D&AD, London, ADC New York, AIGA and the Society of Illustrators.

■

ROY CARRUTHERS, 1938 in Südafrika geboren, studierte am Technical College in Port Elizabeth Werbegraphik und wurde mit der Medaille für den besten Studenten 1956 ausgezeichnet. Er arbeitete für Werbeagenturen in Südafrika und liess sich 1961 in London nieder. Während eines Jahres war er Art Director der Zeitschrift *Town*, bevor er 1968 nach Amerika ging. Ab 1971 war er als freischaffender Illustrator tätig, wandte sich aber 1974 ganz der Malerei zu. Seine Arbeiten wurden in Einzelausstellungen gezeigt, und er erhielt mehrere Auszeichnungen des D&AD, London, des Art Directors Club, New York, der AIGA und der Society of Illustrators.

■

ROY CARRUTHERS, né en Afrique du Sud en 1938. Il étudie au Port Elizabeth Technical College avant de travailler en qualité de directeur artistique pour diverses agences de publicité sud-africaines. En 1961, il arrive à Londres, directeur artistique du magazine *Town*. Installé aux Etats-Unis en 1968, il s'établit à son compte en 1971, fournissant en illustrations un grand nombre de publications américaines de premier plan. En 1974, il abandonne l'illustration pour la peinture. Un grand nombre d'expositions individuelles lui ont été consacrées aux USA. Lauréat de nombreux prix: D&AD (Londres), ADC New York, AIGA, Society of Illustrators.

■

PAUL DAVIS, born in the USA, 1938. He studied at the School of Visual Arts, New York and later joined the *Push Pin Studios*. For many years he has been freelancing, and he specializes in portrait painting, illustration, poster art, and cultural magazine covers. In 1986 his book *Paul Davis: Faces* was published by the *Friendly Press*.

■

PAUL DAVIS, 1938 in den USA geboren. Er studierte an der School of Visual Arts, New York, und arbeitete später für *Push Pin Studios*. Heute ist er seit vielen Jahren freischaffend und hat sich auf Porträtmalerei, Illustrationen, Plakatkunst und Umschläge für Kulturzeitschriften spezialisiert. 1986 wurde sein Buch *Paul Davis: Faces* von der *Friendly Press* herausgegeben.

■

PAUL DAVIS, né aux Etats-Unis en 1938. Ancien élève de la School of Visual Arts, New York. Entré aux *Push Pin Studios*, il s'établit rapidement à son compte, se spécialisant dans la peinture de portraits, l'illustration, l'affiche, les couvertures de magazines culturels. En 1986, les Editions *Friendly Press* lui consacrent une monographie, *Paul Davis: Faces* (Visages).

■

For short biography, see Page 154.
JAN LENICA makes animated films, among them was "Ubu Roi" (King Ubu). He created his characters out of cut-out elements which he manipulated from frame to frame. This illustration is a montage of these original elements from the film, a concise anatomy of his King Ubu.

■

Kurzbiographie Seite 154.
JAN LENICA ist u.a. Trickfilm-Macher, einer seiner Filme ist «Ubu Roi» (König Ubu). Der Künstler macht keine Zeichnungen, sondern er kreiert seine Figuren in Form von ausgeschnittenen Elementen, die er von Bild zu Bild manipulieren kann. Für diesen Umschlag hat Lenica mit diesen Originalelementen eine Montage gemacht, eine gedrängte Anatomie seines Königs Ubu.

■

Voir la notice biographique en p. 154.
Réalisateur de films d'animation (entre autres), JAN LENICA a créé un «Ubu Roi» en découpant ses personnages en éléments qu'il assemble différemment de case en case. Cette illustration regroupe les éléments originaux du film, qui composent une anatomie sommaire du Père Ubu.

■

GÜNTHER KIESER, born in Germany, 1930. He studied at the Werkkunstschule Offenbach and in 1952 went into partnership with Hans Michel in a graphic design studio. Since 1967 he has been a freelance graphic designer. Apart from posters he has done exhibition and stage design, stamps, illustration, book and record covers. In 1972 he held a one-man show at the Lincoln Center, New York. He has participated in numerous international exhibitions and has won many awards. His work is held in MOMA and other important collections. He cites Arcimboldo, Man Ray and Magritte as his models.

GÜNTHER KIESER, 1930 in Deutschland geboren. Er studierte an der Werkkunstschule Offenbach und gründete 1952 zusammen mit Hans Michel ein Graphik-Design-Studio, welches er seit 1967 allein weiterführt. Neben Plakaten kreierte er Bühnenausstattungen und Ausstellungen, Briefmarken, Illustrationen, Buch- und Plattenumschläge. 1972 hatte er eine Einzelausstellung im Lincoln Center. Er hat an zahlreichen internationalen Ausstellungen teilgenommen und für seine Arbeiten viele Preise erhalten. Seine Werke sind u.a. in Sammlungen des MOMA vertreten. Als seine Vorbilder nennt er Arcimboldo, Man Ray und Magritte.

GÜNTHER KIESER, né en Allemagne en 1930. Ancien élève de la Werkkunstschule d'Offenbach, il s'associe en 1952 avec Hans Michel pour ouvrir un studio d'art graphique. Depuis 1967, il travaille à son compte comme graphiste. On lui doit des créations graphiques pour la télévision, des stands d'exposition, des études d'esthétique industrielle, des décors de théâtre, des travaux publicitaires et des maquettes de livres. En 1972, une exposition personnelle lui a été consacrée au Lincoln Center de New York. Il a participé à de nombreuses expositions internationales où il a remporté un grand nombre de prix. Ses œuvres figurent au MOMA, ainsi que dans d'autres collections importantes. Il s'inspire d'Arcimboldo, de Man Ray et de Magritte.

PHIL MARCO, born in Brooklyn. One of America's most outstanding still-life advertising photographers. He was for a time undecided between music and painting. He studied at Pratt Institute and the Art Students League in New York and began to use a camera to record studies for painting – and then became a photographer. He has since divided his time between straight photography and television commercials.

PHIL MARCO, in Brooklyn geboren, gilt als einer der hervorragendsten Stilleben-Photographen in der Werbebranche Amerikas. Anfänglich schwankte er zwischen Musik und Malerei. Während Studien am Pratt Institute und der Art Students League in New York photographierte er jeweils Objekte, die er nachher malen wollte – und wurde dadurch Photograph. Heute teilt er seine Zeit auf zwischen Photographie und Fernseh-Werbefilmen.

PHIL MARCO, né à Brooklyn. L'un des photographes publicitaires américains les plus en vue qui donnent la préférence à la nature morte. A hésité un temps entre la musique et la peinture. Ses études, il les a faites au Pratt Institute et auprès de l'Art Students League de New York. Il est venu à l'emploi de l'appareil photo pour fixer des projets de peintures, puis a cédé au charme d'une photographie sans sophistication abusive. Il partage aujourd'hui son temps entre son activité de photographe et la création de spots télévisés.

HENRYK TOMASZEWSKI, born in Warsaw, 1914. He studied at the Academy of Fine Arts in Warsaw. He worked for Polish publishers as graphic artist before becoming Professor in the department of poster design at Warsaw Academy in 1952. His work has been exhibited worldwide. His awards include Gold and Silver Medals at Warsaw Biennale, first prize at São Paulo Biennale (1963) and Gold Medal at Leipzig Book Fair (1965) among others.

HENRYK TOMASZEWSKI, 1914 in Warschau geboren. Nach seinen Studien an der Kunstakademie Warschau arbeitete er als Graphiker für Verlage und kulturelle Institutionen. 1952 wurde er Professor für Plakatgestaltung an der Akademie in Warschau. Seine Arbeiten wurden in zahlreichen Ausstellungen gezeigt. Er hat Auszeichnungen wie Gold und Silbermedaillen an der Warschauer Biennale erhalten, sowie 1963 den ersten Preis an der Biennale São Paulo und 1965 die Goldmedaille an der Leipziger Buchmesse.

HENRYK TOMASZEWSKI, né à Varsovie en 1914. Ancien élève de l'Académie des beaux-arts de sa ville natale, il a mis se talents de graphiste au service d'éditeurs polonais avant d'accéder à la chaire d'affichisme de l'Académie de Varsovie en 1952. Ses œuvres ont été exposées dans le monde entier. Entre autres récompenses, il a reçu des médailles d'or et d'argent de la Biennale de Varsovie, un Premier Prix de celle de São Paulo en 1963, une médaille d'or de la Foire du Livre de Leipzig en 1965.

ZÉLIO ALVES-PINTO, born in Brazil, 1938. He started work as journalist and illustrator. He worked with several advertising agencies before joining O Cruzeiro magazine in Rio as art assistant. He spent three years in Paris working as press correspondent. When he returned to Brazil he joined the creative department of Denison agency and founded the humorous magazine Urubu. Today he writes short stories and draws cartoons for Brasilian and foreign periodicals. One-man exhibitions of cartoons in Paris in 1961, tapestries in Rio in 1964, graphic works in São Paulo and Rio and in Brussels.

ZÉLIO ALVES-PINTO, 1938 in Brasilien geboren. Er begann als Journalist und Illustrator. Danach arbeitete er für verschiedene Werbeagenturen, bevor er als Art Assistant zur Zeitschrift O Cruzeiro ging. Anschliessend ging er für drei Jahre als Pressekorrespondent nach Paris. Nach seiner Rückkehr nach Brasilien war er bei der Werbeagentur Denison tätig und gründete die humoristische Zeitschrift Urubu. Heute schreibt er hauptsächlich Kurzgeschichten und zeichnet Karikaturen für brasilianische und ausländische Zeitschriften. Einzelausstellungen fanden 1961 in Paris statt (Karikaturen), 1964 in Rio (Wandteppiche), und seine graphischen Arbeiten wurden in São Paolo, Rio und Brüssel gezeigt.

ZÉLIO ALVES-PINTO, né au Brésil en 1938. Il débute comme journaliste et illustrateur, puis passe au service de diverses agences de publicité avant d'entrer au magazine O Cruzeiro de Rio en qualité d'assistant artistique. Correspondant de presse à Paris pendant 3 ans, il retourne au pays pour travailler au département créatif de l'agence Denison et fonde le magazine satirique Urubu. Actuellement il écrit des nouvelles et donne des caricatures à des périodiques brésiliens et étrangers. Des expositions personnelles ont été consacrées à ses caricatures (Paris 1961) et à ses tapisseries (Rio 1964). Ses créations graphiques ont été exposées à São Paulo, Rio et Bruxelles.

For short biography, see Page 172.
One of TADANORI YOKOO's specialities is a type of collage in which he blends material of all sorts in delicately balanced compositions often making use of horizontal stripes and occult symbols. In this instance he has been inspired by Indian motifs and has also applied Japanese brushwork to the title of the magazine – all adding up to a visual unity.

Kurzbiographie Seite 172.
Eine Spezialität TADANORI YOKOOS ist eine Art Collage, wobei ihm in einer Symbiose der ausgefallensten Materialien delikat ausgewogene Kompositionen gelingen. Nicht selten verwendet er horizontale Bänder und okkulte Symbole. Hier liess er sich von indischen Motiven inspirieren, verwendete aber auch japanische Pinselzeichnungen für den Titel, was zusammen zu einer optischen Einheit führt.

Voir la notice biographique en p. 172.
L'une des spécialités de TADANORI YOKOO, c'est un type de collage où il réunit en une composition savamment équilibrée des matériaux de toute sorte en faisant souvent appel à des bandes horizontales et à des symboles occultes. Dans cet exemple, il a été inspiré par des motifs indiens, tout en appliquant la technique japonaise du pinceau au titre du magazine. Il en résulte une forte impression d'unité visuelle.

GÉRARD MIEDINGER, born in Switzerland in 1912. He studied in Zurich and Paris, and worked as a freelance graphic designer for industry doing corporate identity, trademarks, logos, architectural graphics, signage, etc. He has won numerous prizes for his posters and symbols. He was engaged on the design of the Swiss Pavilion in Brussels (1958), Montreal (1967) and on other international trade fairs. He is a former President of the VSG (now ASG) and was jury member for the "Best Posters of the Year".

GÉRARD MIEDINGER, 1912 in der Schweiz geboren. Er studierte in Zürich und Paris und arbeitete dann als freier Mitarbeiter für Industrie- und Dienstleistungsbetriebe, für die er Firmenerscheinungsbilder, Markenzeichen, Logos, Architektur-Design etc. entwarf. Er hat für seine Plakate und Symbole zahlreiche Preise erhalten. Als Ausstellungsgestalter war er für die Schweizer Pavillons in Brüssel (1958) und Montreal (1967) mitverantwortlich, sowie für weitere internationale Industrie- und Handelsmessen. Er war Präsident des VSG (heute ASG) und Jurymitglied beim Wettbewerb «beste Plakate des Jahres».

GÉRARD MIEDINGER, né en Suisse en 1912. Il a étudié à Zurich et à Paris. Graphiste indépendant, il s'est mis au service de l'industrie, a réalisé des programmes d'identité globale de marque, des marques déposées, des logos, des créations graphiques appliquées à l'architecture, des signalisations, etc. Ses affiches et ses emblèmes lui ont valu de nombreux prix. Il a participé à la conception du pavillon suisse de Bruxelles (1958), de Montréal (1967) et d'autres foires-expositions internationales. Président honoraire de l'Association suisse des graphistes, il a siégé au jury du concours de la Meilleure Affiche de l'Année en 1968.

BARRIE TUCKER is an Australian graphic artist with European experience and a former champion discus thrower. He has done a good deal of work for the South Australian Theatre Company, which has its headquarters at the Adelaide Theatre. Within the scope of his work belong in addition the design of calendars and packaging as well as commercial art.

BARRIE TUCKER ist ein australischer Graphiker mit Europa-Erfahrung und ehemaliger Meister im Diskuswerfen. Er hat schon zahlreiche Aufträge für die South Australian Theatre Company ausgeführt, deren Hauptsitz sich im Schauspielhaus von Adelaide befindet. Zu seinem Arbeitsbereich gehören ausserdem die Gestaltung von Kalendern und Packungen sowie Werbegraphik.

BARRIE TUCKER, ancien champion de lancer du disque, est un graphiste australien qui a fait ses premières armes en Europe. Il a réalisé de nombreux travaux pour la South Australian Theatre Company, dont le siège est au théâtre d'Adélaïde (Australie-Méridionale). Font aussi partie de son domaine d'activité la conception de calendriers, les emballages et l'art publicitaire.

For short biography, see Page 174.
When RICHARD HESS was commissioned to paint a likeness of Billie Holiday, he found himself in trouble. After three 16-hour days his portrait was somehow wrong. He was playing her music all the time and the voice contradicted the image. He put his canvas aside, cut out a wooden shelf from his clothes closet – and six and a half hours later the portrait was finished. It still didn't look like Billie Holiday because he'd painted the voice.

Kurzbiographie Seite 174.
Als RICHARD HESS beauftragt wurde, das Konterfei Billie Holidays zu malen, geriet er in Verlegenheit. Nach drei 16-Stunden-Tagen stimmte das Gesicht auf der Leinwand irgendwie nicht. Er hatte sich ständig ihre Lieder angehört, und die Stimme widersprach dem Bild. Er legte die Leinwand zur Seite. Stattdessen schnitt er aus dem Tablar eines Kleiderschrankes ein passendes Stück heraus – und sechseinhalb Stunden später war das Porträt fertig. Es sah immer noch nicht wie Billie Holiday aus, denn er hatte ihre Stimme gemalt.

Voir la notic biographique en p. 174.
Lorsque RICHARD HESS se vit commander un portrait de Billie Holiday, il se trouva vite dans l'embarras. Au terme de 3 journées de travail de 16 heures chacune, quelque chose clochait dans le visage. Tout en travaillant, il avait écouté des chansons de Billie, et la voix de l'artiste était en contradiction flagrante avec son image. Il abandonna la toile, découpa un panneau dans un rayon d'armoire – et six heures et demie plus tard le portrait était achevé. Il ne ressemblait toujours pas à Billie Holiday, car cette fois-ci il avait peint sa voix.

For short biography, see Page 170.
ALAIN LE FOLL has always been set on exploring nature in all its manifestations, particularly in insect and flower life and in the organic details of the human body. In this illustration he has chosen the baboon as a travesty of the human being. He sits and lords it over his family with a self-satisfied air.

Kurzbiographie Seite 170.
ALAIN LE FOLL hat die Natur in allen ihren Erscheinungsformen erforscht, speziell die Lebenssphären von Insekten und Pflanzen sowie die Feinheiten des menschlichen Körpers. Für diesen Umschlag hat er den Pavian gewählt. Sein Pavian ist in vielen Belangen eine Travestie des menschlichen Wesens. Mit selbstgefälliger Miene beherrscht er seinen Klan.

Voir la notice biographique en p. 170.
ALAIN LE FOLL a toujours cherché à explorer la gamme entière des manifestations naturelles, en particulier la vie des insectes et celle des fleurs, ainsi que l'anatomie fine du corps humain. Dans cette illustration, il a choisi le babouin comme parodie de l'homme, qui règne sur le clan familial l'air content de soi.

SOPHIE GRANDVAL, born in Paris. She began designing on silk and this attracted the attention of Hubert de Givenchy and also brought orders from Balenciaga, Dior, Balmain, and Dessès. She was later encouraged to paint in oils by Lucien Durand, and at her first exhibition in his gallery (as well as at a later one in Paris) she sold all her pictures at the preview. She now lives and works in Bath, England, and returns from time to time to Paris.

SOPHIE GRANDVAL wurde in Paris geboren. Als sie 18 Jahre alt war, wurde Hubert de Givenchy auf ihre Seidenmalerei aufmerksam. Dadurch erhielt sie auch Aufträge von Balenciaga, Dior, Balmain und Dessès. Später wurde sie von Lucien Durand ermutigt, in Öl zu malen. An ihrer ersten Ausstellung in seiner Galerie sowie an einer weiteren in der Galerie Delpire, Paris, verkaufte sie alle Bilder an der Vernissage. Heute lebt und arbeitet sie in Bath (England) und kehrt nur gelegentlich nach Paris zurück.

SOPHIE GRANDVAL, née à Paris. Les dessins sur soie qu'elle exécute au début de sa carrière attirent l'attention d'Hubert de Givenchy et lui valent aussi des commandes de la part de Balenciaga, Dior, Balmain, Dessès. Plus tard, c'est Lucien Durand qui l'encourage à se mettre à la peinture à l'huile: elle vend la totalité de ses tableaux lors du vernissage de sa première exposition à la galerie Durand et réitère cet exploit à l'exposition parisienne suivante. Elle habite et travaille aujourd'hui à Bath, dans le sud de l'Angleterre, revenant de temps en temps à Paris.

ALAIN GAUTHIER, born in Paris 1931. He studied under Paul Colin and created hundreds of posters for advertising purposes between 1957 and 1970. During that same period he was awarded the Grand Prix Martini for the best tourism poster. He has participated in numerous poster exhibitions in Japan and the USA. Since 1970 he has concentrated on book illustrations and book-jacket design. He staged one-man shows of his work in Paris in 1975 and in 1980.

ALAIN GAUTHIER, 1931 in Paris geboren. Er studierte bei Paul Colin und entwarf in den Jahren 1957 bis 1970 mehrere hundert kommerzielle Plakate für bekannte Firmen. In diesen Jahren wurde er verschiedentlich ausgezeichnet: 1959 mit dem Martini-Preis für das beste Tourismus-Plakat, 1967 mit dem National Outdoor Advertising Award für ein *Coca-Cola*-Plakat und 1969 mit dem ersten Preis in Essen für sein Plakat «Paris, Antlitz einer Stadt». Seine Plakate wurden in verschiedenen Ausstellungen in Japan und den USA gezeigt. Seit 1970 beschäftigt er sich vermehrt mit Buchillustrationen und Buchumschlägen. 1975 und 1980 hatte er Einzelausstellungen in Paris.

ALAIN GAUTHIER, né à Paris en 1931. Elève de Paul Colin, il a créé des centaines d'affiches publicitaires entre 1957 et 1970. C'est aussi à cette époque qu'il reçoit le Grand Prix Martini récompensant la plus belle affiche touristique. Il a participé à de nombreuses expositions d'affiches tant au Japon qu'aux Etats-Unis. Depuis 1970, il se voue à l'illustration de livres et à la conception de jaquettes. Des expositions personnelles lui ont été consacrées à Paris en 1975 et en 1980.

© 1987 PRO LITTERIS, Zürich

For short biography, see Page 167.
Once Duchamp had caught his nude descending a fourth-dimension staircase, the Cubists did not hesitate to combine two phases of reality in the simultaneity of the picture. If a women in a ROLAND TOPOR drawing has three eyes, it has to do with nightmare. For Topor's province is the abnormal, the frightful world whose bulges behind the curtains of the possible make us quickly turn away our head. On this cover a scary denizen of somebody's unwholesome fancy has been cornered by an incorruptible reporter – surely it is Topor himself!

Kurzbiographie Seite 167.
Seitdem Marcel Duchamp es wagte, 1912 einen Akt eine vierdimensionale Treppe heruntergehen zu lassen, gelang es dem Kubismus, seine Auffassung von der Simultandarstellung als Folge der zerlegenden Strukturprinzipien glaubhaft zu machen. Wenn bei ROLAND TOPOR eine Frauengestalt mit drei Augen auftritt, so hat dies mit der alptraumhaften, hintergründig-schauervollen Welt zu tun, die er uns mit jedem zeichnerischen Schritt eröffnet. Hier ist es dem unerschrockenen Reporter (wohl Topor selbst) gelungen, eine Ausgeburt der «Welt hinter dem Vorhang» in die Enge zu treiben.

Voir la notice biographique en p. 167.
Une fois que Marcel Duchamp eut fait descendre un escalier quadridimensionnel à son nu, le branle était donné pour que les cubistes se lancent dans la combinaison de deux phases du réel en une seule image. Lorsqu'une femme a troix yeux dans un dessin de ROLAND TOPOR, la référence n'est plus à l'analyse structurelle, mais au cauchemar. C'est que le domaine familier de Topor est ce monde aberrant, horrifiant dont les ondulations se devinent derrière les rideaux du possible, nous faisant prestement détourner la tête. Sur cette couverture, un être terrifiant né de quelque imagination débilitante est traquée par un reporter intrépide – Topor en personne!

JACQUI MORGAN, born in Manhattan, 1941. She studied with Richard Lindner at Pratt Institute. She started designing textiles, and since 1967 has done advertising design and illustration. One-man exhibitions were held in New York, Warsaw, and Munich. She has participated in several Biennales and has won many ADC, CA, SI, and AIGA prizes. She teaches art and was on the jury for the Society of Illustrators competitions.

JACQUI MORGAN, 1941 in Manhattan geboren, studierte bei Richard Lindner am Pratt Institute. Sie gestaltete Textilien und beschäftigt sich seit 1967 mit Werbegraphik und Illustrationen. Ihre Arbeiten waren in Einzelausstellungen in New York, Warschau und München zu sehen. Sie hat an verschiedenen Biennalen teilgenommen und Preise des ADC, CA, SI und der AIGA erhalten. Sie unterrichtet an einer Kunstschule und war Jurymitglied bei Wettbewerben der Society of Illustrators.

JACQUI MORGAN, née à Manhattan en 1941. A fait ses études au Pratt Institute avec Richard Lindner. Dessinatrice sur tissus à ses débuts, elle s'oriente à partir de 1967 vers l'art publicitaire et l'illustration. A eu des expositions personnelles à New York, Varsovie et Munich. A participé à plusieurs Biennales et remporté de nombreux prix ADC, CA, SI et AIGA. Professeur d'art, elle a été membre du jury des concours de la Society of Illustrators.

For short biography, see Page 155.
It has long been common knowledge that some sort of an affair is going on between art and writing, especially since advertising has brought them together so much in their lighter moments; but SEYMOUR CHWAST is the first to have caught them in the act. While the scene is delicate in more senses than one, it is hard to feel that the two make very congenial bedfellows, quite apart from the obvious danger that her rather copious lipstick may leave marks on the bedlinen. However, a liaison there evidently is, even though it seems likely to be troubled by all sorts of incompatibilities.

Kurzbiographie Seite 155.
Man weiss schon lange, dass zwischen Graphik und Text eine Liebesaffäre besteht, vor allem seit die Werbung sie so häufig zusammenbringt – aber SEYMOUR CHWAST hat sie als erster in flagranti ertappt. Obwohl er die delikate Szene ganz zart angefasst hat, kann man wohl kaum von zwei harmonischen Partnern reden, abgesehen davon, dass ihr üppiger Lippenstift Spuren auf der Bettwäsche hinterlassen könnte. Die Liaison ist jedenfalls bewiesen, obschon sie von allen möglichen Unverträglichkeiten getrübt scheint.

Voir la notice biographique en p. 155.
Il était depuis longtemps entendu que l'art et l'écriture entretiennent une liaison passionnée, surtout depuis que la publicité les associe si souvent dans des circonstances plutôt légères – mais SEYMOUR CHWAST est bien le premier à les avoir surpris en flagrant délit. Scène délicate à plus d'un titre, et pourtant on ne saurait imaginer partenaires plus inharmonieux, sans parler du risque que la belle laisse des traces de rouge à lèvres sur les draps. Quoi qu'il en soit, le constat même de cette liaison est évident, même si toutes sortes d'incompatibilités risquent de la rendre difficilement vivable.

KAZUMASA NAGAI, born in Osaka, 1929. He studied sculpture at Tokyo University of Art before entering Nippon Design Center in 1960 where he is now President. He won competitions for the symbols of Sapporo Winter Olympics (1966) and Okinawa International Ocean Exhibition. He has gained Silver and Bronze Medals from the Tokyo ADC (1960–67) and numerous other international prizes, including the Gold, Silver and Special prizes at the Warsaw Biennale. One-man shows were held at MOMA (1968), Warsaw and Osaka. He is a member of AGI.

KAZUMASA NAGAI, 1929 in Osaka geboren. Er studierte Bildhauerei an der University of Art in Tokio, bevor er 1960 dem Nippon Design Center beitrat, dessen Präsident er heute ist. Er gewann 1966 und 1972 die Symbol-Wettbewerbe für die Olympischen Spiele Sapporo und die Internationale Ozean Ausstellung Okinawa. Er hat für seine Arbeiten zahlreiche Auszeichnungen erhalten, u.a. Preise des ADC, Medaillen und Spezialpreise an den Internationalen Plakat-Biennalen in Warschau. Einzelausstellungen seiner Werke wurden im MOMA (1968), in Warschau und Osaka gezeigt. Er ist Mitglied der AGI.

KAZUMASA NAGAI, né à Osaka en 1929. A étudié la sculpture à l'Université d'art de Tokyo avant d'entrer en 1960 au Nippon Design Center, qu'il préside aujourd'hui. Vainqueur des concours pour la création des symboles utilisés aux Jeux Olympiques d'hiver de Sapporo (1966) et à l'International Ocean Exhibition d'Okinawa. Il a remporté diverses médailles d'argent et de bronze de l'ADC de Tokyo entre 1960 et 1967, ainsi que de nombreux autres prix internationaux, ainsi des médailles d'or et d'argent et des Prix Spéciaux de la Biennale de Varsovie. Des expositions personnelles lui ont été consacrées au MOMA en 1968, à Varsovie et à Osaka. Il est membre de l'AGI.

JAMES MARSH, born in Yorkshire, England. He studied graphic design at Batley College of Art and Design. After working for several studios and design groups, he founded his own studio under the name of *Head Office* in 1968. Behind this studio name he was able to achieve the freedom to work in various styles and media. This permitted him, in 1975, to become simply James Marsh again. He paints in oil or acrylics, has illustrated numbers of books and works for some of the leading magazines.

JAMES MARSH ist ein englischer Illustrator aus Yorkshire, der seine Graphiker-Ausbildung am Batley College of Art and Design erhielt. Nachdem er für verschiedene Studios und Design-Gruppen tätig war, gründete er 1968 sein eigenes Atelier, das *Head Office.* Unter diesem Namen konnte er anonym bleiben und sich die Freiheit nehmen, in verschiedenen Stilarten und Medien zu arbeiten, was ihm 1975 erlaubte, wieder James Marsh zu sein. Er malt Öl- und Acrylbilder, illustriert Bücher und ist für führende Zeitschriften tätig.

JAMES MARSH, né dans le Yorkshire anglais. A étudié l'art graphique au Batley College of Art and Design. Après avoir travaillé pour divers studios et groupes de design, il fonde en 1968 un studio qu'il baptise *Head Office.* Ce pignon sur rue lui permet de créer en toute liberté dans différents styles et médias. En 1975, il se personnalise en redevenant James Marsh. Des éditeurs et des grands magazines se disputent ses illustrations (huile ou acrylique).

ANNEGERT FUCHSHUBER, born in Germany. Illustrator and writer of children's books. Because this was the two-hundredth issue and appeared in 1979 – "The Year of the Child", it was natural to make it a Special Issue and devote it entirely to children's book illustration. The features included illustrations from: USA, Britain, France, Germany, Switzerland, Japan, Poland, and Czechoslovakia.

ANNEGERT FUCHSHUBER, in Deutschland geboren, Illustratorin und Autorin von Kinderbüchern. Weil dies die zweihundertste Ausgabe von *Graphis* war und sie im Jahr des Kindes erschien (1979), war es naheliegend, eine Spezialausgabe herauszugeben und sie ausschliesslich der Kinderbuchillustration zu widmen. In den Artikeln wurden Illustrationen aus den USA, England, Frankreich, Deutschland, Polen und der Tschechoslowakei vorgestellt.

ANNEGERT FUCHSHUBER, née en Allemagne. Illustratrice et auteur de livres pour enfants. La parution du n° 200 en 1979 coïncidait avec l'Année de l'Enfance. Aussi ce numéro d'anniversaire a-t-il été entièrement consacré à l'illustration de livres d'enfants. Sont représentés les illustrateurs américains, britanniques, français, allemands, suisses, japonais, polonais et tchèques.

© 1987 PRO LITTERIS, Zürich

For short biography, see Page 160.
The motif of this cover is taken from TOMI UNGERER's book "Abracadabra". It was suggested by him to advertise the services of an advertising agency and design studio. Ungerer sees advertising as a battle. The agency must be armed for combat while the visual communications it provides must have a keen cutting edge. The broadsword comes in handy as a T-square.

Kurzbiographie Seite 160.
Das Motiv dieses Umschlags stammt aus TOMI UNGERERS Buch «Abracadabra». Es wurde für die Eigenwerbung einer Agentur entworfen. Werbung ist eine Schlacht, will Ungerer hier mitteilen. Eine Agentur, welche für die Kunden in Schranken tritt, muss von Kopf bis Fuss gewappnet sein. Ein Schwert fungiert als Reissschiene.

Voir la notice biographique en p. 160.
Le sujet de cette couverture est tiré du livre «Abracadabra» de TOMI UNGERER, où il figure au titre d'une campagne promotionnelle pour une agence de publicité disposant de son propre studio de design. Ungerer a une vision guerrière de la pub: l'agence doit être armée de pied en cap; les communications visuelles qu'elle établit doivent avoir le tranchant d'un sabre, qui figure ici l'équerre.

ROBERT GIUSTI, was born in Zurich in 1937 and raised in New York (he has dual citizenship). He studied at Tyler School of Fine Arts, Philadelphia, and graduated from Cranbrook Academy of Art, Michigan. He first joined *Random House* as art director and designer before becoming freelance in 1973. Since then he has been engaged in editorial illustrations, record-cover design, TV, film art, and advertising art. He has participated in numerous group shows in the USA. Among other awards, he has gained AIGA Awards of Excellence and Silver Awards from the New York ADC.

ROBERT GIUSTI, 1937 in Zürich geboren, ist in New York aufgewachsen und ist Bürger beider Länder. Er studierte an der Tyler School of Fine Arts, Philadelphia, und schloss seine Studien an der Cranbrook Academy of Art, Michigan, ab. Bevor er 1973 freiberuflich tätig wurde, arbeitete er als Graphiker und Art Director beim Verlag *Random House*. Sein Arbeitsbereich umfasst Illustrationen und Graphik für redaktionelle und Werbezwecke, Schallplattenhüllen, Film und Fernsehen. Er hat an verschiedenen Gruppenausstellungen in den USA teilgenommen. Nebst anderen Auszeichnungen gewann er AIGA-Preise und wurde vom New York ADC und von der Society of Illustrators ausgezeichnet.

ROBERT GIUSTI, né à Zurich en 1937, aujourd'hui citoyen américain et suisse. A fait ses études à la Tyler School of Fine Arts de Philadelphie et obtenu son diplôme à la Cranbrook Academy of Art (Michigan). D'abord directeur artistique et designer aux Editions *Random House*, il reprend son indépendance en 1973. Actif dans l'illustration de presse, la conception de pochettes de disques, la création graphique appliquée à la télévision et au cinéma, l'art publicitaire, il a participé à de nombreuses expositions collectives sur le territoire des Etats-Unis. A reçu entre autres des Prix d'excellence de l'AIGA et diverses médailles d'argent de l'ADC de New York.

KIYOSHI AWAZU, born in Tokyo, 1929. He studied at Hosei University and worked first in the publicity department of a film-distributing company before founding the *Awazu Design Institute* in 1964. In 1967 he devized the basic concept for the recreation area at Expo '70 in Osaka. He has created posters for anti-war and liberation movements. Included in his scope are: film-making, exhibition design, murals, serigraphy, calligraphy, etc. He has won several prizes.

KIYOSHI AWAZU, 1929 in Tokio geboren. Nach seinen Studien an der Hosei University arbeitete er in der Werbeabteilung eines Filmverleihs und gründete 1964 das *Awazu Design Institute*. 1967 entwarf er das Basiskonzept für die Erholungsplätze der Expo '70 in Osaka. Er hat Plakate für Antikriegs- und Freiheitsbewegungen kreiert, Filme gedreht und Ausstellungen, Wandbilder, Siebdrucke und Kalligraphien gestaltet. Für seine Arbeiten hat er zahlreiche Auszeichnungen erhalten.

KIYOSHI AWAZU, né à Tokyo en 1929. A fait ses études à l'Université Hosei. D'abord attaché au département publicitaire d'une société de distribution cinématographique, il fonde en 1967 l'*Awazu Design Institute*. En 1967, il met au point la conception de base pour l'aménagement de l'aire récréative de l'Expo 70 d'Osaka. Il est l'auteur d'intéressantes affiches pacifistes ou encourageant les mouvements de libération. Awazu est aussi cinéaste, concepteur d'expositions, peintre de murals, sérigraphe, calligraphe, etc. Il est lauréat de divers prix.

■ ■ ■ ■

WALTER BALLMER, born in Switzerland, 1923. He studied at the Kunstgewerbeschule in Basle. In 1947 he went to Italy and worked in the Boggeri design studio in Milan. In 1956 he began working for *Olivetti* and has been instrumental in their extensive corporate image and exhibition design, including the design of large-scale decorative murals. Among his many awards is a Gold Medal at the Ljubljana Bio 5 for his *Olivetti Image* Exhibition. He has been a member of AGI since 1970. Since 1971 he is very successfully managing his own studio *Unidesign*.

■

WALTER BALLMER, 1923 in der Schweiz geboren, studierte an der Kunstgewerbeschule in Basel. 1947 liess er sich in Mailand nieder, wo er für das Design Studio Boggeri arbeitete. 1956 kam er zu *Olivetti* in die Abteilung für Öffentlichkeitsarbeit, Produktgestaltung und Werbung, wo er sich mit Prestige- und Produkt-Werbung befasste, weltweit Ausstellungen konzipierte und die dekorative Gestaltung von Monumentalwänden ausführte. Unter den zahlreichen Auszeichnungen befindet sich auch eine Goldmedaille, die ihm an der Bio 5 in Ljubliana für seine Ausstellung *Olivetti Image* verliehen wurde. Seit 1970 ist er Mitglied der AGI, und seit 1971 führt er sehr erfolgreich sein eigenes Studio Unidesign.

■

WALTER BALLMER, né en Suisse en 1923. Ancien élève de l'Ecole des arts décoratifs de Bâle. Part en 1947 en Italie, où il travaille dans un studio de design milanais. Entré chez *Olivetti* en 1956, il a puissamment contribué à l'image globale de marque de l'entreprise, à la conception de ses expositions et notamment à la réalisation de murals décoratifs de grandes dimensions. Récipiendaire de nombreux prix, il est médaille d'or de la Bio 5 de Ljubljana pour son exposition vouée à l'image publique d'*Olivetti*. Il est membre de l'AGI. En 1971 il ouvre son propre studio, *Unidesign*, à Milan.

■

For short biography, see Page 141.
In order to measure the size of distant objects, one can use the method of outstreched arms and held up thumbs or pencils. However, on the cover of ANDRÉ FRANÇOIS this method will become alienated from its purpose. The fingernail becomes a screen out of which a baldhead answers us and a mouth, imbedded in the thumb folds, appears to conjure away the one who actually wants to look in the distance. The clock has no hands. The time stands still. The outgoing activity of our once inquiring minds has been reversed.

■

Kurzbiographie Seite 141.
Um die Grösse von weit entfernten Objekten zu messen, kann man die Methode des ausgestreckten Armes und aufgerichteten Daumens oder Zeichenstiftes verwenden. Auf dem Umschlag von ANDRÉ FRANÇOIS jedoch wird diese Methode zweckentfremdet. Der Fingernagel ist zum Bildschirm geworden, von dem aus uns ein Kahlkopf Befehle erteilt, und ein Mund, eingebettet in eine Daumenfalte, scheint dem, der doch eigentlich in die Ferne schauen wollte, beschwörend zuzureden. Die Uhr hat keine Zeiger. Die Zeit steht still. Der Geist forschender Aktivität von ehedem ist nach innen gerichtet.

■

Voir la notice biographique en p. 141.
On détermine communément les dimensions d'un objet éloigné en tendant le bras et en plaçant le pouce ou un crayon dans la ligne de mire. Sur sa couverture, ANDRÉ FRANÇOIS dénature sensiblement cette méthode. L'ongle du pouce s'est transformé en écran de télévision; le personnage chauve qui y apparaît donne des ordres, et une bouche insérée dans les plis de la jointure semble adjurer le propriétaire du pouce, qui devrait en somme porter son regard au loin. La montre est dépourvue d'aiguilles. Le temps s'est arrêté. L'activité extravertie de l'esprit s'est inversée: c'est désormais l'exploration de la vie intérieure qui compte.

■

JAY MAISEL, born in Brooklyn, 1931. He studied graphic art at Lincoln High School and went on to study painting at Cooper Union. He took his BFA at Yale (1953). He switched to photography and took courses with H. Matter and A. Brodovitch. Since 1954 he has been a freelance photographer working for magazines, advertising agencies and some of the major corporations. He has taught color photography at the School of Visual Arts and at Cooper Union and he still lectures. In 1978 he received the American Society of Magazine Photographers award for outstanding achievement. He has held numerous one-man exhibitions.

■

JAY MAISEL, 1931 in Brooklyn geboren. Er studierte Graphik an der Lincoln High School und anschliessend Malerei an der Cooper Union. 1953 schloss er in Yale mit einem BFA ab. Erst dann wechselte er zur Photographie und nahm Kurse bei Herbert Matter und Alexey Brodovitch. Seit 1954 arbeitet er als freischaffender Photograph für Zeitschriften, Werbeagenturen und Industrieunternehmen. Er war Lehrer für Farbphotographie an der School of Visual Arts und an der Cooper Union und ist auch heute noch häufig als Dozent tätig. 1978 erhielt er eine Auszeichnung der American Society of Magazine Photographers für seine hervorragenden Leistungen in der Photographie.

■

JAY MAISEL, né à Brooklyn en 1931. A étudié l'art graphique à la Lincoln High School, la peinture à Cooper Union. Obtient son BFA à Yale en 1953. Passé à la photographie, il suit les cours de H. Matter et A. Brodovitch. Depuis 1954, il est photographe indépendant au service de magazines, d'agences de publicité et de certaines grosses entreprises. Il a enseigné la photographie en couleurs à la School of Visual Arts et à Cooper Union et est un conférencier écouté. En 1978, il a reçu le prix de l'American Society of Magazine Photographers pour ses réalisations hors pair. De nombreuses expositions individuelles lui ont été consacrées.

ALAN PECKOLICK / ERNIE SMITH / TONI DISPIGNA. The three were co-workers of Herb Lubalin and formed: *Herb Lubalin Associates, Inc.* Alan Peckolick, born in New York, 1940, was a graduate of Pratt Institute. He became Herb Lubalin's assistant in 1964. In 1968 he opened his own studio in New York. In 1974 he designed a Gold Medal for the NY ADC – and won it himself. Ernie Smith graduated from the Art Center School, Los Angeles. He became partner and Vice President of *Herb Lubalin, Inc.* in 1967. Toni DiSpigna was born in Italy, 1943. He graduated from Pratt Institute. In 1973 he opened his own studio and joined the group in 1978.

■

ALAN PECKOLICK, ERNIE SMITH, TONI DISPIGNA arbeiteten mit Herb Lubalin als Partner in der New Yorker Design-Firma *Herb Lubalin Associates Inc.* zusammen. Alan Peckolick wurde 1940 in New York geboren und ist Absolvent des Pratt Institute. 1964 wurde er Assistent von Herb Lubalin. 1968 eröffnete er sein eigenes Studio in New York. Für den ADC New York entwarf er 1974 eine Goldmedaille, die er prompt selbst erhielt. Ernie Smith ist Absolvent der Art Center School, Los Angeles, und wurde 1967 Partner und Vize-Präsident bei *Herb Lubalin, Inc.* Toni DiSpigna, 1943 in Italien geboren, studierte am Pratt Institute. 1973 gründete er sein eigenes Atelier und stiess 1978 zur Herb-Lubalin-Gruppe.

■

ALAN PECKOLICK / ERNIE SMITH / TONI DISPIGNA. Ces trois artistes se sont associés à Herb Lubalin au sein de *Herb Lubalin Associates, Inc.* Alan Peckolick, né à New York en 1940, est diplômé du Pratt Institute. Assistant de Herb Lubalin en 1964, il ouvre son propre studio à New York en 1968. En 1974, il crée pour l'ADC de New York une médaille d'or qu'il est le premier à remporter. Ernie Smith est diplômé de l'Art Center School de Los Angeles. Il devient associé et vice-président de *Herb Lubalin, Inc.* en 1967. Toni DiSpigna, né à Ischia (Italie) en 1943, est diplômé du Pratt Institute. Il s'installe à son compte en 1973, rejoint le groupe d'associés en 1978.

■

For short biography, see Page 162.
This illustration by ETIENNE DELESSERT is one of eight he did for a book of poems by Jacques Prévert. Delessert's work, in a way falls into two categories, for behind the beautifully smooth-textured scenes that delight children with their somehow larger-than-life magic there is a hinterland of more private work that is gloomier, more scathing, occasionally lethal. The three matches must obviously appeal to an artist who has painted a whole cycle of things on fire.

Kurzbiographie Seite 162.
Diese Illustration von ETIENNE DELESSERT ist eine von acht, die er für einen Gedichtband von Jacques Prévert machte. Delesserts Arbeit lässt sich in zwei Kategorien einteilen: den lieblich zarten Szenen, welche die Kinder entzücken, steht eine andere, verborgenere Welt gegenüber, die eher düster, ironisch und zuweilen vernichtend ist. Die drei Streichhölzer entsprechen offensichtlich dem Temperament eines Künstlers, der einen ganzen Bilderzyklus zum Thema Flammen gemalt hat.

Voir la notice biographique en p. 162.
Cette illustration d'ETIENNE DELESSERT est l'une des huit qu'il a réalisées pour un recueil de poèmes de Jacques Prévert. L'œuvre de Delessert a deux faces, l'une mieux connue du public – les scènes aux doux coloris qui enchantent les enfants par leur magie envahissant le réel –, l'autre plus secrète, âpre, ténébreuse, parfois meurtrière. Les trois allumettes semblent convenir au tempérament d'un artiste qui a réalisé un cycle entier de peintures mettant en scène des objets embrasés.

For short biography, see Page 158.
HEINZ EDELMANN's illustration refers to his new undertaking at the time to design all the books for the *Klett-Cotta* Publishers in Stuttgart. All the year he had a flow of urgent jobs that he has depicted here as "hot potatoes". By the way the potatoes themselves are not photographed – which would have saved him time – but lovingly and meticulously painted.

Kurzbiographie Seite 158.
Während HEINZ EDELMANN mit der Gestaltung der gesamten Bücher des *Klett-Cotta*-Verlags beschäftigt war, hatte er die Inspiration zu diesem *Graphis*-Umschlag. Er fühlte sich mit so viel Arbeit konfrontiert, dass er dringende neue Aufgaben als «heisse Kartoffeln» bezeichnete. Trotz des Zeitaufwandes hat er diese heissen Kartoffeln für *Graphis* nicht photographiert, sondern liebevollst gezeichnet.

Voir la notice biographique en p. 158.
L'illustration de HEINZ EDELMANN se rapporte à l'énorme travail qu'il venait d'entreprendre à l'époque pour les Editions *Klett-Cotta* de Stuttgart: dessiner les maquettes de toutes les nouveautés de la maison. Il était tellement submergé de travail que toute nouvelle commande équivalait pour lui à des «patates bouillantes». Et pourtant, il a pris le temps de peindre méticuleusement les deux pommes de terre au lieu de se contenter d'une photo vite faite.

JAN SAWKA, born in Poland, 1946. He studied architecture and art. In 1970 he was made Director of the STU Theater in Cracow and in 1972 Director of the Barn Gallery in Warsaw. He was one of the cooperators on the Georges Pompidou Centre in Paris (1975). He moved to the USA in 1977 and has participated in numerous international group and one-man shows. His many awards include the Oscar of Painting awarded by the French President (1975) and a Gold Medal at the Warsaw Biennale in 1978.

JAN SAWKA, 1946 in Polen geboren. Er studierte Architektur und Kunst. 1970 wurde er Direktor des STU-Theaters in Krakau und 1972 Direktor der Barn-Galerie in Warschau. Er hat am Centre Georges Pompidou Paris (1975) mitgearbeitet. 1977 übersiedelte er in die USA und war dort in zahlreichen Gruppen- und Einzelausstellungen vertreten. Zu seinen zahlreichen Auszeichnungen gehören der vom französischen Präsidenten verliehene Oskar für Malerei (1975) und eine Goldmedaille an der Warschauer Biennale 1978.

JAN SAWKA, né en Pologne en 1946. A étudié l'architecture et l'art. En 1970, il est nommé directeur du Théâtre STU de Cracovie, en 1972 directeur de la Galerie Barn de Varsovie. En 1975, il figure parmi les coopérateurs qui mettent en route le Centre Georges-Pompidou sur le plateau Beaubourg. Installé aux Etats-Unis dès 1977, il a participé à de nombreuses expositions individuelles et collectives. La série de prix importants dont il est récipiendaire comprend l'Oscar de la peinture reçu des mains du président de la République en 1975, ainsi qu'une médaille d'or de la Biennale de Varsovie en 1978.

FRANÇOIS ROBERT, born in Switzerland, 1946. He first went to Milan and spent 3 years as graphic designer with *Pirelli*. In 1971 he joined *Unimark Int.* in Johannesburg and moved to Chicago with the same firm. He founded *François Robert Associates* in 1974 and soon won major clients, including *Santa Fe, Raychem, Borg-Warner* and *Inland Steel*. Apart from advertising art, photography, illustration, packaging, book design, etc., he also acts as design consultant. Since 1972 he has gained some 100 awards.

FRANÇOIS ROBERT, 1946 in der Schweiz geboren. In Mailand arbeitete er drei Jahre als Graphik-Designer für *Pirelli*. 1971 ging er zu *Unimark Int'l* in Johannesburg und übersiedelte später mit dieser Firma nach Chicago. 1974 gründete er *François Robert Associates* und hatte bald so bedeutende Kunden wie *Santa Fe, Raychem, Borg-Warner* und *Inland Steel*. Zu seinem Arbeitsbereich gehören neben Werbegraphik, Photographie, Illustration, Verpackungen, Buch-Design etc. auch Design-Beratung. Seit 1972 hat er einige Hundert Auszeichnungen erhalten.

FRANÇOIS ROBERT, né en Suisse en 1946. En début de carrière, il passe trois années comme graphiste chez *Pirelli* à Milan. En 1971, il entre chez *Unimark Int.* à Johannesburg et suit cette société à Chicago. En 1974, il fonde *François Robert Associates* dont la clientèle compte bientôt des noms importants, *Santa Fe, Raychem, Borg-Warner, Inland Steel*, etc. Il est à la fois conseiller en design et réalisateur de travaux publicitaires, de photographies, d'illustrations, d'emballages, de maquettes de livres. Depuis 1972, une centaine de prix sont venus récompenser ses œuvres.

HERBERT MATTER, Switzerland, 1907-1984. He studied at the Ecole des Beaux-arts, Geneva, and Académie Moderne, Paris, under Fernand Léger. He worked with A.M. Cassandre on posters and Le Corbusier on architecture. In 1932 he returned to Zurich where he designed posters for the Swiss National Tourist Office. He went to the USA and was design consultant to *Knoll Associates Inc.* In 1949 he made the film *The Works of Calder* for MOMA. He was professor of photography at Yale (1952-76). In 1977 he was taken into the Hall of Fame of ADC New York and in 1980 he received a Guggenheim Foundation Fellowship in photography.

HERBERT MATTER, Schweiz, 1907-1984. Er studierte an der Ecole des Beaux-arts, Genf, und an der Académie Moderne, Paris unter Fernand Léger. Er arbeitete mit Cassandre (Plakate) und Le Corbusier (Architektur) zusammen. 1932 kehrte er nach Zürich zurück und entwarf hier Plakate für das schweizerische Verkehrsbüro. Später übersiedelte er in die USA und arbeitete dort als Design-Berater für *Knoll.* 1949 machte er für das MOMA den Film *The Works of Calder.* 1952-76 war er Professor für Photographie an der Yale University. 1977 wurde er in die Hall of Fame des ADC New York aufgenommen und 1980 erhielt er ein Stipendium der Guggenheim-Stiftung für Photographie.

HERBERT MATTER, Suisse, 1907-1984. Il a étudié à l'Ecole des beaux-arts de Genève et à l'Académie moderne de Paris sous la direction de Fernand Léger. Réalise des affiches en collaboration avec A.M. Cassandre, des projets d'architecture en collaboration avec Le Corbusier. Rentré à Zurich en 1932, il y crée des affiches pour l'Office National Suisse du Tourisme. Installé aux Etats-Unis, il est conseiller en design chez *Knoll Associates Inc.* En 1949, il réalise le film *The Works of Calder* pour le MOMA. Il a enseigné la photo à Yale de 1952 à 1976. Admis au Hall of Fame de l'ADC de New York en 1977, il a été bénéficiaire d'une Fellowship de la Fondation Guggenheim en photographie en 1980.

JAMES McMULLEN, born in China, 1934. He was educated in China, India, Canada, and the USA. He studied at Pratt Institute, and at the start of his career he worked for *Push Pin Studios* (1965-68). He now runs his own studio which specializes in film art and animation, theater decor, advertising art, book design and illustration. Together with Seymour Chwast he designed an exhibition for AIGA (1973). He has held numerous one-man exhibitions. In 1976-77 he was Vice President of AIGA. He has gained Silver and Gold Medals from the Society of Illustrators.

JAMES McMULLEN, 1934 in China geboren. Er wurde in China, Indien, Kanada und in den Vereinigten Staaten ausgebildet, bevor er am Pratt Institute in New York studierte. 1965-68 war er Mitglied der *Push Pin Studios.* Er hat jetzt ein eigenes Studio, das auf Filmkunst und Trickzeichnungen, Bühnenbilder, Werbegraphik, Buch-Design und Illustration spezialisiert ist. Zusammen mit Seymour Chwast konzipierte er 1973 eine Ausstellung für die AIGA. Er hatte zahlreiche Einzelausstellungen. 1976-77 war er Vizepräsident der AIGA. Er wurde mit Gold-und Silbermedaillen der Society of Illustrators ausgezeichnet.

JAMES McMULLEN, né en Chine en 1934. A été à l'école en Chine, en Inde, au Canada et aux Etats-Unis. Ancien élève du Pratt Institute, il a d'abord travaillé pour le *Push Pin Studios* (1965-68). Il dirige aujourd'hui son propre studio spécialisé dans la création graphique pour le cinéma, le film d'animation, les décors de théâtre, l'art publicitaire, la conception de livres et l'illustration. Avec Seymour Chwast, il a réalisé en 1973 une exposition pour l'AIGA. De nombreuses expositions personnelles lui ont été consacrées. Il a été vice-président de l'AIGA en 1976-77. La Society of Illustrators lui a décerné des médailles d'or et d'argent.

GILBERT STONE, who has made more of elongation than anybody since El Greco, holds a foremost place among America's painters and illustrators. Educated at the Parsons School and New York University, he worked for many US publications so that his unmistakable style has become familiar to the reading public. He had numerous one-man shows and his work is in many permanent collections. Among the hundred or more awards he won are three Gold Medals from the Society of Illustrators. Stone lectured widely and gave courses at the School of Visual Arts for twenty years. The Visual Art Museum staged a retrospective of his illustration in 1980.

GILBERT STONE, der wie niemand seit El Greco seine Figuren in die Länge zieht, nimmt unter den amerikanischen Malern und Illustratoren einen führenden Platz ein. An der Parsons School und der Universität New York ausgebildet, arbeitete er für zahlreiche bekannte US Zeitschriften. Seine Arbeiten sind in zahlreichen Ausstellungen gezeigt worden und in vielen Sammlungen zu finden. Unter den etwa hundert Auszeichnungen befinden sich drei Goldmedaillen der Society of Illustrators. Stone unterrichtete während zwanzig Jahren an der School of Visual Arts, New York. Das Visual Art Museum zeigte 1980 eine Retrospektive seiner Arbeiten als Illustrator.

GILBERT STONE, qui a plus que tout autre depuis le Greco allongé ses figures, occupe une place enviée parmi les peintres et illustrateurs américains. Formé à la Parsons School et à l'Université de New York, son travail pour un grand nombre de magazines américains l'a fait connaître, lui et son style spécifique, d'un vaste public. Ses œuvres figurent dans une foule de collections. La bonne centaine de prix qu'il a remportés comprend trois médailles d'or de la Society of Illustrators. Pédagogue de choc, il a enseigné pendant 20 ans à la School of Visual Arts de New York. En 1980, le Visual Art Museum a consacré une rétrospective à ses illustrations.

BRALDT BRALDS, born in Holland. He studied art history and typesetting at Rotterdam and first worked as a typesetter. He became a freelance graphic designer in 1971 and then turned toward illustration. He moved to New York in 1980 where his work is constantly in demand. He has received numerous Society of Illustrators awards.

BRALDT BRALDS, in Holland geboren, studierte Kunstgeschichte und Buchdruck in Rotterdam und arbeitete vorerst als Schriftsetzer. 1971 wurde er freischaffender Graphiker, später Illustrator. 1980 zog er nach New York, wo er bald grossen Erfolg hatte. Er hat zahlreiche Preise der Society of Illustrators erhalten.

BRALDT BRALDS, né en Hollande. Après ses études de l'histoire de l'art et de la typographie à Rotterdam, il travaille comme compositeur-typographe. Etabli à son compte en 1971, il réalise des travaux graphiques, puis des illustrations. En 1980, il s'installe à New York, où ses productions sont très demandées. Il est lauréat de nombreux prix de la Society of Illustrators.

 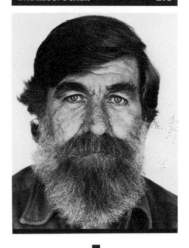 

For short biography, see Page 141.
ANDRÉ FRANÇOIS is a sort of visual philosopher. The seemingly simple signs that he uses - fish and butterflies, flowers, clock dials, eggs, and eyes - are ciphers for more abstract concepts. They may at first glance appear childishly obvious, but the longer you look at them, the deeper they get. The artist's eye contemplates the world - and there springs the idea, the creative spark, the new life - which is also a new eye looking at a new world.

Kurzbiographie Seite 141.
ANDRÉ FRANÇOIS könnte man einen visuellen Philosophen nennen. Seine vermeintlich einfachen Zeichen - Fische und Schmetterlinge, Blumen und Zifferblätter, Eier und Augen - sind Sinnbilder für abstrakte Ideen, die er zu Thesen entwickelt. Die Thesen erscheinen vorerst kindlich einfach, aber je länger man sie betrachtet, desto tiefer gehen sie. Vom Auge des Künstlers, das die Welt betrachtet, entspringt die Idee, der kreative Funke, das neue Leben, das auch ein neues, in eine neue Welt blickendes Auge ist.

Voir la notice biographique en p. 141.
ANDRÉ FRANÇOIS est une espèce de philosophe visuel. Les signes simples en apparence qu'il emploie - poissons, papillons, fleurs, cadrans, œufs, yeux - servent à coder des concepts plus abstraits. On peut les trouver tellement évidents qu'ils en paraissent enfantins. Pourtant, plus on les étudie, plus ils acquièrent de profondeur. L'œil de l'artiste contemple l'univers - et c'est de cette contemplation qui naît l'idée, l'étincelle créatrice, une vie nouvelle - qui est comme un œil nouveau ouvrant sur un monde nouveau.
© 1987 PRO LITTERIS, Zürich

For short biography, see Page 163.
No youth ever won more acclaim than David, no work of art is more famous than Michelangelo's dream of youth. But what MILTON GLASER has come up with here (photographed by Matthew Klein) is just the eye, meaning vision. It is an exhibit, to be hung on a wall as an object of contemplation and a stimulus for creativity.

Kurzbiographie Seite 163.
Noch nie hat ein Jüngling so grossen Ruhm erworben wie David, kein Kunstwerk ist so berühmt wie Michelangelos Interpretation seiner Jünglingsfigur. Doch was MILTON GLASER auf diesem Umschlag zeigt (photographiert von Matthew Klein), ist nur das Auge, das Sehen bedeutet. Das Ganze ist in ein Ausstellungsstück verwandelt, das als Gegenstand der Betrachtung und als Stimulus für den kreativen Geist an der Wand hängt.

Voir la notice biographique en p. 163.
Aucun adolescent n'a jamais atteint la réputation de David, aucune œuvre d'art n'a jamais éclipsé la gloire du rêve de jeunesse que Michel-Ange cisela dans la pierre. Mais ce que MILTON GLASER en a retenu (et fait photographier par Matthew Klein), c'est l'œil seul, soit la vision. Il en a fait une pièce d'exposition à accrocher à la cimaise comme objet de contemplation et source d'inspiration créatrice.

JOHN PAUL ENDRESS/PAULA SCHER. This illustration is from a series of record covers. All of the covers depicted magnified shots of small objects, and they were all photographed by John Paul Endress. Paula Scher was Art Director for CBS Records and she designed about 80 record covers and 50 posters a year. Today she is a partner of Koppel & Scher, New York. She has taught at various schools and has won numerous medals including a Gold Medal from the Art Directors Club and a Silver Medal from the Society of Illustrators.

JOHN PAUL ENDRESS/PAULA SCHER. Dieser Umschlag gehört zu einer Reihe von Schallplattenhüllen. Es handelte sich bei allen um Vergrösserungen von kleinen Objekten, die John Paul Endress photographierte. Paula Scher war Art Director für CBS Records, für die sie über 80 Schallplattenhüllen und 50 Plakate pro Jahr entwarf. Heute ist sie Partnerin des Studios Koppel & Scher in New York. Sie hat an verschiedenen Kunstschulen unterrichtet und zahlreiche Auszeichnungen erhalten, darunter eine Goldmedaille des Art Directors Club und eine Silbermedaille der Society of Illustrations.

JOHN PAUL ENDRESS/PAULA SCHER. Cette illustration est tirée d'une série de pochettes de disques. Toutes ces pochettes montrent des vues agrandies de petits objets photographieés par John Paul Endress. Paula Scher a été directrice artistique de CBS Records, où elle a réalisé 80 pochettes et 50 affiches par année. Elle s'est associée avec l'artiste Koppel au sein de Koppel & Scher, New York. Elle a aussi créé des maquettes de livres et travaille indépendamment comme graphiste. Diverses écoles d'art l'ont eue comme professeur. Ses nombreux prix comprennent une médaille d'or de l'Art Directors Club et une médaille d'argent de la Society of Illustrators.

For short biography, see Page 166.
On this cover by JOSSE GOFFIN there is an unusual being who observes us through triple eye-glasses. The shape of the shoulders of this being and the coordinates on his jacket make it seem likely that it is Mr. World gazing at us, in three different lights: incendiary red, environmentalist green and royal blue. No wonder then that the color of his face changes accordingly!

Kurzbiographie Seite 166.
Auf dem Umschlag von JOSSE GOFFIN ist ein menschliches Wesen dargestellt, das uns durch eine dreiglasige Brille betrachtet. Die Form der Schultern dieses Wesens und die Koordination auf der Jacke deuten wahrscheinlich auf Mr. Welt hin, der uns im Schein von drei farbigen Lichtern anstarrt: Feuerrot, Umweltgrün und Königsblau. Kein Wunder, dass jeweils auch seine Gesichtsfarbe ändert!

Voir la notice biographique en p. 166.
Sur cette couverture de JOSSE GOFFIN, un humain nous fixe à travers des lunettes trioculaires. Le contour de ses épaules et les coordonnées figurant sur son veston nous font supposer qu'il s'agit de M. Monde qui nous observe sous trois éclairages chromatiques différents: le rouge incendiaire, le vert écologique, le bleu royal. Pas étonnant alors qu'il change visiblement de couleur!

LEO LIONNI, born in Amsterdam, 1910. He moved to Italy at fourteen and settled in the USA in 1939. He was one-time art director of *Fortune* magazine. He has taught at various schools and universities. In 1960 he returned to Italy to devote himself to painting and sculpture. He created an imaginary botany: *La botanica parallela* - an illustrated "scientific fantasy" published in Italy. All texts, drawings, tables, and facts were Lionni's own invention.

LEO LIONNI, 1910 in Amsterdam geboren. Im Alter von 14 Jahren kam er nach Italien, 1939 übersiedelte er dann in die USA. Er arbeitete für die Agentur *N.W. Ayer*, war Art Director bei *Fortune* und unterrichtete an Kunstschulen und Universitäten. 1960 kehrte er nach Italien zurück und widmete sich der Malerei und Bildhauerei. Er kreierte eine imaginäre Botanik: *La botanica parallela* - ein illustrierter «wissenschaftlicher Hokuspokus», bei Adelphi Edizioni, Mailand, erschienen. Text, Zeichnungen, Tabellen usw. sind von A bis Z von Lionni erfunden.

LEO LIONNI, né à Amsterdam en 1910. Arrivé en Italie à l'âge de 14 ans, il s'installe aux Etats-Unis en 1939. Il a été directeur artistique du magazine *Fortune* et a enseigné dans diverses écoles et universités. De retour en Italie en 1960, il se voue à la peinture et à la sculpture. Créateur d'une botanique imaginaire, *La botanica parallela*, chef-d'œuvre de fiction scientifique publié en Italie. Les textes, les dessins, les tableaux et les données qui y figurent ont tous été inventés par Lionni.

ROMAN CIEŚLEWICZ, born in Poland, 1930. He graduated from Cracow Academy of Arts and in 1963 he moved to Paris. He became a French citizen in 1971. His scope includes posters, lettering design, murals, exhibition design, packaging, and illustration. He won a Grand Prix at the 1972 Poster Biennale and numerous cinema poster prizes. In more recent years he has done a great deal of collage and photomontage in the fine art field and has had numerous one-man shows in famous European Museums.

ROMAN CIEŚLEWICZ, 1930 in Polen geboren. Er ist Absolvent der Krakauer Kunstakademie, 1963 zog er nach Paris und wurde 1971 französischer Staatsbürger. Sein Arbeitsbereich umfasst Plakatgestaltung, redaktionelles Design, Wandbild, Ausstellungskonzeption, Verpackungen und Illustration. Er erhielt den Grand Prix der Plakatbiennale 1972 in Warschau sowie verschiedene Preise für seine Kinoplakate. In den letzten Jahren machte er vor allem Collagen und Photomontagen, und seine Arbeiten wurden in zahlreichen Einzelausstellungen in bedeutenden europäischen Museen gezeigt.

ROMAN CIEŚLEWICZ, né en Pologne en 1930. Diplômé de l'Académie des Arts de Cracovie. En 1963, il part pour Paris. Naturalisé Français en 1971. Son œuvre comprend des affiches, des caractères, des murals, des stands d'exposition, des emballages, des illustrations. Il a remporté le Grand Prix de l'affiche du cinéma en Tchécoslovaquie 1964 et le Grand Prix de la Biennale de l'affiche de Varsovie en 1972. Des expositions lui ont été consacrées dans son pays natal, en France et à l'étranger.

PIERRE MENDELL, born in Essen, 1929. He studied under Armin Hofmann at Basle in 1958-60, then worked with Michael Engelmann in Munich till he founded a studio with Klaus Oberer in 1961. KLAUS OBERER, born in Basle, 1937. He studied at the College of Design there under Armin Hofmann in 1955-59. For the next two years he worked with Michael Engelmann in Munich before founding a studio with Pierre Mendell in 1961.

PIERRE MENDELL, 1929 in Essen geboren. Er studierte bei Armin Hofmann in Basel (1958-60) und arbeitete dann mit Michael Engelmann in München, bis er 1961 zusammen mit Klaus Oberer ein Studio gründete. KLAUS OBERER, 1937 in Basel geboren. Er studierte an der dortigen Kunstgewerbeschule unter Armin Hofmann (1955-1959). In den nächsten beiden Jahren arbeitete er mit Michael Engelmann in München, bevor er dort 1961 mit Pierre Mendell ein Studio gründete.

PIERRE MENDELL, né à Essen (RFA) en 1929. Il étudie à Bâle sous la direction d'Armin Hofmann de 1958-60, puis s'en va travailler à Munich avec Michael Engelmann jusqu'à ce qu'il fonde son propre studio en s'associant avec Klaus Oberer en 1961. KLAUS OBERER, né en 1937 à Bâle, où il étudie le design sous la direction d'Armin Hofmann de 1955 à 1959. Il collabore ensuite durant deux ans avec Michael Engelmann à Munich avant de cofonder un studio avec Pierre Mendell en 1961.

For short biography, see Page 158.
HEINZ EDELMANN's many posters and his illustrations for children's books have encouraged a sense of fun in his work which has left one of its expressions on our cover. Every designer's pencil knows it only has to make the slightest mistake and the eraser will be on its tail in hot pursuit. Edelmann has captured these two eternel antagonists, in the role of hunter and hunted, fugitive and bully, in a little scene of great verve and vitality.

Kurzbiographie Seite 158.
HEINZ EDELMANNS Arbeiten haben oft eine humorvolle Note. Auf diesem Umschlag flüchtet ein dünner, schreiender Bleistift vor einem hämisch lachenden, dicken Radiergummi. Der Zeichenstift des Graphikers weiss sehr wohl, dass ihm beim geringsten Fauxpas der Radiergummi wie ein Racheengel auf den Fersen folgt. Flüchtender und Verfolger, Ausführender und Auslöschender, die gegensätzlichen Komponenten – im Kopf des Zeichners sind sie im ewigen Kampf vereint.

Voir la notice biographique en p. 158.
Les nombreuses affiches de HEINZ EDELMANN et ses illustrations de livres d'enfants ont fait connaître son sens de l'humour. Notre couverture en porte la marque. Le crayon du designer sait d'instinct qu'au moindre déraillement la gomme correctrice va se lancer à ses trousses tel un ange vengeur. Edelmann a saisi ces deux éternels antagonistes dans le rôle du chasseur et du gibier, du gendarme et du voleur, en une petite scène vibrante de verve et de vitalité.

MICHEL DUBRÉ, born in Paris, 1942. He studied at the Ecole Estienne and the Ecole des Arts Appliqués and became an art teacher in 1966. His scope encompasses painting, collage, graphics, animated films, posters, stage decor and costumes. Since 1972 he has devoted his time to drawing and painting. His work has appeared in magazines and is used by corporations including *Air France, Goodyear, Crédit Agricole* and *IBM*. In 1978 he did a sculpture for the Centre Pompidou. He has won many awards and has held exhibitions in Paris, London, and New York.

MICHEL DUBRÉ, 1942 in Paris geboren. Er studierte an der Ecole Estienne und der Ecole des Arts Appliqués. 1966 wurde er Kunstlehrer. Seine Tätigkeit umfasst Malerei, Collagen, Graphik, Trickfilme, Plakate, Bühnenbilder und Kostüme. Seit 1972 widmet er sich dem Zeichnen und Malen. Seine Arbeiten sind von Zeitschriften und Firmen wie *Air France, Goodyear, Crédit Agricole* und *IBM* verwendet worden. 1978 schuf er eine Plastik im Auftrag des Centre Pompidou. Er wurde verschiedentlich ausgezeichnet und hatte Ausstellungen in Paris, London und New York.

MICHEL DUBRÉ, né à Paris en 1942. Ancien élève de l'Ecole Estienne et de l'Ecole des arts appliqués, il est professeur d'art dès 1966. Ses activités comprennent la peinture, le collage, les travaux graphiques, le film d'animation, l'affiche, les décors et costumes de théâtre. Depuis 1972, il consacre son temps au dessin et à la peinture. Ses créations ont paru en magazine et sont utilisées par des grandes sociétés telles qu'*Air France, Goodyear,* le *Crédit Agricole* et *IBM*. En 1978, il a réalisé une sculpture pour le centre Georges-Pompidou. Lauréat de nombreux prix, il a eu des expositions à Paris, Londres et New York.

MARVIN RUBIN, born in 1928. He graduated from UCLA in 1950 after studying art education and theater. Up to 1965 he worked primarily as a designer and art director for various firms: *Chevrolet, Capitol Records, Suzuki,* etc. He later turned to illustrating books and magazines and also worked on exhibition design, films and TV. He has taught design and illustration for many years.

MARVIN RUBIN, 1928 geboren. Er studierte Kunsterziehung und Theaterwissenschaft an der UCLA. Nach seinem Abschluss 1950 arbeitete er bis 1965 vorwiegend als Graphiker und Art Direktor für verschiedene Firmen: *Chevrolet, Capitol Records, Suzuki* etc. Dann wandte er sich hauptsächlich der Illustration von Büchern und Zeitschriften zu und arbeitete auch für Ausstellungen, Filme und Fernsehen. Er ist Lehrer für Graphik und Illustration.

MARVIN RUBIN, né en 1928. Diplôme de l'UCLA en éducation artistique et art du théâtre. Jusqu' en 1965, il travaille surtout comme designer et directeur artistique pour diverses sociétés: *Chevrolet, Capitol Records, Suzuki,* etc. Il s'oriente par la suite vers l'illustration de livres et magazines, réalise des stands d'expositions, travaille pour le cinéma et la télévision. Pendant de longues années, il a enseigné le design et l'illustration.

ZENJI FUNABASHI, born in Japan, 1942. He has worked in Canada and in the USA on animated films. He returned to Japan in 1980 and is active in many fields of graphic design. He specializes in "paper cutouts" for illustration in magazines and for advertising, posters, and animated films. He also does wood sculpture and murals.

ZENJI FUNABASHI, 1942 in Japan geboren, studierte Graphik an der Tama Fine Art University. In Kanada und den USA machte er Zeichentrickfilme und kehrte 1980 nach Japan zurück. Er ist auf zahlreichen Gebieten der Graphik und Holzplastik tätig, u. a. hat er sich auf eine Ausschneidetechnik spezialisiert, und diese Illustrationen werden für Werbung, Plakate und Trickfilme verwendet.

ZENJI FUNABASHI, né au Japon en 1942. A travaillé au Canada et aux Etats-Unis à la réalisation de films d'animation. De retour au Japon en 1980, il y multiplie ses activités de designer, se spécialisant dans l'illustration à base de papiers découpés pour les magazines, la publicité. On lui doit aussi des affiches et des films d'animation, ainsi que des sculptures sur bois et des murals.

For short biography, see page 161.
EUGENE HOFFMAN's last cover for *Graphis* (125) showed a fanciful vintage locomotive beautifully assembled from fragments of rusty iron and tin plate. His highly individual style of three-dimensional assemblage had not changed much in the meantime, but it is perhaps significant that the locomotive, symbol of dynamism and progress, has given place to the crab, scavenging crustacean "scuttling across the floors of silent seas". Crabs live, he says, on the dross and detritus on the ocean bottom, and he thinks that man may well end up doing much the same.

Kurzbiographie Seite 161.
EUGENE HOFFMANS letzter Umschlag für *Graphis* (125) zeigte eine phantasievolle Nostalgie-Lokomotive aus Fragmenten von rostigem Eisen und Metallplättchen. Es handelt sich, wie häufig bei Hoffman, um eine dreidimensionale Assemblage, aber statt einer Lokomotive, Symbol für Dynamik und Fortschritt, ist hier ein Krebs dargestellt, ein rückwärtsgehendes Krustentier. Krebse leben auf Schutt und Unrat in den Gründen des Ozeans, meint Hoffman, und er glaubt, dass auch der Mensch soweit kommen könnte.

Voir la notice biographique en p. 161.
La couverture précédente d'EUGENE HOFFMAN pour *Graphis* 125 représentait un ancien modèle de locomotive magnifiquement reconstitué à partir de fragments de fer rouillé et de fer-blanc. Depuis, le style très individuel qu'il confère à ses assemblages tridimensionnels n'a guère varié. Il est certainement significatif que la locomotive, symbole du dynamisme et du progrès, est remplacée ici par un crabe, ce crustacé balayeur des bas-fonds de l'océan. Ce genre d'animal vit, nous dit Hoffman, des déchets et détritus de toute sorte qui s'accumulent au fond de la mer, préfigurant ainsi le sort de l'humanité à venir.

For short biography, see page 135.
The illustration by JACQUES N. GARA-MOND was used in a calendar published by the Imprimeries Martin, Paris. Under a title "Villa Mon Rêve" that suggests a close lipped irony, it shows the severe lines and shadows of modern cubic architecture, here somehow reminiscent of de Chirico. Is the artist poking gentle fun at a common human dream? The question hangs unanswered in the air. The observer is left to make up his own mind.

Kurzbiographie Seite 135.
Die Arbeit von JACQUES N. GARAMOND heisst «Villa Mon Rêve» und wurde in einem Kalender der Imprimeries Martin, Paris, verwendet. Der Titel suggeriert eine versteckte Ironie. In strengen Linien und Schatten wird eine moderne kubistische Architektur dargestellt. Die einsamen, bedeutungsträchtigen Szenen erinnern an de Chirico. Ist dies eine «Traumvilla» oder eine «Villa für meinen Traum»? Die Antwort hängt in der Luft, und der Betrachter kann sich seine eigene Meinung dazu bilden.

Voir la notice biographique en p. 135.
L'illustration de JACQUES N. GARAMOND figure dans un calendrier des Imprimeries Martin de Paris. Intitulé un tant soit peu ironiquement «Villa Mon Rêve», elle exhibe les lignes sévères et les ombres de l'architecture cubiste moderne, avec un rappel de Giorgio de Chirico dans les scènes solitaires chargées de signification. S'agit-il de la «villa de mes rêves» ou d'une «villa pour mes rêves»? La réponse reste en suspens. A l'observateur d'en décider.

HOLGER MATTHIES, born in Hamburg, 1940. He studied color lithography in Hamburg and has been a freelance graphic artist since 1965. He is best known to the public through his theater poster design, but he also includes advertising art, photography, postage stamps, symbols, book and record cover design in his métier. He has earned international repute for his work (well over 500 posters bear his name) and he has been widely exhibited in Germany, Japan and the USA. He was awarded (among many other prizes) the Gold Medal at the Poster Bienale, Warsaw (1978) and the Toulouse-Lautrec Medal in Silver in Essen (1984).

HOLGER MATTHIES, 1940 in Hamburg geboren. Er studierte an der Werkkunstschule und an der Hochschule für Bildende Künste in Hamburg. Seit 1965 arbeitet er freischaffend. Bekannt wurde er hauptsächlich durch seine Theaterplakate, doch hat er auch Briefmaken, Symbole, Buch- und Plattenumschläge entworfen und Photographien gemacht. Sein Ruf ist international (weit über 500 Plakate tragen seinen Namen) und seine Arbeiten wurden in Ausstellungen in Deutschland, Japan und den USA gezeigt. Nebst vielen anderen Preisen erhielt er 1978 die Goldmedaille der Plakat Biennale Warschau und 1984 die silberne Toulouse-Lautrec-Medaille in Essen.

HOLGER MATTHIES, né en 1940 à Hambourg, où il étudie la litho couleur. Artiste indépendant depuis 1965, ce graphiste est surtout connu du grand public par ses affiches de théâtre. Il réalise pourtant aussi des travaux publicitaires, des photos, des timbres-poste, des emblèmes, des couvertures de livres et d'albums de disques. Ses travaux lui ont valu une réputation internationale (plus de 500 affiches portent son nom!). Un grand nombre d'expositions lui ont été consacrées en Allemagne, au Japon, aux Etats-Unis. Sa collection importante de prix comprend la médaille d'or de la Biennale de l'affiche de Varsovie en 1978 et la médaille d'argent Toulouse-Lautrec à Essen en 1984.

For short biography, see page 141.
This motif recalls a design YUSAKU KAMEKURA once used in a very effective poster for an exhibition of his own work: square and more complex rectangular shapes lunge forward from a black background with the three-dimensional force to form a near-kinetic pattern that might almost serve as a symbol of our technical age.

Kurzbiographie Seite 141.
Das Umschlagmotiv von YUSAKU KAMEKURA erinnert an eines seiner ausdrucksstarken Plakate für eine Einzelausstellung seiner Arbeiten: quadratische und komplexere rechteckige Teile schnellen mit grosser dreidimensionaler Kraft aus dem schwarzen Hintergrund hervor, um ein nahezu kinetisches Muster zu bilden, das als Symbol unseres technischen Zeitalters dienen könnte.

Voir la notice biographique en p. 141.
Le motif rappelle une composition dont YUSAKU KAMEKURA fit jadis une affiche très remarquée pour présenter l'une de ses expositions personnelles: des sections carrées et rectangulaires, ces dernières plus complexes, se projettent en avant depuis un arrière-plan noir avec assez de vigueur tridimensionnelle pour évoquer une structure quasi cinétique qui pourrait bien servir de symbole à notre époque technologique.

PAUL BRÜHWILER was born in Lucerne in 1939, where he also began his professional training. In 1960 he went to Paris to continue his studies, working there for Création Hollenstein and for Editions Condé Nast. From 1965 to 1973 he lived in Los Angeles, where he served as an art director under Saul Bass, Charles and Ray Eames and Carson/Roberts. He founded his own design studio in Los Angeles in 1969 but in 1973 he returned to Switzerland. He has since freelanced from his studio in Küsnacht near Zürich. He teaches graphic art and visual communication at the School for Applied Arts in Lucerne.

PAUL BRÜHWILER wurde 1939 in Luzern geboren und erhielt dort seine erste berufliche Ausbildung. Zur Weiterbildung ging er 1960 nach Paris und arbeitete unter anderem bei Création Hollenstein und Editions Condé Nast. Von 1965 bis 1973 lebte er in Los Angeles, war vier Jahre Art Director bei Saul Bass, Charles und Ray Eames sowie Carson/Roberts. 1969 gründete er sein eigenes Design-Studio in Los Angeles. 1973 kehrte er in die Schweiz zurück und arbeitet jetzt in seinem Studio in Küsnacht bei Zürich. Er unterrichtet Graphik und visuelle Kommunikation an der Schule für Gestaltung in Luzern.

PAUL BRÜHWILER est né en 1939 à Lucerne, Suisse, où il a reçu sa première formation professionnelle. Parti se perfectionner à Paris, en 1960, il y travaille entre autres pour Création Hollenstein et Editions Condé Nast. De 1965 à 1973, on le trouve à Los Angeles, en particulier quatre ans comme directeur artistique chez Saul Bass, Charles et Ray Eames, ainsi que chez Carson/Roberts. Il fonde en 1969 son propre studio de design à Los Angeles. Rentré en Suisse en 1973, il installe un studio indépendant à Küsnacht près de Zürich. Enseigne les techniques du graphisme et de la communication visuelle à l'Ecole d'Art Appliqué à Lucerne.

HANS HILLMANN, born 1925 in Germany. He studied at first in Kassel and finally in Italy. Since 1953 he worked as a freelancer specializing in film posters and illustrations. In 1982 a book appeared under the title *Fliegenpapier*, in which Hillmann tells in pictures the criminal story *Flypaper* by Dashiell Hammett. He has taken part in many exhibitions, e.g. in the documenta III in Kassel (1964), in the Poster Biennale in Warsaw (four times between 1966-72) as well as in the Venice Biennale (1972). He is a Professor at the Art College, Kassel and President of the AGI Germany. He has been honored for his work many times.

HANS HILLMANN, 1925 in Deutschland geboren. Er studierte zuerst in Kassel und anschliessend in Italien. Seit 1953 arbeitet er freiberuflich und hat sich auf Filmplakate und Illustrationen spezialisiert. 1982 erschien unter dem Titel *Fliegenpapier* ein Buch, in dem Hillmann die Kriminalgeschichte *Flypaper* von Dashiell Hammett in Bildern erzählt. Er hat an vielen Ausstellungen teilgenommen, so z.B. an der documenta III Kassel (1964), an der Plakatbiennale Warschau (viermal zwischen 1966-72) sowie an der Biennale Venedig (1972) Er ist Professor an der Kunsthochschule Kassel und Präsident der AGI Deutschland. Für seine Arbeiten ist er mehrfach ausgezeichnet worden.

HANS HILLMANN, né en Allemagne en 1925. A terminé en Italie ses études commencées à Kassel, en RFA. Etabli à son compte en 1953, il se spécialise dans l'affiche de cinéma et dans l'illustration. Dans l'ouvrage paru en 1982 sous le titre de *Fliegenpapier* (Papier tue-mouches), il met en images le roman policier de Dashiell Hammett, *Flypaper*. A participé à de nombreuses expositions, ainsi à la documenta III de Kassel (RFA) en 1964, à la Biennale de l'affiche de Varsovie (quatre fois, entre 1966 et 1972), à la Biennale de Venise en 1972. Professeur à l'Université des arts de Kassel, il préside la section allemande de l'AGI. Ses travaux lui ont valu toute une série de récompenses.

STEPHEN TARANTAL studied at Cooper Union and the Tyler School of Art. He works freelance for magazines and corporations such as *Smith Kline, AT&T, Insurance Company of North America, Macmillan, Univac* etc. Most of his work is 3-dimensional - a combination of canvas covered forms, painted and bolted, but he also adds carved wood, colored wire and other various elements. He has taught since 1969 at Philadelphia College of Art and his work has won him a number of major awards, including Gold Medals from the Philadelphia ADC.

STEPHEN TARANTAL studierte an der Cooper Union und der Tyler School of Art und ist seither freischaffend tätig für Zeitschriften und Firmen wie *Smith Kline, AT&T, Insurance Company of North America, Macmillan, J.C. Penney und Univac*. Die meisten seiner Arbeiten sind dreidimensional, vielfach bestehend aus geformter und mit Acryl bemalter Leinwand. Seit 1969 lehrt er am Philadelphia College of Art. Seine Arbeiten wurden regelmässig ausgestellt und brachten ihm eine Anzahl wichtiger Preise, darunter Goldmedaillen des Philadelphia ADC.

STEPHEN TARANTAL a étudié à Cooper Union et à la Tyler School of Art. Il travaille à son compte pour des magazines et des sociétés telles que *Smith Kline, AT&T, Insurance Company of North America, Macmillan, Univac*, etc. La plupart de ses travaux sont tridimensionnels - une combinaison de formes recouvertes de toile, peintes et boulonnées, auxquelles il ajoute aussi du bois sculpté, du fil de couleur et divers autres éléments. Depuis 1969, il enseigne au Philadelphia College of Art. Ses travaux lui ont valu de nombreuses récompenses de poids, dont des médailles d'or de l'ADC de Philadelphie.

UTE OSTERWALDER, born in Allenstein, Germany, 1939. She currently teaches illustration and design at the Hamburg School of Applied Art (Fachhochschule Hamburg). Her illustrations have won her international acclaim and have appeared in *Twen, Zeit-Magazin,* and *Stern*. She also works with the *Suhrkamp* publishers. She lives in Hamburg.

UTE OSTERWALDER, 1939 in Allenstein, Deutschland, geboren. Sie lebt und arbeitet in Hamburg, wo sie an der Fachhochschule einen Lehrauftrag für Illustration hat. Mit ihren Illustrationen, die unter anderem in den Zeitschriften *Twen, Zeit-Magazin* und *Stern* erschienen sind, hat sie sich einen internationalen Namen geschaffen. Viele ihrer Arbeiten sind durch den deutschen *Suhrkamp*-Verlag publiziert worden.

UTE OSTERWALDER, née à Allenstein (Allemagne) en 1939. Enseigne l'illustration et le design à la Haute Ecole des arts appliqués (Fachhochschule) de Hambourg. Ses illustrations, publiées dans *Twen, Zeit-Magazin* et *Stern*, lui ont valu une flatteuse réputation internationale. Elle travaille aussi pour les Editions Suhrkamp. Ute Osterwalder habite Hambourg.

BRAD HOLLAND, born in Ohio, 1944. Painter and illustrator. He moved to Chicago in 1961 and began publishing cartoons in local newspapers. In 1965 he created *Asylum Press* in Kansas City to publish posters, newspapers for the underground press and pamphlets. He moved to New York in 1967 and started illustrating books. In 1971 he began political drawings for *The New York Times*. His work has been exhibited in Bordeaux, the Louvre, Teheran and Washington DC. His work has been published worldwide and he has gained many awards, including numerous Gold Medals.

BRAD HOLLAND, 1944 in Ohio geboren. Maler und Illustrator. Er zog 1961 nach Chicago und begann in lokalen Zeitungen Cartoons zu veröffentlichen. 1965 gründete er die *Asylum Press* in Kansas City für die Veröffentlichung von Plakaten, Untergrundzeitungen und -Pamphleten. 1967 zog er nach New York und begann, Bücher zu illustrieren; 1971 kamen politische Zeichnungen für die *New York Times* hinzu. Seine Arbeiten wurden u.a. in Bordeaux, im Louvre, in Teheran und Washington DC ausgestellt. Bedeutende Zeitschriften in aller Welt haben seine Arbeiten veröffentlicht, und er erhielt zahlreiche Auszeichnungen einschliesslich vieler Goldmedaillen.

BRAD HOLLAND, né dans l'Ohio en 1944. Peintre et illustrateur. Installé à Chicago en 1961, il y commence une carrière de dessinateur d'humour dans les journaux du coin. En 1965, il crée à Kansas City les Editions *Asylum Press*, qui vont publier des affiches, des journaux de l'underground, des pamphlets. Arrivé à New York en 1967, il se voue à l'illustration de livres. C'est en 1971 qu'il commence sa série de dessins politiques dans le *New York Times*. Il a eu des expositions à Bordeaux, au Louvre, à Téhéran et à Washington. De nombreuses médailles d'or sont venues récompenser son œuvre, qui lui a valu une foule d'admirateurs.

JAN MLODOZENIEC, born in Warsaw, 1930. He studied at the Warsaw Academy of Fine Arts under Prof. Henryk Tomaszewski. He is renowned for his cultural posters, book illustrations, graphics, satirical cartoons. About twenty one-man shows have been devoted to him and he has participated in numerous collective exhibitions. Included on his list of awards is a Silver Medal at the International Book Illustration Exhibition in Leipzig, a Gold Medal at the Biennale in Katowice and a Gold Medal at the Poster Biennale in Warsaw in 1980.

JAN MLODOZENIEC, 1930 in Warschau geboren. Er studierte bei Prof. Henryk Tomaszewski an der dortigen Kunstakademie. Er wurde vor allem durch seine kulturellen Plakate, Buchillustrationen, graphischen Arbeiten und satirischen Karikaturen bekannt. Er hatte zahlreiche Einzelausstellungen und nahm an vielen Gruppenausstellungen teil. Unter seinen Auszeichnungen befinden sich eine Silbermedaille der Buchkunst-Ausstellung in Leipzig, eine Goldmedaille der Plakat-Biennale in Kattowitz und eine Goldmedaille der Poster-Biennale in Warschau (1980).

JAN MLODOZENIEC, né à Varsovie en 1930. Elève d'Henryk Tomaszewski à l'Académie des beaux-arts de Varsovie. Artiste renommé pour ses affiches culturelles, ses illustrations de livres, ses créations graphiques, ses dessins satiriques. Une vingtaine d'expositions personnelles lui ont été consacrées, et ses œuvres ont figuré dans un grand nombre d'expositions collectives. Il tire quelque fierté de nombreux prix dont une médaille d'argent de l'Exposition internationale de Leipzig consacrée à l'illustration de livres, une médaille d'or de la Biennale de Katowice et une médaille d'or de la Biennale de l'affiche de Varsovie en 1980.

RUDOLF BECK. Designer, Stuttgart. The cover illustration relates to a feature on the international furniture corporation *Knoll International*. It is a shot of a chair designed for *Knoll* by Ettore Sottsass. Rudolf Beck has been working for *Knoll* as freelance graphic-designer since 1969.

RUDOLF BECK, Graphik-Designer, Stuttgart. Der von ihm gestaltete Umschlag bezieht sich auf einen Artikel über die internationale Möbelfirma *Knoll International*. Es handelt sich um eine Detail-Aufnahme eines von Ettore Sottsass für *Knoll* entworfenen Stuhls. Rudolf Beck ist seit 1969 als freier Graphik-Designer für *Knoll* tätig.

RUDOLF BECK. Designer, Stuttgart. L'illustration de couverture qu'il a réalisée se rapporte à un article traitant de la maison internationale d'ameublements *Knoll International*. Il s'agit de la photo d'un siège créé pour *Knoll* par Ettore Sottsass. Rudolf Beck œuvre en qualité d'artiste indépendant pour les communications et l'image graphique de *Knoll* depuis 1969.

For short biography, see Page 174.
The drawings of EUGÈNE MIHAESCO always have a hidden dimension. However, on this cover the second dimension seems not even to be hidden, but present as a sort of mirror image. Its upper half shows a stone tower with a pennon flying from its summit. It stands on terra firma in the red glow of the extrovert day, embodying authority, force, the establishment, the hard facts of the powers that be. Its reflection, however, has become a nib, dipping into the introvert night of the waters, a symbol of the non-material world.

Kurzbiographie Seite 174.
Die Zeichnungen von EUGÈNE MIHAESCO haben immer eine versteckte Dimension. Auf diesem Umschlag jedoch scheint diese zweite Dimension nicht einmal versteckt zu sein, sondern gegenwärtig als eine Art Spiegelbild. Seine obere Hälfte zeigt einen Steinturm mit flatterndem Fähnchen. Der Turm steht auf solidem Fundament, umgeben vom Abendglühn des extrovertierten Tages, Autorität, Kraft, Althergebrachtes, die harten Tatsachen der herrschenden Mächte versinnbildlichend. Sein Spiegelbild ist jedoch zu einer Feder geworden, welche in die introvertierte Nacht der Gewässer eintaucht: ein Symbol der nichtmaterialistischen Welt.

Voir la notice biographique en p. 174.
Les dessins d'EUGÈNE MIHAESCO ont toujours une dimension cachée. Sur notre couverture, cette autre dimension n'est pas occultée, mais présente sous forme d'une espèce de reflet de miroir. Le haut est un donjon au fier gonfanon, solidement construit sur la terre ferme, baigné de la splendeur crépusculaire du jour extraverti et incarnant l'autorité, la puissance, la tradition, les réalités d'airain de l'ordre établi. Par contraste, le miroir le transforme en bec de plume trempant dans l'obscurité et l'introversion des profondeurs marines – symbole d'un monde soustrait au matérialisme ambiant.

HARALD SCHLÜTER, creative director and photographer. He has his own advertising agency in Essen-Kettwig, West Germany. This illustration is taken from a sheet in the successful 1985 calendar which Schlüter designed for a German lithographer. The title of the calendar is *Agency Art*. By specific choice of the photographed section of a layouter's drawing-board base, with its doodling and experimentation fragments, the visual language of the advertising agency is recorded.

HARALD SCHLÜTER, Kreativ-Direktor und Photograph in seiner eigenen Werbeagentur in Essen-Kettwig, BRD. Dieser Umschlag ist eines der zwölf Blätter eines Kalenders, den Schlüter für den Lithographen Dannhöfer gestaltete. Der Titel des Kalenders ist *Agency Art*, Spuren der täglichen Arbeit im Atelier. Durch die Wahl des photographierten Ausschnitts brachte er die völlig zufälligen Schnittlinien und Materialfragmente auf den Pappen in eine bewusste Form.

HARALD SCHLÜTER, directeur créatif et photographe. Dispose de son propre agence publicitaire à Essen-Kettwig (RFA). Cette illustration est tirée d'un feuillet du calendrier à succès pour l'année 1985 que Schlüter a réalisé pour un atelier de lithographie allemand sous le titre de *Agency Art*. Par un choix déterminé du détail à photographier sur la planche à dessin d'un maquettiste, il réussit, à travers les gribouillis et les fragments d'expérimentation, à évoquer le langage visuel de l'agence de publicité.

■

MINORU MORITA, born in Manchuria, 1943. When quite young he went to America and he is now settled in New York. He is a designer, art director and teacher and also President of *Creative Center Inc.* His work is held in the permanent collection of the Hiroshima Museum of Modern Art. This issue coincided with the forty years' commemoration of the Hiroshima disaster and a feature inside was devoted to the "Images for Survival" peace posters by American and Japanese artists for the Hiroshima Appeals Campaign.

■

MINORU MORITA, 1943 in der Mandschurei geboren. Er kam schon früh nach Amerika und liess sich in New York nieder. Er ist Designer, Art Direktor, Lehrer und auch Inhaber des *Creative Center Inc.* Seine Arbeiten befinden sich in der permanenten Sammlung des Museums für moderne Kunst in Hiroshima. Im Gedenken an die Katastrophe von Hiroshima erschien in dieser Ausgabe ein Artikel über «Images for Survival» (Überlebensbilder), eine Serie von Friedensplakaten (Hiroshima-Appeals-Kampagne), die von amerikanischen und japanischen Künstlern stammen. Moritas Hiroshima-Plakat wurde als Umschlag verwendet.

■

MINORU MORITA, né en Mandchourie en 1943. Parti très jeune en Amérique, il habite aujourd'hui New York. Designer, directeur artistique et enseignant, il est aussi président du *Creative Center Inc.* Ses œuvres figurent dans les collections permanentes du Hiroshima Museum of Modern Art. Ce numéro du magazine est sorti lorsque l'on commémorait le 40e anniversaire de la catastrophe d'Hiroshima. C'est pourquoi l'un de ses articles était consacré aux affiches pacifistes par lesquelles, sous le titre d' «Images for Survival» (Images de survie), des artistes américains et japonais ont répondu à l'Hiroshima Appeals Campaign.

■

ROSMARIE TISSI, born in Switzerland, 1937. She followed a one-year elementary course at the School of Applied Art (Kunstgewerbeschule) in Zürich with a four-year graphic-design apprenticeship, several times gaining federal scholarships for applied art. Her partnership with Siegfried Odermatt dates from 1968. They have won numerous prizes at international graphic-design contests. Their work has been exhibited in several museums and shown in various publications in Switzerland and abroad. They have been members of the AGI since 1974.

■

ROSMARIE TISSI, 1937 in der Schweiz geboren. Sie absolvierte nach einem einjährigen Elementarkurs an der Kunstgewerbeschule Zürich eine 4jährige Graphikerlehre. Sie erhielt mehrmals eidgenössische Stipendien für angewandte Kunst. Seit 1968 arbeitet sie als Partnerin mit Siegfried Odermatt. Sie wurden seit ihrem Zusammenschluss mit zahlreichen Preisen an internationalen Design-Wettbewerben ausgezeichnet. Sonderausstellungen ihrer Arbeiten wurden im In- und Ausland gezeigt. Seit 1974 sind sie Mitglied der AGI.

■

ROSMARIE TISSI, née en Suisse en 1937. Elle a étudié une année à l'Ecole des arts appliqués de Zurich avant de faire un apprentissage de design graphique en quatre ans. Elle a bénéficié de plusieurs bourses fédérales d'art appliqué. Son association avec Siegfried Odermatt date de 1968. Tous deux ont remporté de nombreux prix dans des concours internationaux d'art graphique appliqué. Leurs travaux ont été exposés dans divers musées et ont été présentés dans un certain nombre de publications en Suisse et à l'étranger. Ils sont membres de l'AGI depuis 1974.

■

ANDRZEJ DUDZIŃSKI, born in Poland, 1945. He studied art and architecture in Gdansk and Warsaw. He spent two years working in London before returning to his native country where he quickly became famous for his creation of "Dudi" – a satirical cartoon "watchbird" – which appeared in magazines, books, and later, on the radio. In 1977 he moved to New York where he now contributes to The *New York Times, Newsweek, Vogue,* and many other leading publications. His one-man show «The Spectators» was held at London's National Theatre in 1983. He currently teaches at the Parsons School of Design.

■

ANDRZEJ DUDZIŃSKI, 1945 in Polen geboren. Er studierte Kunst und Architektur in Danzig und Warschau. Er arbeitete zwei Jahre in London, bevor er nach Polen zurückkehrte, wo er u.a. bekannt wurde durch die Kreation von «Dudi», einem satirischen «Aufpasser-Vogel», der in Zeitschriften erschien und später am Radio auftrat. Seit 1977 lebt er in New York und arbeitet für die *New York Times, Newsweek, Vogue* und andere führende Publikationen. Seine Ausstellung "Die Zuschauer" wurde 1983 im National Theatre, London, gezeigt. Dudziński lehrt an der Parsons School of Design.

■

ANDRZEJ DUDZIŃSKI, né en Pologne en 1945. A étudié l'art et l'architecture à Gdansk et à Varsovie. Part travailler deux années à Londres, puis revient au pays où il s'impose rapidement par son caractère de B.D. satirique «Dudi», l'oiseau persifleur qui a d'abord les honneurs des magazines, puis de la radio. En 1977, il s'installe à New York où il apporte dorénavant ses contributions au *New York Times,* à *Newsweek,* à *Vogue* et à bien d'autres publications de premier plan. Son exposition personnelle intitulée «Les Spectateurs» a été organisée au National Theatre de Londres en 1985. Dudziński enseigne à la Parsons School of Design.

■

MARSHALL ARISMAN, born in New York, 1938. He graduated from Pratt Institute in 1960. He is co-chairman of the media department at the School of Visual Arts and has been regularly contributing his drawings to the most prestigious US magazines. He is committed to humanistic concerns and to nuclear disarmament. (His *"The Last Tribe"* series included 90 paintings, masks and monoprints on this theme). One-man shows of his work have been staged in the USA, Europe and Japan. Among the many awards conferred on him by the Society of Illustrators and the New York ADC is the Illustrator of the Year Award *(Playboy)* in 1979.

■

MARSHALL ARISMAN, 1938 in Jamestown, New York, geboren, ist Absolvent des Pratt Institute (1960). Er ist zur Zeit Vorsitzender der Media-Abteilung der School of Visual Arts. Seine Zeichnungen erscheinen regelmässig in den wichtigsten amerikanischen Zeitschriften. Er engagiert sich für Menschenrechte und nukleare Abrüstung. (Sein Epos «The Last Tribe» umfasst 90 Gemälde, Masken und Monotypien zu diesem Thema). Einzelausstellungen seiner Werke fanden in den USA, in Europa und Japan statt. Unter den zahlreichen Auszeichnungen, die er von der Society of Illustrators und dem New York ADC erhalten hat, befindet sich auch der Illustrator of the Year (1979) des *Playboy.*

■

MARSHALL ARISMAN, né à New York en 1938. Diplômé du Pratt Institute en 1960. Coprésident du département des médias de la School of Visual Arts, il alimente régulièrement en dessins les magazines américains les plus prestigieux. Fortement engagé dans la cause de l'humanisme et du désarmement nucléaire. (Sa série intitulée «La Dernière Tribu» traite ce sujet en 90 peintures, masques et monotypes.) Des expositions personnelles lui ont été consacrées aux Etats-Uni, en Europe et au Japon. Il a été de nombreuses fois lauréat de la Society of Illustrators et de l'ADC de New York et récipiendaire, en 1979, du Prix de l'Illustrateur de l'Année *(Playboy).*

■

For short biography, see Page 150.
A characteristic of KURT WIRTH's posters is a suggestive and significant abstract form perfectly combined with a concise message whereby the typography is inseparable from the pictorial motif. For this cover he has succeeded eloquently and with full impact in composing the title letters of *Graphis* in a similar manner.

Kurzbiographie Seite 150.
Hauptmerkmal der Plakate von KURT WIRTH ist die weitgehend abstrahierte Bildform mit knapper Wortbotschaft, wobei er Typographie und Bildmotiv zu einer untrennbaren Einheit verbindet. Auf diesem Umschlag ist es ihm überzeugend und mit verblüffender Wirkung gelungen, die Titelschrift *Graphis* auf diese Weise zu integrieren.

Voir la notice biographique en p. 150.
Ce qui caractérise les affiches de KURT WIRTH, c'est leur forme abstraite suggestive et significative qui se combine à merveille avec un message concis de manière à rendre la typo inséparable du motif visuel. Dans cette couverture, il a réussi de manière très convaincante à réaliser une intégration semblable du titre de *Graphis,* d'où l'impact de la composition.

TAKENOBU IGARASHI, born in Japan, 1944. He studied and taught in the USA. Today he heads his own design team in Tokyo. His work extends from graphic design to sculpture. The signal feature of Igarashi's work is this pioneering advance into the still little reconnoitered world between the dimensions. His architectural alphabets and numerals, an example of which has been used for the cover (for once with all the supporting lines and points) suggest architecture of considerable structural differentiation, even if it appears in two dimensions only. His work has been widely exhibited.

TAKENOBU IGARASHI, 1944 in Japan geboren. Er studierte und unterrichtete in den USA. Heute führt er ein eigens Design-Studio in Tokio. Sein Arbeitsbereich erstreckt sich von Graphik-Design bis zu Bildhauerei. Hauptmerkmal für seine Arbeit ist das pionierhafte Vordringen in die immer noch wenig erkundete Welt zwischen den Dimensionen. Seine Architektur-Alphabete und -Zahlen, von denen ein Beispiel (für einmal mit allen Hilfslinien und Punkten) für den Umschlag verwendet wurde, weisen eine bemerkenswerte strukturelle Differenzierung auf, auch wenn sie wie hier nur in zwei Dimensionen erscheinen. Die Arbeiten wurden in zahlreichen Ausstellungen gezeigt.

TAKENOBU IGARASHI, né au Japon en 1944. A étudié et enseigné aux Etats-Unis. Est aujourd'hui à la tête de sa propre équipe de design à Tokyo. Sa gamme créative va du design graphique à la sculpture. La caractéristique de l'œuvre d'Igarashi, c'est son travail de pionnier dans l'exploration de l'univers interdimensionnel encore peu connu. Ses alphabets et nombres architecturaux, dont un spécimen a été utilisé pour cette couverture (en y incluant pour une fois tous les points et lignes de repère), impliquent une différenciation structurelle considérable au sein d'une trame pourtant réduite aux deux dimensions. Ses travaux ont été présentés dans de nombreuses expositions.

STASYS EIDRIGEVIČIUS, born in Lithuania, 1949. He graduated from the Fine Arts Institute in Vilnius. In 1970 he started producing bookplates and miniatures and in 1976 decided to devote his time to graphic art. His first book illustrations were published in 1977. Since then he has illustrated some 30 books for children and adults. More recently he has turned toward larger formats especially for his drawings and poster designs. He has participated in numerous exhibitions in Europe and the USA. He lives and works in Warsaw.

STASYS EIDRIGEVIČIUS wurde 1949 in Litauen geboren und promovierte am Staatlichen Kunstinstitut in Wilna. 1970 begann er Exlibris und Miniaturen zu entwerfen, und 1976 beschloss er, sich ganz der Graphik zu widmen. Seine ersten Buchillustrationen wurden 1977 veöffentlicht, und seither hat er ca. 30 Bücher für Kinder und Erwachsene illustriert. Neuerdings wendet er sich auch grösseren Formaten zu, im besonderen für seine Zeichnungen und Plakatentwürfe. Seine Arbeiten wurden in zahlreichen Ausstellungen in Europa und den USA gezeigt. Er lebt und arbeitet in Warschau.

STASYS EIDRIGEVIČIUS, né en Lituanie en 1949. Diplômé de l'Institut des beaux-arts de Vilnious. Dès 1970, il crée des ex-libris et des miniatures. En 1976, il décide de se consacrer exclusivement à l'art graphique. Ses premières illustrations de livres paraissent en 1977. Depuis, il a illustré une trentaine de livres pour enfants et adultes. Ces derniers temps, il a découvert le grand format, en particulier pour ses dessins et ses affiches. Il a participé à de nombreuses expositions en Europe et aux Etats-Unis. Il habite et travaille aujourd'hui à Varsovie.

GRAPHIS
GRAPHIS
GRAPHIS
GRAPHIS
GRAPHIS
GRAPHIS
GRAPHIS
GRAPHIS
GRAPHIS
GRAPHIS
GRAPHIS
GRAPHIS
GRAPHIS
GRAPHIS

ORDER FORM / BESTELLSCHEIN / BON DE COMMANDE

□ 9/10	□ 37	□ 72	□ 108	□ 167	□ 199	□ 224
□ 13	□ 38	□ 73	□ 109	□ 168	□ 200	□ 225
□ 14	□ 39	□ 74	□ 110	□ 170	□ 201	□ 226
□ 15	□ 40	□ 75	□ 111	□ 171	□ 202	□ 227
□ 16	□ 41	□ 76	□ 112	□ 175	□ 205	□ 228
□ 17	□ 43	□ 77	□ 113	□ 176	□ 206	□ 229
□ 18	□ 45	□ 78	□ 114	□ 178	□ 207	□ 230
□ 19	□ 46	□ 79	□ 115	□ 179	□ 209	□ 231
□ 20	□ 49	□ 80	□ 116	□ 180	□ 210	□ 232
□ 23	□ 52	□ 81	□ 117	□ 183	□ 211	□ 233
□ 25	□ 54	□ 82	□ 123	□ 184	□ 212	□ 234
□ 26	□ 56	□ 83	□ 129	□ 185	□ 213	□ 235
□ 27	□ 60	□ 85	□ 132	□ 186	□ 214	□ 236
□ 28	□ 61	□ 86	□ 141	□ 187	□ 215	□ 237
□ 29	□ 62	□ 92	□ 142	□ 189	□ 216	□ 238
□ 30	□ 64	□ 94	□ 148	□ 190	□ 217	□ 239
□ 31	□ 65	□ 97	□ 150	□ 191	□ 218	□ 240
□ 32	□ 66	□ 98	□ 151	□ 193	□ 219	□ 242
□ 33	□ 67	□ 99	□ 152	□ 195	□ 220	□ 243
□ 34	□ 68	□ 101	□ 154	□ 196	□ 221	□ 244
□ 35	□ 70	□ 104	□ 161	□ 197	□ 222	□ 245
□ 36	□ 71	□ 107	□ 166	□ 198	□ 223	□ 246

	WORLD	CH	BRD	USA	CAN	U.K.	FRANCE
Price per issue	Sfr. 24.00	Sfr. 22.00	DM 29.00	US$ 12.00	$16.50	£9.20	FF 95.00
Preis pro Ausgabe	Sfr. 24.00	Sfr. 22.00	DM 29.00	US$ 12.00	$16.50	£9.20	FF 95.00
Prix par numéro	Sfr. 24.00	Sfr. 22.00	DM 29.00	US$ 12.00	$16.50	£9.20	FF 95.00

□ Check enclosed (For Europe, please make Sfr-checks payable to a Swiss bank)
□ Amount paid into your account at the Swiss Bank Corp. in New York, London or Zurich.
□ Amount paid to Postal Cheque Account Zürich 80-23071-9 (through your local postoffice)
□ Send invoice

□ Scheck liegt bei (Sfr.-Scheck bitte auf eine Schweizer Bank ziehen)
□ Betrag überwiesen auf Ihr Konto bei der Schweizerischen Bankgesellschaft. 8021 Zürich
□ Betrag überwiesen auf PC Zürich 80-23071-9/PschK Frankfurt a.M. 3000 57-602
□ Bitte stellen Sie Rechnung

□ Chèque bancaire ci-joint (prière de tirer les chèques en FS sur une banque Suisse)
□ Règlement adresseé à votre compte auprès de l'UBS. 8021 Zürich
□ Règlement adressé au CCP Editions Graphis. Zürich 80-23071-9
□ Facture demandée

NAME/NOM

STREET/STRASSE/RUE

ZIP/PLZ/CEDEX

CITY/ORT/LIEU

COUNTRY/LAND/PAYS

DATE/DATUM

SIGNATURE/UNTERSCHRIFT

GRAPHIS PRESS CORP., 107 DUFOURSTRASSE, CH-8008 ZURICH (SWITZERLAND)

GRAPHIS HAS A LOT TO OFFER YOU

GRAPHIS POSTERS – the only yearbook in the world that concerns itself with poster creation on an international level.

PHOTOGRAPHIS – presents a dynamic, complex, and rich display of outstanding achievements in different fields of photography.

GRAPHIS DESIGN ANNUAL – an outstanding collection of today's trends in the international scene of graphic arts, design and illustration.

GRAPHIS – the most distinguished, international journal of advertising and design. A GRAPHIS subscription guarantees you an overview of international creative works in graphic design throughout the whole year.

GRAPHIS – 6 times a year a catalyst for new, creative ideas.

GRAPHIS HAT IHNEN VIEL ZU BIETEN

GRAPHIS POSTERS – ist weltweit das einzige Jahrbuch, das dem Plakatschaffen auf internationaler Ebene Rechnung trägt.

PHOTOGRAPHIS – bietet ein vielseitiges, komplexes Bild hervorragender Leistungen aus verschiedenen Bereichen der internationalen Photographie.

GRAPHIS DESIGN ANNUAL – eine Zusammenstellung repräsentativer Arbeiten aus Graphik, Design und Illustration aus aller Welt.

GRAPHIS – die anspruchsvolle, internationale Zeitschrift für Werbung und Design. Ein GRAPHIS-Abonnement gewährt Ihnen über das ganze Jahr eine Übersicht über das internationale kreative Schaffen.

GRAPHIS – 6mal jährlich, Zündstoff für neue, kreative Ideen.

GRAPHIS VOUS EN OFFRE D'AVANTAGE

GRAPHIS POSTERS – est le seul annuel au monde qui tienne compte de la création d'affiches au niveau international.

PHOTOGRAPHIS – présente un tableau varié et complexe des meilleurs réalisations au service de la publicité commerciale et de la photographie rédactionnelle.

GRAPHIS DESIGN ANNUAL – entreprend de réunir les réalisations exceptionnelles au plan international. Un classic de la littérature publicitaire.

GRAPHIS – la revue prestigieuse et internationale d'art publicitaire et d'art appliqué. Un abonnement GRAPHIS vous procure tout au long de l'année une vue d'ensemble de l'activité créatrice internationale.

GRAPHIS – 6 fois par an, une source explosive d'ideé créatrices, nouvelles.

□ I would like to have some more information about your publications.
□ Ich würde gerne mehr über Ihr Verlagsprogramm erfahren.
□ J'aimerais recevoir un supplément d'informations.

NAME/NOM

STREET/STRASSE/RUE

ZIP/PLZ/CEDEX   CITY/ORT/LIEU

COUNTRY/LAND/PAYS

GRAPHIS PRESS CORP., 107 DUFOURSTRASSE, CH-8008 ZURICH (SWITZERLAND)

A unique chance

GRAPHIS BACK-ISSUES 1944–1986

Profit from our offer and order now the desired issues.

There is only a limited quantity available.

■

Eine einmalige Gelegenheit

GRAPHIS ARCHIV-AUSGABEN 1944–1986

Profitieren Sie von unserem Angebot und bestellen Sie jetzt die gewünschten Ausgaben. Es sind nur noch wenige Exemplare erhältlich.

■

Une occasion unique

GRAPHIS NUMÉROS D'ARCHIVES 1944–1986

Profitez de notre offre et commandez aussitôt les numéros que vous désirez. Nous ne disposons que d'un nombre limité.